Of sons and skies

Flying through World War Two

Robert Arley

Splash TV

First published in 2018

Splash TV Limited

Copyright © 2017 by Robert Arley

Robert Arley reserves the moral rights to
be identified as the author of this work

ISBN: 978-1-9998944-0-5

www.ofsonsandskies.com

Chapters:

Preface: *One night*

One night

You wanted the war to end. And until that came about, you wanted a reliable plane - which has been carefully gone over since its last mission by the most attentive ground crew. They should have patched up any damage caused by enemy guns, tested the engines and all other mechanical parts, to hand over to the skipper a machine fit for purpose.

You want your fellow crew members to be fit and well, and to have a decent attitude to the task that lies before them. No moaning about bad workmanship or leadership or routes or target hazards.

You want a precise, positive briefing from your bosses. The Squadron Commander should give you a strong sense of the purpose for this sortie - why it's important and how it's going to help bring the war to an end.

You want the weather officer to dish out a clear picture of conditions on your route over the next ten hours. And what sort of weather do you want? Not storms, not fog, not heavy rain. But cloud versus clear skies? That's a hard one. A full moon and no cloud means you can see where you're going, but so can everyone else. Enemy flak guns can spot you a mile off. And the night-fighters know where you are, so can come in from any angle. Cloud gives you cover, but now you're reliant on the navigation aids that are available - starting with your own navigator.

You want your plane to remain mechanically sound throughout its journey and not develop problems somewhere along the way, especially over the North Sea. You want to be part of a big fleet of planes on this mission. At least three hundred, preferably four. Because the bigger bunch of bombers flying across enemy territory, the less likely your particular craft gets picked on by those night-fighters.

You want the route to be one that avoids the biggest batteries of flak guns. You want the target to have some understandable military purpose and for it to lie at a distance from housing and other civilian facilities.

You always appreciate aircraft factories as an aiming point because damage to these structures must surely lessen the capacity of the enemy to pursue the battle against you.

You don't want the final approach to the target dense with shells blasting from below. You want your skipper to stay calm and in control, but have the capacity to hurl the crate away from immediate danger

*and drop out of gun-sight line from approaching fighters - but not fall
into barrages of flak.*

*You don't want your pilot shot. You don't want to crash-land. You
don't want to try to clamber out of a falling, flaming plane and hope
your parachute will work. You don't want to land in Germany and have
local people find you and beat you up as an enemy of the state doing
them harm.*

*You don't want to discover that a fellow crew member has been hit by
flak and might be dead or just badly wounded, and needs to be patched
up and laid down carefully in the fuselage in the hope he will make it
back alive.*

*You don't want any disruption to the fuel delivery from the tanks -
leakage of precious juice which could mean the machine cannot re-
cross the North Sea and instead will come down in the drink.*

*You want the dinghy to work and for everyone to manage to get in it
and for the carrier pigeon to be given a decent grid reference of your
current position, and for the little bird to fly back to its home and so
alert Air-Sea Rescue of your whereabouts.*

*You want your navigator to find the way back to your airfield and for
your pilot to declare that the undercarriage seems sound and that the
runway hasn't been bombed and is not full of holes.*

*You want to learn that all the other crews on that night's mission have
also successfully got back to base.*

That's what you wanted.

*Sometimes, you got most of that, but never, of course, night after
night.*

* * * * *

If you are unfamiliar with the trajectory of military flying from 1939 to 1945, you will be astounded to discover the extraordinary activity that took place in the skies before you were born - the challenges of handling relatively primitive machines in difficult conditions; every aerial journey being a matter of life or death for those aboard, and frequently also for those underneath.

Thousands of courageous young men learned to fly the troublesome craft, to take them across land and sea to face their enemies. Often at the core of our story is the flight path of RAF Bomber Command, Britain's biggest organisation devoted to military flying; with the most airfields, planes and pilots. But we will visit also other air forces and consider their strengths and weaknesses in different arenas around the globe as the aggression spread.

And we will occasionally skim through the headlines of the major newspapers to see how they presented the problems and solutions to an anxious readership.

We will dip in and out of a cross-section of the formidable endeavours pursued by intelligent people to impose dismay on others.

At the end of all that conflict, the world became relatively peaceful. Europe especially has mostly flourished since the termination of hostilities.

This book is designed to encourage people to appreciate how lucky they are; to never have suffered the fears, dangers and drastic violence of those years.

Chapter One

SOMETHING IN THE AIR

As we taxi out for take-off, let us briefly reflect on what came before. The Wright Brothers first flew a powered craft through the air in 1903: the concept of a manned machine that could travel above the ground was realised. Six years later Louis Bleriot managed to propel a fragile contraption over the English Channel. Then a bi-plane ambitiously flew from London to Manchester. To clarify its route, ground teams along the way laid out big white sheets marked with giant numbers and fired coloured flares into the air so the pilot could look down to see what point he had reached.

The Great War began five years later. Pioneering aircraft teetered over the trenches examining the movement of forces below. A few pilots tried hurling grenades from their cockpits on to the soldiers beneath: bombing began. The Germans developed airships – held aloft by hydrogen – which could slowly meander across the North Sea and decant ordnance on Britain. Meanwhile planes with guns started to harass each other above the battle lines – aerial warfare. And blokes in the trenches took pot shots at those enemy machines above - defence. Eventually the war came to an end; but there is always bitterness following international conflict, and in 1918 the Germans were particularly gloomy at the terms of the treaties imposed by the Allies. The losers bore a grudge which would smoulder through the 1920s.

In 1919 Alcock and Brown made the first non-stop crossing of the Atlantic in an aircraft - sixteen chilly hours. In the same year the first ever passenger flight took place: two people in a cramped cabin - below the pilot's exposed cockpit - journeyed from London to Paris.

Through the 1920s British Empire routes began to be established: Cairo in Egypt was a popular destination; only took a couple of days from Croydon, with decent hotels and fine suppers each evening. A longer series of elegant hops would eventually get one as far as India or South Africa. Meanwhile the Schneider Trophy annual aircraft races were advancing aeronautical design, endurance and speed. A British seaplane won in 1931, having covered the 220 mile course at an average speed of 340 mph.

In the USA postal services took to the air. In 1932 Amelia Earhart was the first woman to fly solo across the Atlantic, then Boeing launched their Model 247, capable of conveying ten passengers at 180 mph. The Americans also devised 'blind-flying' aids – instruments and systems that would allow a plane to travel in bad weather and the dark. But mostly flying was confined to daylight hours and good conditions.

Those post-war treaties prohibited Germany from having military aircraft; however there was nothing to stop them developing passenger planes. Lufthansa began commercial flights in 1926 and ten years later had the largest passenger network in Europe. The grievances which were annoying many Germans started to find a focus in the rantings of Adolf Hitler, who expounded a heated, distorted narrative that blamed Jews, communists, trade unions, any social minority, and most adjoining nations for all the country's troubles. This insignificant but vitriolic survivor of the Great War was soon supported by a gang of racist thugs who propelled him centre stage in regional politics. Eventually about a third of the German nation voted for the Nazi party in 1933 and, on the basis of that proportion of the electorate, Hitler was able to gain power.

View from above

"The Egyptian is a chicken-hearted savage whose resistance will collapse at the sound of the first bomb."

Foreigners held no fear for the man who became known as 'the father of the RAF'. Hugh Trenchard had not found it easy to commence a career in the armed forces, yet he eventually rose to the highest rank in a military service that had not even been thought of when he was born - in Somerset in 1873.

What should we know about this formidable fellow? He was good with guns – thanks to his parents giving him one for his eighth birthday, so he could shoot small mammals in the fields around Taunton. This preparation later helped him win a rifle championship amongst army officers in India.

Hugh struggled to pass exams, hindered by what would one day be described as dyslexia. The army and navy rejected him as a cadet, but his parents paid for him to go to a cramming college, which eventually squeezed him into the Scots Fusiliers. He then deployed three qualities highly advantageous in a military world: he liked sport, had a loud voice and was extremely tall. This got him into a polo team where he played with another keen young soldier, one Winston Churchill, who would prove a valuable contact.

Hugh's battalion was sent to South Africa to help suppress the natives and challenge the Boers. The latter soon wounded him, which resulted in a convalescence trip to Switzerland where, despite his injuries, he took up bobsleighing and swiftly won the 1901 St. Moritz Tobogganing Novices Cup. Next he had a spell in Nigeria 'managing' troublesome locals and surveying undocumented swathes of the British Empire.

He returned to England, where the activity of flying was in its hazardous infancy, and took lessons at Brooklands. Hugh proved not to be a great pilot, possibly due to partial blindness in one eye, but his mighty presence and military track record got him an administration job at an air training school. His career now took off, and by the start of the First World War Lieutenant-Colonel Trenchard was in charge of Britain's Royal Flying Corps.

No-one was quite sure how planes overhead might function in conjunction with armies on the ground, but some generals thought it

11

could be a fruitful experiment. Within a few months Hugh was managing major aerial operations in France, particularly the tactical bombing of enemy troops. He relished this capacity for causing alarm and damage over battlefields, and he also dabbled with offensive action, dispatching bombers behind German lines, even though such outings often resulted in the loss of the machines and men. He patently impressed Field Marshall Haig who later reckoned the most important military discoveries of the war had been barbed wire and Hugh Trenchard.

At the end of hostilities, Winston Churchill, as Secretary of State for Air, assigned Hugh the role of Chief of Air Staff. Good old polo. But the newly-created Royal Air Force had to be severely downsized - by around 90%. However Hugh was determined to maintain a structure that would constitute an independent national fighting force for Britain's future interests, so he established some essential elements, not least, an officer training school at Cranwell in Lincolnshire, and engineering apprenticeship schemes with promises to the best students for future consideration as aircrew. He also fought off frequent attempts by the Army and Navy to absorb the remaining planes, pilots and premises.

As luck would have it, an uprising in Somalia lent itself to aerial suppression, which Trenchard master-minded. Next Mesopotamia (now forming much of Iraq) became agitated, and the RAF was given the task of policing the region in a manner far cheaper and easier than deploying troops. Flying a plane in a menacing manner above an angry bunch of natives would generally be sufficient to disperse them. Firing a few rounds from the cockpit or dropping a hand grenade would certainly scatter the stragglers.

At home, for a much more civilised constituency, Hugh launched the Hendon Air Displays, a great national celebration of Britain's capacity to flourish in the skies. Prior to the miner's strike he suggested to Winston that the RAF could be used to deal with "industrial disturbances or risings" in the UK. His polo pal told him this would not be appropriate.

But in shaping the RAF through the 1920s Air Marshall Trenchard became an ace at public relations, ordering rules and regulations to be drafted on every topic of air policy and practice, which his wife would then help turn into finished form. The great man wrote little but was occasionally required to make a speech. Amongst his more memorable observations were:

"The aeroplane is the most offensive weapon ever invented. Although it is necessary to have some defence to keep up the morale of your own people, it is infinitely more necessary to lower the morale of the people against you by attacking them."

Getting serious

Imagine the party political broadcast on behalf of the Nazi Party – presented to the whole family round their little telly. My view is that had television been invented a bit earlier - so that every European living room had one in its corner by 1930 - then the German electorate would have first seen Hitler on the small screen, in the comfort of their own homes, and quickly concluded that he was a nasty piece of work, best given a wide berth. But where democracy relied on public meetings in public places – such as beer halls, and later in the streets – Adolf and his gruesome gang could frenzy a sour crowd by festering racism and resentment.

The Nazi regime immediately began to build military aircraft - secretly at first, later openly. German officials visited the United States to buy planes and attempt to recruit experienced pilots. The French monitored their neighbours' progress and commenced to build shadow factories far away from Paris, hopefully out of reach of future bombers. In 1936 Germany's Third Reich announced to the world that they had an aircraft element within their Armed Forces. The regime was soon able to give everyone a demonstration of that capacity by contributing to the Spanish Civil War the following year. Guernica proved a convenient showcase for the devastating power of bombing from the air. It was also an ideal training ground for German air crews and flying technology. Picasso presented the ugly outcomes in oil. Four hundred people died in this assault on communist forces in northern Spain.

The fear of aerial bombing had already been elevated by newspaper pundits, while H. G. Wells and other novelists petrified readers with descriptions of future Wars of the Worlds: huge aircraft dropping huge bombs wiping out whole populations at a stroke. At intervals, Westminster debated scenarios for devastation from the air impinging on Britain's safety and security. One Liberal MP estimated that a

European power could drop 600 tons of ordnance on London daily, causing 35,000 deaths each time. A Labour Member took a more strategic approach:

> "When the Germans attack us, they will not bomb London. They will go straight to the aerodromes and to the petrol tanks. Once our aerodromes have been put out of action, the country will be absolutely at the mercy of the enemy."

A Conservative provided a degree of comfort:

> "We have a machine today which can go four miles up in the air within seventeen minutes of the alarm being given. To be able to do that is one of the most amazing achievements of modern engineering."

Prime Minister Stanley Baldwin considered that "the bomber will always get through". Seemingly there was no effective means of universally inhibiting the approach of such a fearsome weapon. In parallel, everyone realised how horrible things turned out if a plane crashed. In the 1920s there were a dozen fatal accidents involving passenger aircraft – six dead here, seven dead there - because that was how many individuals the machines carried. Through the 1930s, fatalities from troubled civilian flights rose to three hundred.

Showing off

"Aren't planes great! Look what they can do."

The annual Royal Air Force Display at Hendon in 1933 took place a few months after Hitler had declared himself Chancellor of Germany. The illustrated programme for the event on Saturday 24th June reveals a touching naivety about the capacity of the Force's planes and the circumstances in which they might be used. All the craft were bi-planes, the fuselage sandwiched at right-angles between a pair of wings. The crowd would be admiring magnificent men in their flying machines, thanks to a buoyant industry spread across England: A.V. Roe and Blackburn in the north; Saunders-Roe and Supermarine on the south coast; Boulton & Paul and Short Bros eastward; The Bristol Aircraft Company and Westland to the west; Armstrong Whitworth and Gloster in the Midlands; De Havilland, Handley Page and Vickers around London. Their marketing messages conveyed the essential agenda: brilliant engineering capable of extraordinary achievement:

'The General Purpose Biplane that flew twice over Mount Everest'

These bearings form the accepted standard for aviation duty, used in the overwhelming majority of cases where reliability is of the utmost importance'

'A very high all-round performance, but in spite of its high top speed it is extremely easy to fly or land'

'World's Non-Stop Flight Record (5,340 miles in 57.5 hours) and the World's Altitude Record (43,975 feet, over eight miles) were both achieved on K.L.G. sparking plugs'

'When Supreme Reliability is Essential'

Visitors could witness a succession of aerial exercises; even mock battles. Demonstrations included Supply Dropping, Low Flying Attacks and Message Picking-up:

'The message is placed in a bag and attached to a loop of cord suspended from two light uprights. The pilot flies so that a grapnel hook, which can be lowered from below the aircraft, passes between the uprights and the message is collected.'

Concluding the flying displays was the Set Piece, an aerial drama wherein belligerent REDLAND, 'in disregard of her covenants', has commenced a war against benign BLUELAND – and is attacking the latter's vital sea communications:

'An air raid warning is received, the siren is sounded and the Fighter Squadron is dispatched to intercept.'

'...the raiders appear from the opposite direction, having made use of cloud formations in order to deceive the Defence, and are immediately engaged by the Anti-Aircraft Guns.'

'In spite of their utmost endeavours, the outnumbered defending aircraft are unable to prevent the attackers' bombing activities, and the Base is destroyed.'

Could the moral of this story be that BLUELAND needed more and better aircraft? Hugh Trenchard often hovered around the Royal enclosure to provide an unofficial commentary on the implications of these scenarios for the King. And doubtless parties of Germans would have discreetly alighted from the London Electric Railway at Colindale

Station to attend the show and evaluate what the Brits could currently achieve. Certainly domestic plane designers realised there was room for improvement. Both the Hurricane and the Spitfire began to be developed soon after this distinguished festival of flight.

Perhaps the most poignant panel in the charming souvenir booklet is the half-page allocated to a flying school based at Heston Airport, Hounslow:

> 'Today you are seeing many breath-taking stunts in the air. "If that's flying", perhaps you say, "I'd rather stay on terra firma". But please do remember that the stunts are for your entertainment. Flying, straightforward everyday flying, is a practical safe pastime; and there is no earthy reason why YOU shouldn't fly. Hundreds of people, for business and social reasons, have made up their minds to learn. To them we say, "Come down to Heston –have lunch or tea in our restaurant – watch the flying – talk to our pilot instructors – learn how simple and safe aviation actually is."

Who knows how many of the readers explored that offer and so invested some of their disposable income to learn to fly, and thus became pilots who would swiftly be absorbed by the RAF when huge numbers were suddenly needed - as REDLAND's aggression approached the white cliffs.

Peace in our time?

Early in the 1930s, Hugh Trenchard, aged 57, chose to retire from the top Air job and instead entered the House of Lords. However he kept a quasi-official role in the RAF hierarchy which allowed him to continue lobbying for what he saw as the Force's interests, even to the point of persuading the Air Ministry to redeploy senior personnel when he considered their performance inadequate.

An American journalist, Hubert Knickerbocker, after an investigative tour of 'the European capitals', concluded that:

> 'The armaments race is on. Germany, France, Britain, Russia, Japan and Italy are off on the race that ends in the Olympic games of death.'

From the mid-1930s, defying the appeasement lobby, the RAF rapidly acquired swathes of farmland on which it contracted the laying down of long strips of concrete or tarmac and the erection of buildings to house staff and machines. Pits were dug - well away from the over-ground structures - for securing the weaponry soon to be delivered to each embryonic aerodrome. More than 400 air stations were established, to accommodate one or more squadrons, each with 16 or so serviceable aircraft on stand-by, supported by 2,000 personnel. Airfields close to the coast had shelters built for ground crew to occupy in the face of direct attacks by the Luftwaffe (German for Air Force). Elsewhere 60,000 hospital beds were being set aside to receive the possible casualties from the first weeks of aerial bombardment.

As a belligerent Germany flexed its muscles and pushed into adjoining territory, how did the balance of air forces look? The Luftwaffe had grown fast – with many powerful aircraft and keen, capable pilots, who had discreetly developed their training aboard gliders. Britain, France, Poland, Russia and Italy also had home grown air forces but none were a match for the German air fleets. By 1939 the Luftwaffe had more than 1,000 fighter aircraft – fast planes bristling with machine guns – and 2,000 bombers. The dreaded Stuka dive-bomber design had been based on studies of American stunt flying. It could roar steeply down towards a target releasing its ordnance at the last moment then veer upward out of harm's way.

Britain possessed 600 fighters and 500 bombers, mostly out-dated and not all ready for action. The Royal Air Force had no wish to put its limited assets to any serious test. The Air Ministry in Whitehall received almost daily memoranda from senior RAF personnel requesting bigger commitments to better aircraft. Whether Trenchard's successors did enough to beef up the Force through the 1930s would remain a moot point for many years. As an elderly statesman of military flying, his Lordship visited many British air stations. Crews recall a big man with a handlebar moustache offering kindly encouragement in a booming voice. The esteemed visitor would make jokes about the Luftwaffe and point out that it was reasonable to:

"...terrorise munitions workers into absenting themselves from work."

* * * * * *

The Second World War as conducted in the air was one of the most widespread, complicated, dangerous and deadly activities ever undertaken by mankind. It saw the construction of half a million aircraft, the deaths of a quarter of a million Allied airmen, and the killing of millions of people below, mostly civilians.

The fundamental principle was for armed machines to dominate the skies and deliver abrupt and arbitrary violence to enemies - all designed to encourage the surviving recipients to surrender. Tragically, the blood spilled, injuries sustained, lives lost, structures destroyed, only stimulated the opponents to pursue acts of retaliation. Hence the staggering enormity of the aggressive endeavours.

And, of course, for everyone who managed to live through those years, no-one knew how or when it might end. Only we, with hindsight, can view the arc of the events. At the time, at home or away, almost all of it was absolutely terrible, and it went on and on and on; and generally got worse and worse and worse.

1939

WHAT A START

Keep your seat belts fastened while we gain height. First, the good news: all the major nations signed an agreement to say they would not bomb civilians. As we now know, this honourable intention would become a bit dented, then badly damaged, then abandoned, in a school-playground-style process of tit-for-tat. But that was some way off.

After Prime Minister Chamberlain declared war on Germany at 11.00 am on Sunday 3rd September 1939, how long before the RAF suffered its first casualty? In accordance with Sod's Law, less than two hours. Twenty-eight year old John Issac was undertaking his second solo training flight on a Blenheim from Hendon. But his engine cut out, and the plane came crashing down close to the Town Hall south-east of the airfield. Pilot Officer Issac died, as did a member of the public on a Sunday lunchtime walk.

John Issac was a young partner at a London solicitors' practice, who had learned to fly as a hobby, then joined a Hendon squadron as a part-timer. Issac is commemorated in Golders Green Crematorium with a single line inscription on a Commonwealth War Graves plaque. He was the first of more than 70,000 young men who died flying for the RAF during the war. Tragically, the thick law of Sod had merely opened its first page.

Meanwhile Bomber Command (BC) was sending an aircraft across the North Sea to undertake some reconnaissance on the movements of the German navy. Eventually the plucky crew spotted some naval vessels at sea. Did they radio back to base to call up further planes – craft that could attack the military shipping? They thought they could, and they thought they had. But the radio messages never reached their destination in one piece. The receivers merely picked up a long garbled noise. Only when the exploratory crew returned did their colleagues acquire the news of the enemy ships at sea.

Something disconcerting here. Operational commanders knew war was on the cards. Yes, they had a spotter plane ready to roll, but the radio system back to their ground base would not work. Regrettably, things not working properly, or breaking down at the worst possible moment, would happen frequently in the months ahead.

From other British airfields 27 planes were dispatched to find the German fleet off the coast of Denmark. They couldn't. In parallel 10 aircraft took off on a mission to drop propaganda leaflets over northern Germany. The planes crossed the North Sea, but one failed to get beyond France. Due to engine problems it was forced to land in a field of cabbages, some of which were propelled into the aircraft as it shuddered to a halt. Mercifully, no crewman was injured by flying vegetable. Wouldn't that have been embarrassing! But now the Royal Air Force had one valuable machine stuck on a French farm, unable to contribute in the foreseeable future to the defence of Britain or to menace her enemies.

Next day, following another frustrating failure of radio communication, 29 aircraft set off to assault ships in the vicinity of the German naval base at Wilhelmshaven – halfway along the coast between Holland and Denmark. But they were met by fearsome anti-aircraft fire and a bunch of highly effective German fighter planes. Most of the British bombs dropped fruitlessly into the sea, a few bounced across the armour-plated deck of a battleship and splashed into the water. Some aircraft were shot down by ship or shore guns. Several were damaged by Messerschmitt fighter planes. One British aircraft crashed onto a German warship killing some of the sailors as well as the airmen.

The barrage of defensive effort rapidly resulted in seven British bombers being lost; that is, being unable to return to base. They were sufficiently damaged to catch fire and crash to the ground, or be forced to land in the vicinity of the air battle. That is a lousy decision for a pilot to have to make. Your aircraft is not up to re-crossing the North Sea. Do you try to bring it down? In which case it, and you, fall into enemy hands. Or should everyone jump out to allow the plane to crash some way off, while you and your colleagues hope for a smooth, safe parachute descent, well away from the nearest German soldier?

The statistics don't reveal the hasty decision-making in the cockpit. They simply tell us that 25 British aircrew died that day. And two relatively-lucky crew members who landed in one piece became the first British prisoners-of-war: Sergeant Booth and Aircraftsman Slattery. In anyone's fight, that would be described as a bloody nose. Twenty-five RAF airmen dead. And no discernible damage to any German ships.

The Second World War had begun.

Don't hurt anyone

It would be a terrible thing to drop a bomb somewhere and so accidentally injure, or even worse, kill an innocent member of the public. Before the war there had been many anguished discussions as to what constituted appropriate targets: would it be okay to bomb enemy airfields, troops on the ground, a moving armoured column? What about railway stations, road junctions, bridges? Could you define and isolate an area populated by people in uniform as opposed to civilians? What about factories making arms for the war? Were the workers innocent bystanders or guilty of war-mongering?

As the RAF fellows first flew across the North Sea with their early generation bombs slung below, the plan was to avoid civilian deaths. Of course, boats in harbours might have civilians aboard - as guests, or workers from the dockyards undertaking maritime maintenance. Hence the chaps in the sky were looking down for German naval vessels under power. If they could spot such Third Reich representatives out on the high seas, then that was fair game. They could drop a bomb on the ship. Or could they?

It proved damned difficult to see any vessels anywhere across all that water, and the big boats that did appear on the horizon, when you got close to them, looked mostly like fishing or merchant craft. Chances of happening upon a real German Navy steamer were extremely low. And if you did see one beneath, could you decant your weapon to reach it? The sailors had guns on the deck which they started firing in your direction as soon as you approached their vicinity. You needed to estimate the precise moment you should release your ordnance from any particular height to have half a chance of its trajectory taking it anywhere near the vessel sailing forward at maybe 15 miles an hour while you're doing 150 mph. Almost impossible. And you only have a couple of chances, because your plane is only carrying a couple of bombs (that was all it was ever designed to carry), and each time you try to pass over the ship, the men on the guns get better at controlling the arc of their ammunition and so become more likely to reach your craft – which is not what you want when you are up in the air and a long way from home.

Fact was, many senior air officers had not really comprehended just how problematic such a simple-sounding exercise would prove to be in practice. Any schoolboy with a toy aeroplane can envisage the manoeuvre that results in a bomb from a plane dropping on the deck of a ship and blasting the latter to smithereens. And almost all politicians were once schoolboys with toy weaponry. So they imagined this should be a piece of cake. In practice it was staggeringly difficult. But how does a man in uniform, who has received an enormous slice of the country's military budget, break the news to his bosses that destroying enemy ships at sea is not really something the Force currently has the means to accomplish? (A scientific solution to the tricky ambition of hitting a specific ship in a specific place with one particular weapon was decades away: to be demonstrated with Exocet missiles at the Falkland Islands in the 1980s.)

Only bright spot: as long as the UK directed its efforts to bombing German naval vessels at sea, the chances of unintended civilian casualties were low indeed.

The sun was in my eyes
Rudimentary radar – that was going to give the Brits a big advantage – if it worked, and if we knew how to use it. A series of first generation radio-direction-finding (RDF) devices had been erected along the south-east corner of the British coast, facing out to sea. Patently it was essential that the manning and comprehension of the screens was well managed: trained personnel able to assess flickering electronic smudges representing objects in the perimeter skies to determine which might be enemy planes on the move.

Co-ordinating reports of possible airborne breaches of our borders was critical, as was all decision-making about the deployment of our fighter aircraft to attempt to approach and challenge those alien planes.

Understandably it takes a bit of time to get the system working properly. The chaps at those lovely new aerodromes were eager to give the Hun a bloody nose, but initial endeavours went a bit pear-shaped. On Wednesday 6th September, just three days on from the Declaration of War, one of the RDF squads on the Essex coast registered some aircraft high in the sky. They phoned in a report and soon a dozen RAF fighter planes were sent up to investigate. Several more aircraft joined them shortly afterwards from other East Anglian airfields.

In bright sunlight, different bunches of planes were now heading towards each other, manned by pilots attracted to the prospective glory of being first to resist the intruders. A couple of our brave boys start to shoot at approaching aircraft. One plane was damaged and a pilot was killed. But these were not Luftwaffe invaders; they were other RAF units which had come into the area from a different direction without liaison with the squadron already on their way there. And now an eager anti-aircraft battery managed to fire a few rounds into the fuselage of what turned out to be another British plane – which would hence require some serious attention from mechanics before being airworthy again.

Naturally the incident was covered up. Highly hush-hush. Wags who later found out about this unfortunate misunderstanding and its fatal consequences would cruelly refer to it as the Battle of Barking Creek. However this was an incredibly useful lesson. The teams needed better monitoring and analysis of those radio direction screens; improved identification, sharper reporting, smarter flight management and clearer aerial procedures. Fighter Command learned a lot. Secretly, several officers were sacked, and the story was kept out of the papers for many years. This must not happen again; we will call it teething troubles.

Aiming high

'Flying is not one of those arts which can be acquired by self-tuition. There is no recognised system of study which will give the would-be pilot knowledge enough to take a machine into the air without practical experience. It is certainly true that in the pioneering days flying had to be self-taught and that even recently there have been cases of people taking a chance by flying a machine without previous experience or instruction. These latter exploits have generally ended very unhappily, which is in itself proof that expert guidance at the beginning of a pilot's career is very necessary.'

...from a 1930s Introduction to Aviation.

Following the deaths of those Bomber Command airmen on the 4th September, questions were asked about the adequacy of training. However much preparation the chaps had had through the summer months, clearly it was not enough. In fact, in the two years prior to the war BC pilots had found it necessary to make a number of forced landings whilst on training flights across the UK. They had bumpily come down because they had got lost and were running out of fuel. Nearly 500 such incidents were recorded.

On 5th September, a Pilot Officer on a training flight over Yorkshire in his Hampden bomber misjudged a turn - the speed, the angle, the wind - or something went wrong with the plane - and he crashed into a field and died. Mercifully he was alone. But the force had lost another pilot and another aircraft. Was the problem classroom syllabus, cockpit technique or mechanical issues - perhaps yet to be identified?

8th September, another training flight, this time in Suffolk: a bomber inexplicably flew into trees and killed the crew of five. There goes another valuable aircraft and out must go letters of commiseration to the families of the unfortunate victims.

A few days later, on a leafleting mission, a Whitley bomber crashed south of Hamburg, but the crew survived and so raised the RAF's prisoner-of-war numbers to seven. Next day in Somerset, a Blenheim on a training flight fell from the sky. Next day a Whitley was taking off from a French aerodrome and it crashed. The war had been going on for just a week and the UK had lost thirteen aircraft, three on training flights, resulting in 34 dead airmen and seven fellows banged up in German prisons.

William Chorley's sober volumes, documenting the final flight of every BC craft and crew, reveal the portfolio of tragic circumstances when endeavours in the sky took a turn for the worst and terminated the life of someone's son: crashes into cloud-covered hills, crunches into hills clearly visible ahead. Slicing into high voltage cables strung between steel towers. Had they seen those brutal wires? Collisions with other aircraft on take-off; a crash landing because the undercarriage jammed. Elsewhere a deadly descent due to elevator locks 'wrongly positioned'.

Frequently the people making the biggest errors - or discovering, when it's too damned late to do anything about it, that there is a fatal flaw in the design or build or servicing of a particular aircraft - those pilots who died at the joystick - didn't learnt a lesson that would be much use to them. They and their shocking experience were lost. And this was in the days before flight recorders; prior to when a couple of engineers could dig around in wreckage and extract black boxes that might allow them to theoretically re-construct the final minutes of that doomed flight and so discover what had been going horribly wrong.

After three further weeks of training, the Force was left with eight less aeroplanes, 37 fewer men.

Encountering the enemy

Through the autumn Bomber Command undertook numerous reconnaissance missions. Some were to compensate for the force's frustrating lack of maps of north-west Europe, but most of it was just flying at a safe height over the Germans on the ground trying to spot what they were up to. Old hands from the Great War had made similar expeditions. You could learn a lot.

Was this more hazardous than training? In September, on reconnaissance trips, ten aircraft were lost. Five were shot down by Messerschmitts (speedy, nippy fighters, armed with high-powered guns); the other five crashed for reasons we don't know. In terms of fatalities, 15 airmen died on those flights.

What about operations? The first aerial engagement between British and German fighter planes took place over the German coast on 20th

September. Three craft on each side. This would be a good test. It resulted in two of the RAF machines being shot up and crashing to the ground. But six days later, Britain got her own back. A German plane was flying close to the Scottish coast. An RAF patrol fired at the intruder and caused it to fall into the sea, where Royal Navy sailors rescued the survivors. Now a new problem: what do we do with the captured German airmen?

On 29th September, five British bombers headed for Heligoland, the bay in the western neck of the Danish peninsula. All five were shot down; sixteen crewmen died, four became prisoners of war. 16th October, German planes attack British naval vessels in the Firth of Forth. Spitfires intercept and three intruding craft splash into the sea, only one crewman surviving. The Spitfire showed its stuff. But another prisoner of war. Where to put them? How to treat them?

Next day, more Luftwaffe planes cross the North Sea. These make for Scapa Flow and one drops the first German bomb to land on the United Kingdom. It hits the island of Hoy where it does no more than make a hole in the ground; but nevertheless an unpleasant event - an uneasy feeling about what those nasty things can do. Someone needs to check that nothing dangerous remains within the scattered fragments before they are cleared up and carted away - probably by the military, who want to take a good look at the bits of bomb to see what can be learned about German munitions technology.

Meanwhile, the Luftwaffe were proving a key component in advancing German forces across Poland - blasting everything a few miles in front of the ground troops to ease their progress. Warsaw, the Polish capital, needed to be overwhelmed. The invaders bombed and strafed it, killing 25,000 people in a fortnight. Now the German Air Force really could brandish a fearsome reputation.

By the end of November – three months into the war - as a result of problems and challenges during Operations, 50 BC aircraft had been lost. But alongside that, in training and other non-operational flights, 70 planes were destroyed.

What do we know about the last minutes of those terrifying flights? There were undercarriage problems: some wouldn't go up, others wouldn't come down; others collapsed whilst taxying. One aircraft landed on the runway, then its brakes failed so it skewed ferociously into the side of a hanger. One aircraft crash-landed on top of a hangar, killing the airmen, and maiming engineers in the building. Another aircraft stalled on take-off and fell on top of the Officer's Mess killing the pilot and two chaps who were taking a break.

Perhaps worst were mid-air collisions: one plane crunches into another. If you are teaching people to fly, best to have a great big cube of airspace dedicated exclusively to that one aircraft and its crew - no other planes anywhere near that giant invisible box. You don't want two planes travelling through the same bit of sky, with one of them, at least, full of folk who are not absolutely sure what they're doing. They're concentrating on something else - maybe wondering what a certain handle is for, or what a particular switch does. Then, out of the blue, when it's far too late, someone looks up and sees another plane heading straight for them – perhaps piloted by someone also struggling to command their craft.

Now what? Is there time for evasive action? Changing tack can work quite well with boats in the sea, because they move very slowly, so there's plenty of time to steer a fresh course to avoid a collision. Planes – different matter: one pilot swerves left and the other pilot swerves right, so they're still heading towards each other – at maybe 300 hundred miles an hour. Bang. Two aircraft lost in a horrific moment. Plus all aboard.

Those were cases wherein one could understand what had happened. Even more alarming were inexplicable terminations: over the fields of east Anglia, Kent, Yorkshire, no enemy in sight – an aircraft suddenly yaws up in the air, or spins wildly, or hurtles down straight into the soil. People couldn't even imagine what might have caused such violent aberrations from a viable trajectory. Additionally, many planes just disappeared without trace. No one ever learnt what became of the craft or the fellows at the controls. They must have gone into the sea. Or were wrecked amidst remote hills – the remains not discovered for months.

Mercifully there were sometimes tales of survival: Sergeant Griffin was a rear gunner on a Whitley bomber over France on 27th October. It was cold and miserable and lonely down at that back end of the plane. Just the intercom to keep you updated on the pilots' actions and plans. The weather was terrible; freezing cold. The aircraft engines started to ice up. The skipper decided it was impossible to fly back to Britain, so he told everyone to bale out.

Sergeant Griffin didn't get the message: intercom malfunction. He sat there unaware of the situation as his colleagues floated down on to French soil. The aircraft had been left heading westward. Despite the icing, it crossed the North Sea, then it started to drop and eventually reached an English farmer's field. It didn't turn over or catch on fire. It bumped and banged and skidded and shuddered before eventually coming to a clumsy halt, roughing up the Sergeant no end. He climbed out of his turret and braced up to discuss with the skipper why they had all suffered such a lousy landing. But no sign of the pilot, or the rest of the crew. Griffin was mystified. Only days later did he learn they were all in France.

Another rear gunner was less lucky. On 15th November at RAF Heyford, a bomb mission training flight. The crew of three – pilot, navigator and rear gunner – were conveying a 20 pound bomb – just for practice. Flight went okay, so they came in to land. Touched down, started to brake - and the bomb fell off. It exploded immediately – destroying the tail of the plane and killing the rear gunner who, of course, was horribly close to the deadly device when it impacted with the concrete. The pilot and navigator would fly another day. In this case they had learnt an applicable lesson – at the cost of the rear gunner's life.

Not every crash was fatal. One aircraft which overturned when it touched down was examined carefully and judged to be damaged "beyond economical repair", but, the report explained, the crew merely "suffered a bad shaking". Doubtless the top brass at the Air Ministry had their own sort of bad shaking when they contemplated the statistics emerging from the first three months of endeavour – a painful and death-peppered learning curve.

Where the hell is Heligoland?
Every few days Bomber Command aircraft would try to negotiate the long, cold, wet and windy North Sea in order to spot and spit at some vessel that was surely a military menace designed to sooner or later do the Allies harm. Germany did not have a huge length of coastline adjacent to the Atlantic; just the short, north-west-facing stretch between Holland and Denmark. So not many convenient places to harbour naval vessels. One vital spot was Heligoland, near the mouth of the River Elbe. Up river, travelling south-east, one would find Hamburg – a juxtaposition that would prove critical for future air strikes.

Lots of the German Navy's best ships were docked around Heligoland, amidst dedicated resources, well defended. So it was a suitable destination for BC, as there were plenty of sailors and not too many civilians. During October and November, as the days shortened and the weather worsened, minor missions against enemy ships were intermittently tackled and often aborted or defeated.

On 14th December, BC braced up for a bigger trip towards Heligoland, despatching a dozen planes, but the Luftwaffe were ready to confront them. However, half the British aircraft got back: a better proportion of returns compared with earlier sorties, but still a painful outing. Four days later, they tried again. 22 planes set off; 12 were shot down and three crashed on their return flight; more than 50 crew lost. The airmen now hated Heligoland. The hierarchy tried to lay the blame for the grim fatality figures on inadequate formation flying and poor squadron leadership.

Three RAF bombers went back to the hellish bay on 2nd January. Two were shot down by a dozen Messerschmitts, three of which were lost in the encounter. You can look at those numbers in various ways: three-quarters of the German squadron survived; 67% of the RAF's complement failed to return; more German planes were lost than British. As we shall see, newspaper editors would soon find ways to present uncensored data to cheer their readership, dismay opponents.

The next big attempt to tackle the enemy fleet would be on 12th April 1940, when 83 British bombers went out and 74 returned. This was a healthier statistic. There was virtue in travelling in numbers. The German fighters could only pick off a limited proportion of your planes.

The more craft, the lower the percentage lost. That had to be better, surely? Accountancy-wise, yes; fatality-wise, not necessarily.

Mass communication

From the off, Bomber Command directed planes into German airspace to distribute messages from the British Government to enemy citizens. The first million leaflets fluttered across the roofs of Hamburg and Bremen - and doubtless plenty of farmers' fields and patches of the North Sea:

> *Attention, (Achtung!) Germans, note that, in spite of the German blood which has been shed in the Polish war...*
> *One. Your Government's hope of successful Blitzkrieg has been destroyed by the British Cabinet's decision to prepare for a three years' war.*
> *Two. In the west, British troops are already standing shoulder to shoulder with their French Allies.*
> *Three. Our fleets have swept German merchant shipping from the oceans.*
> *Four. Night after night the British Air Force has demonstrated its power by flights far into German territory.*

The recipients of the literature knew this last bit was true. How else could the paper have reached their back garden in the dark? But would such information stimulate the average Hamburger into second thoughts? Cause him or her to question the legitimacy of the Nazi regime? Seek to overthrow political leadership?

That leadership was not democratic, and soon imposed harsh penalties on citizens found in possession of enemy propaganda. By harsh, this could be all the way up to hanging, with the rest of the family banged up in a concentration camp. It was making an example of the guilty party in order to deter others. Generally worked immensely well.

Nevertheless, a dedicated team in the UK War Office saw great virtue in bulk dissemination of info by aircraft. On 1st October three million leaflets sprinkled from the European sky pointing out that many Nazi party leaders had siphoned off their financial assets to South America or Japan for the moment when the regime collapsed and they needed to make a quick but comfortable getaway.

Later in the autumn 26 cities received selected quotes from 'Mein Kampf' exposing Adolf Hitler's alarming values, including:

> *The most effective weapon to replace reason – intimidation and physical force.*

Of course, many Germans knew this by now, but did not necessarily anticipate the full nature of the prospects ahead.

On Christmas Eve 700,000 unseasonable leaflets were scattered in 'nickel' raids above urban Germany, quoting passages from Prime Minister Chamberlain's BBC broadcast speech of November 26th about the capacity of the British to face up to nasty Nazi aggression wherever and however.

Start of the New Year, our boys supplied fresh thoughts:

Hamburg – ruined by the Nazis – young upstarts without education, practical knowledge or experience. Hamburg is a dead city.

That outcome lay some way off. The tone and look of the pamphlets came to resemble leader articles from popular newspapers. One included photographs taken by RAF cameras over Hamburg, thus confirming the Force's capacity to fly above the city in daylight. This leaflet was headed:

The Lion has wings.

The Command found the flights useful for practicing navigation technique. But unloading the cargo was a challenge. Someone had to untie the packages and hurl the paperwork down the flare chute. Station officers warned crew of the dangers of failing to cut the strings. A heavy packet of leaflets might drop toward the ground and hurt someone. However it was all good training, and who knows, those messages might have dismayed enough Germans to shorten the war in some way. They surely sowed seeds of doubt in the minds of the population they reached, and certainly telegraphed potential trouble ahead for your average Hamburg citizen.

A later RAF Commander dismissed the sheaves of advocacy as merely providing Germans with free toilet paper, but I contend they had greater value. Assuming someone had the nerve to show their boss what was falling from the skies, the harsh critiques must have wrong-footed Hitler – perhaps the first time he would have encountered meaty, intelligent overseas resistance to his ugly agenda.

More than a hundred leaflet missions were flown - long journeys in very cold conditions, wherein propellers might ice up and flick daggers of ice into the side of the plane. Everyone aboard was in danger of

31

frostbite, however only a small percentage of aircraft were lost on these sorties. And some planes brought all their correspondence back because they couldn't find the required location for their distribution. The Daily Express identified a gap in official recognition of the communication efforts:

> 'There are some heroes missing from the latest list of R.A.F. awards. They are the men who have carried out our air leaflet raids in Germany. So far during the war not one member of a bomber crew has been decorated for leaflet raiding. If the full stories of the leaflet raids could be told they would be appreciated as some of the epic flights of this war.'

Yes, there was a long way to go. The "white bombs" had not brought the Third Reich to its knees. But what would?

Four frightful months

Patently a huge proportion of early endeavours in the air had the capacity to go horribly wrong. The planes were nothing like as reliable as people were led to believe. And the crew often did not know what to do for the best when something went wrong - all before encountering anything that could be described as opposing forces.

The Polish air force had been more or less eliminated by the Blitzkrieg tactics of the Luftwaffe in September, though a few of the Polish planes made an escape to Romania, and some of those pilots joined the RAF to help out. Hermann Goering, the big, blingy, Luftwaffe boss, loudly grumbled about the loss of 200 aircraft and more than 100 pilots from Germany's assault on her neighbours.

Toward the end of October a German intruder over Scotland was engaged by the RAF, causing the enemy plane to crash not far from Edinburgh, killing all aboard. As soon as word got round, hundreds of sight-seers turned up to peer at the wreckage. Additional problems: what do we do with foreign planes and bodies that have crunched down on home turf? And how do we keep the crowds at bay?

Other UK war administration was making headway: by November the Women's Auxiliary Air Force had recruited more than 8,000 personnel and revealed that it was willing to take on females aged up to fifty providing - they had experience of radar plotting. The Commonwealth Air Training Scheme had started in Canada: wide, open spaces; no more prangs between two planes above the same busy British airfield.

Over in Scandinavia, fierce little Finland was now in the process of eliminating 500 Russian aircraft as the nation attempted to protect its borders from the communist invaders.

On 3rd December, during another BC attempt to hit warships around Heligoland, a bomb failed to release from its lugs and as the pilot continued forward he briefly travelled over the mainland, at which point the bomb popped off, hence delivering the first item of British ordnance on to German soil.

By now some friends had started to lend a hand: an Indian Prince paid for a fleet of aircraft: the Hyderabad Squadron; and a whole Australian air contingent turned up to share the load. There would be many invaluable inputs from overseas to come.

By the end of the year a total of 68 Bomber Command aircraft had been lost on Operations, while a stinging 78 had been destroyed in non-operational duties. Almost 300 RAF air crew had been killed, and 27 were in German prison camps.

What lay ahead? Everyone in the UK connected with the principles and practice of aerial warfare was sobered by the alarming statistics so far. From the humblest factory worker churning out multiple parts for aircraft engines to every individual in every squadron – the trainers, engineers, support staff, flyers – all realised they needed to do better. So too, the executive officers in Whitehall: try harder, work smarter, find better solutions, systems, strategies. Keep at it. There was no alternative but to get out there and improve performance, whatever the cost.

No-one knew this now but, of the air crew available to the Royal Air Force at the commencement of the war, 90% would be dead before it was over.

1940

LUFTWAFFE OVERHEAD

'What is the nation's main task in the coming year?'

... was the question asked in the Daily Express Opinion column on Monday 1st January 1940. The answer:

> 'The development of our Empire and the mobilisation of its resources. The Empire is giving us freely of men and wealth. More Canadian troops arrive – the French Navy co-operating in bringing them across the Atlantic, for the first time. The Empire is our strength in the hour of battle, and it must be our glory when peace returns.'

The proprietor of the Express was a Canadian, Max Aitken, elevated to the title Lord Beaverbrook. He took a special interest in aeronautical matters and would soon have a formal role in the advancement of aerial capacities in Britain. His first edition of the New Year included a summary of the state of play:

> 'Aircraft production is 100% greater than January 1, 1938, and planes are being turned out faster than the R.A.F. can absorb them. Britain has very large secret reserves of aircraft.'
>
> 'America is building more than 6,000 warplanes for the Allies. The merits of our warplanes have been proved. The German Messerschmitt is shown as a failure. Nothing has as yet beaten our Spitfires and Hurricanes.'

Not much to worry about then. If Hitler had this translated, he would realise that mighty forces lay across the Channel.

No news of recent R.A.F. combat activity, but a double-sided dig at the Russians. On the front page, we learn they are a menace:

REDS BOMB 12 TOWNS

'Squadron after squadron of Russian planes flew over Finland yesterday, unloading hundreds of bombs on a dozen towns. It was one of the worst air-raid days Finland had known.'

While on the back page we discover:
SOVIET ARMADA SHAM EXPOSED
'The Allied High Command have received details of the much-vaunted Red Air Force, which shows it to be a bigger sham than the Red Army. For her 4,000 mile wide continent Russia has a first line strength of little more than 4,465 machines. Compared with the latest products of the chief Western European powers 65% of the Red machines are obsolete.'

The Fuhrer must have found these revelations encouraging. The Express allocated a few column inches to the Reich Minister of Propaganda's New Year message:
"Germany is prepared politically, economically and spiritually to defy the attacks of her enemies. Only one thing is certain about the New Year. It will be a hard one, and we will have to keep a stiff upper lip."

So not just a British posture. The diabolical Nazi propaganda guru, Goebbels (hereinafter to be referred to as PGG), continued:
"There is no longer any doubt that the war-mongers in Paris and London want to tear Germany apart and annihilate the German people. In vain they repeat the cant that they only wish to destroy Hitlerism. We know that kind of talk from the past. Our Reich of 90,000,000 people stands in the way of their plans to rule the world. They hate our people because it is decent, brave, diligent, conscientious, and intelligent."

The Express reported that PGG had mounted exhibitions in Berlin and Munich designed to show how Britain has always "stolen the spoils of the world."

Next day, under a banner proclaiming '122nd day of the war against Hitlerism', the Express featured a front page report of our boys' New Year endeavours in the sky:
R.A.F. SEND BOMBER DOWN IN FLAMES
'For half an hour yesterday three British Coastal Command planes fought two German Heinkels over the sea 130 miles off the East Scottish coast. Officially admitting the loss of a plane, the Germans last night explained that "before the fight the machine developed a technical hitch and was thus not fully ready for combat". They claimed that one British plane was

so damaged that "it certainly failed to reach its home station." The British Air Ministry say all three R.A.F. planes "resumed their patrol".'

The back page provided re-assuring news from the Shetland Isles:
NAZI PLANE DIVES AT WARSHIP
'Result of Field-Marshall Goering's first air raid on Britain in 1940 was: One Nazi plane shot down; three British sheep killed.'

The 'World's largest selling daily' reckoned:
'Europe is now faced again with a renewal of Hitler's war of threats, with its prediction every other day of a "great offensive" or "terrible blows" against the Western Powers. This may be just a part of Hitler's war of nerves and war of boredom. On the other hand, there may be something behind it this time.
Whichever it is, the people Who Should Know say that nothing of a very spectacular nature is to be expected before February. Most possible action by Hitler would be an attempt to avoid France's Maginot Line in the north by a drive through Holland and Belgium. This would give Goering air bases nearer to Britain, so that his fighter planes could escort bombers on air raids on Britain.'

Sitting ducks

When you have acquired, checked and prepared for combat a squadron of planes and positioned them appropriately close to the runway, there's nothing worse than for those valuable machines to be damaged, and so not be able to take-off. Unfortunately this happened, far too often. The Germans came over and bombed and strafed aircraft, breaking them up or setting them on fire. And some had never even flown in action.

The Luftwaffe relished this alarming intervention: reaching an enemy airfield to find aircraft dotted about with almost no defences to inhibit the intruders. In minutes a few German fighters could do massive amounts of damage. Sweeping down to rattle bullets and propel ordnance into everything below only occurred intermittently, but the annoyance factor was enormous.

British airmen first tasted such humiliation after they took squadrons of planes across the Channel to help the French resist the advance of the German army. Over a few days in May 1940, the RAF lost hundreds of aircraft on temporary airfields. The planes that managed to take off and attempt to tackle the enemy fared little better. The machines were out-manoeuvred and out-gunned by the German invaders and so were shot down by the dozen.

The best craft that France and Britain could muster first faced the Luftwaffe on 10th May when 400 of them were lost. Next day, the destruction tally totalled 300; same number the day after that, followed by a hundred more every day for the next week - in all a loss of around 2,000 planes, which cost the Luftwaffe 1,100 craft in the engagements. Sixty per cent of the UK's contribution to the combined Allied fleets was eliminated.

Time for a quick exit. Air men could fly back to Britain – albeit severely overloading their transport in the process - but the army needed shipping to return to home shores. As we know, the Navy was generously supplemented by hundreds of small boats – fishing and leisure vessels – that crossed the English Channel to spend a few perilous minutes in the shallows at Dunkirk in order to take on board as many men as possible who had waded out for a ride home.

Senior strategist Lord Gort made several well-intentioned but poorly-received speeches from a vantage point on the sand dunes, thanking all the chaps for what they had done so far and ensuring them that there would be marvellous opportunities ahead to tackle those terrible German soldiers again. His pep talks were interrupted by the scattering of men in all directions whenever an aircraft approached, because this was likely to be a lone Luftwaffe plane attempting to assault those below.

Hundreds on the beaches were wounded, dozens died. Many escaping troops blamed the RAF for failing to protect them, but in fact British airmen widely succeeded in keeping the skies above Dunkirk free of enemy planes. Hermann Goering had told Hitler that he could destroy the remaining British troops on the ground, but the Luftwaffe was drained from its commitments over the previous month - seriously short of fit pilots and operational craft. The RAF kept most of the aerial snipers at bay, although it was many years before this vital undertaking was recognised and respected. One veteran of Dunkirk told me, with tears in his eyes, how he had helped a wounded pal aboard a boat and had nursed his sickly colleague across the choppy waters. Reaching Dover, locals lifted the injured soldier out of the vessel, whereupon his stomach broke open from the weight of shrapnel lodged inside his body.

Once the Luftwaffe had taken over the airfields along the French coast, they could prepare to mount assaults on England, and RAF facilities would obviously be high on their hit list. Unfortunately many British airfields at this time were poorly protected; often just a few gun emplacements around their perimeters.

The embryonic UK radar systems were all outward facing – alerting their operators that planes might be approaching the British coast. If those aircraft proved to be German and got beyond the coastal monitoring, there was no comprehensive mechanism to determine their positions over British soil. So they could easily arrive at a destination with total surprise. And if that address was an RAF airfield, then anything on the ground at that moment was a sitting duck.

The Luftwaffe destroyed many aircraft on stations across the south of England. On 13th August Detling in Kent was attacked, which eliminated 22 planes and killed 67 staff on the ground. In all that day 47 RAF craft were broken up on British airfields.

German crews also flew from Norway to Yorkshire: on 15th August nine bombers were blown to bits at Driffield; three hangars were also damaged and the runway was left full of craters.

Next day Luftwaffe planes managed to reach the training base at Brize Norton in Oxfordshire and obliterated 46 aircraft there, while more German craft swooped over from Cherbourg to attack radio detection towers on the Isle of Wight, and rough up the Tangmere RAF station east of Portsmouth. In just 20 minutes the raiders messed up most hangars, workshops and power systems. Forty vehicles were destroyed, along with fourteen planes. A proportion of the home squadron got into the air and fought back, reckoning they saw off 25 intruders. Ten service personnel and three civilians were killed. The commanding officer logged the exchanges:

'The depressing situation was dealt with in an orderly manner and it is considered that the traditions of the RAF were upheld by all ranks. In conclusion it must be considered that the major attack launched on this Station by the enemy was a victory of the RAF.'

Memo from No 10

On the very day that the Luftwaffe first blasted British aircraft in France, Churchill took over as Prime Minister and swiftly pulled in his pal Max Aitken from the Daily Express to become Minister of Aircraft Production. Churchill's Second World War history profiles his recollections combined with correspondence from the time, mostly from the PM's office to key players. Terse notes cover every aspect of the affairs of state and overseas issues. He dictated his concerns, then sought action on every front. Of matters aerial, first note to the Secretary of State for Air on 27th May addressed confusing terminology: he wanted clarification on the distinction between "put out of action" and "destroyed." Then on 3rd July, making clear he has studied previous correspondence and statistics, he asked why there was a shortage of pilots.

Other recipients of PM memos were the Chief of Air Staff and Aitken (aka Lord Beaverbrook). No 10 demanded immediate responses regarding the lack of available fighter squadrons, the unnecessary storage of spares, slow repair programmes, statistics being revealed publicly that might aid the enemy, and the viability of firing blanks from Ack-Ack guns to reassure nearby civilians that defensive action was being pursued whilst not hazarding RAF craft above.

He wanted reports on the interrogation of German aviator prisoners-of-war; he was frustrated by the poor growth of the available bomber force, by the low numbers of gas-filled bombs in store, and long delays in fitting better bomb sights. Some documents clearly expose his determination to pursue the war with maximum vigour. To Beaverbrook on 8th July:

> '... when I look round to see how we can win the war I see that there is only one sure path.... there is one thing that will bring him (Hitler) down, and that is an absolutely devastating, exterminating attack by very heavy bombers from this country upon the Nazi homeland. We must be able to overwhelm them by this means, without which I do not see a way through. We cannot accept any lower than air mastery. When can it be obtained?'

On 25th July the British Prime Minister wrote to U.S. President Roosevelt that:

'...we must subject Germany and Italy to a ceaseless and ever-growing aerial bombardment. These measures may themselves produce an internal convulsion or collapse.'

The American didn't live to receive a complimentary copy of Churchill's war memoirs. If Roosevelt had been around in 1949, perhaps their author would not have described the theme of Volume II as:

'How the British people held the fort alone till those who hitherto had been half blind were half ready.'

Turned out bad again

Many air war veterans considered that, on balance, their biggest enemy was bad weather. Prior to the war, aircraft had been generally kept on the ground in the face of inclement conditions. It was unnecessarily dangerous to manoeuvre a plane through storms.

As we know, the prevailing weather in northern Europe is determined by westerlies - fronts blowing in from the Atlantic to the UK, before continuing across the North Sea to the continent. So when heading towards Germany, the Brits had it all in their favour: the wind was behind them. There might be benign conditions en route, but would those isobars remain favourable long enough to make a trouble-free return to British bases?

75 years ago meteorologists did not have all the data sources that allows today's broadcasters to show us well informed images of what's likely to happen in the next few days. It was crude stuff back then. A sprinkling of weather reports were transmitted and collated from friendly Atlantic shipping or via detectors in Northern Ireland, but these did not add up to a comprehensive forecast - merely a rough evaluation of what might evolve in the skies in the forthcoming 24 hours.

On the basis of such rudimentary science, BC men and machines were assigned tasks that could lead them into very difficult conditions. Good weather going out was critical. You've got a great big beast of an aircraft, known to have a number of curiosities regarding performance at the best of times. Now it's loaded up with heavy bombs and as much fuel as is needed for the anticipated flight. Lifting it off the runway is challenging enough. But, hopefully, you get in the air and you're heading east.

Reaching mainland Europe, there's every chance you will have to spend time orientating yourself to your whereabouts. If there is dense cloud, that means zig-zagging over enemy territory looking for a landmark or three. Avoiding Ack-Ack fire and patrolling fighters uses up more of that finite quantity of fuel.

Assuming you manage to release your payload approximately in the required location, you now want to head back. So more critical navigation work: if we follow this compass course, we ought to pass over Great Yarmouth in about three hours' time. That assumes the weather allows you to stick to the route. Perhaps stormy conditions drifting across the sea soon force you north or south of that desired path.

Inevitably, fuel is getting very low. Will this aircraft ever reach land? Factored into every flight plan was the concept of the PLE point: Prudent Limit of Endurance. Having loaded up the plane with a certain weight of bombs and a precise quantity of fuel, how far can it fly? On the way back the wind's in your face, so more petrol required. Records and recollections suggest that the PLE was scrimped on, not just occasionally, but far too frequently. Of course, if an aircraft has been shot at by the enemy and this has caused a hole to appear in the fuel feeds or tanks, there could be an insurmountable power problem.

So many British airmen commenced their return journey with a big question mark over whether they would reach England. If there was patently not enough juice, the pilot might decide to land in occupied Europe. But frequently, rather than falling into enemy hands – murdered by angry bomb victims' families, shot by the military or becoming a prisoner of war, and allowing your machine to be examined by the Luftwaffe which could use that knowledge against your fellow servicemen – the pilot would head for home on a wing and a prayer, as they say. Maybe the weather would be kind, and a gap in the approaching low pressure allowed you to make it to East Anglia and peer out for something below which could be Great Yarmouth, albeit mostly blacked out. But frequently that trickle in the bottom of the tanks was quickly absorbed by your spluttering engines, and instead of making it to any old airfield, or even just a field, the aircraft smacked

41

into the sea, where piloting and luck determined the next few minutes of everyone's lives.

Hit a high wave at the wrong angle at 90 miles an hour and there's a screech of metal ripping against water, tearing the plane and its contents into pieces, all of which will sink without trace in seconds, quite possibly sucking men down with it. Is there time for everyone to scramble to the inflatable dinghy? Where are we? Which way to paddle? Can we keep this tiny rubber boat upright, and avoid it being swamped by big waves?

Such was the conclusion for a large number of Bomber Command flights. No firm figures for splash downs in the North Sea; there was never a report from the crews that died. But from the few survivors we know that such horrors formed the final moments of the flights that failed to return and didn't land or crash in another country.

The Few

Hitler had always been intrigued by Paris. It looked so lovely, seemed so grand. But he only had pictures, films and the tales of others to go on. Until now he had never managed to visit the capital. But as soon as he overcame the French, taking a look became irresistible.

Might he mount a grand parade through the streets? Could you trust those sour Parisians not to take a pot shot? Very risky. On top of that, there was the awful prospect that, if you publicised it in advance, the English flyers might send over some of their damn bombers and spoil the day for everyone. That wasn't really on. Bad PR!

Instead the Fuhrer had to make do with a short, sneaky visit with as few people as possible knowing about it. Adolf flew with some pals (including his pet architect Albert Speer - wearing German military uniform, so he'd fit in) to Le Bourget airport at half past five in the morning on 28th June, four days after the French Armistice was signed. A fleet of Mercedes was standing by to take the conqueror on his sight-seeing tour. First stop was the glorious Opera building which he had always admired. A glum employee shuffled the invader-in-chief through the elaborate facilities. Speer later recalled that his boss had been thrilled to pop in to Paris. Adolf confided to Albert that it was fortunate he hadn't had to destroy the city. The architect was instructed to make Berlin even more magnificent.

As Adolf meandered through the French capital, did he muse on future prospects, such as saluting admiring throngs from the balcony of Buckingham Palace, the previous occupants confined to the Tower of London, or worse? The ferocious Luftwaffe triumphs in Spain, Poland, France and Holland had taken place within a relatively modest amount of airspace. The German fighters and bombers had set off from airfields close to the places they were targeting, not using up much petrol to inflict their terror. And after causing mayhem, it was an easy ride back to base for re-fuelling, re-arming and a sandwich. But the English Channel required at least 21 miles of flying over the sea before a German aircraft could bring its weaponry to bear: time-consuming, fuel-heavy and potentially dodgy.

This was early days in aircraft design and construction. Now we assume 100% reliability from our planes - superbly perfected, to undertake their journeys successfully, and to land where they are meant to, in one piece. Seventy-five years ago, no aircraft enjoyed such standards of performance. Out of every hundred machines that emerged from a factory some would become troublesome quite quickly.

To send a fleet of planes across 42 miles of sea in 1940 meant a proportion would never be seen again. But the Luftwaffe had hundreds of confident, clever, brave pilots, eager to climb into their machines, rise into the air and travel to where the targets lay, there to dismay and damage their foes. These young men were not necessarily Nazis. They were just capable fellows pursuing careers in the Armed Forces, smart enough to handle a flying machine, use it in the air, and to bring it back again. Everyone knew that this was a high risk occupation: some percentage of participants would fail in the tasks.

The challenges for the RAF's Fighter Command were similar. Here, equally, there were plenty of young men simply excited at the prospect of having a go. But the English airfields were judiciously distributed across Kent and adjoining counties, so the British boys did not have far to travel to encounter intruders. In fact, they could wait until Jerry got close, then take off and attack him. If a Brit survived those skirmishes, then with their last bit of fuel, they might get back to their own air station or, if not that, then another one. And if they couldn't make it to an airfield? Well, any field offers a feasible landing, where a sympathetic farmer and his wife would come running over to help them

43

out of the cockpit and tend to any wounds and give them a cup of tea while an official rescue party will have been telephoned from the farmhouse thanks to the magic of modern technology. Why, this system worked so well for the home side, that some of those British or Commonwealth pilots who crash-landed on domestic soil could be back at their own airfield by the afternoon and might go up again in a different kite and have another stab at the enemy before supper; whereas German pilots who came down in English fields might get tea and bandages but would soon be taken to a prisoner-of-war camp.

Similar contrast for the planes: German machines hitting the deck in Britain – scrap metal for recycling. But British planes could be recovered, brought back to base and possibly repaired, or certainly scavenged for spares. And bear in mind the Luftwaffe had already lost quite a number of their best pilots and aircraft. Those vicious sorties against the Poles, Dutch and French had eliminated many old hands from the Great War and a proportion of ambitious newcomers.

This is the prospective scenario wherein Hitler considers he could be in a viable position to invade England. So he starts to muster boats and barges along his long array of occupied Channel ports in France, Belgium and Holland. But patently for his invasion fleet to have a decent chance of edging towards the UK, they need the skies to be completely free of RAF planes.

Was this a realistic aspiration? Applying Blitzkrieg principles to the whole southern edge of a huge island, several hundred miles long with dozens of towns and harbours dotted along its coast-line, behind which are a scatter of bristling air stations?

There was a fairly even balance of prospects when the two sides came out on to the pitch – okay, we've got here at last – the footballing analogy. Not a lot in it. The Luftwaffe had more machines, but the home side had that better recovery capacity. Furthermore, the Germans were frequently fielding more than one man per plane – bigger bomber aircraft with a crew of three which could be picked off by a lone Hurricane handler.

There are two determining factors to this battle: the front line: the pilots and their planes, and the back-up: systems producing more airmen and aircraft. Each part needs to function superbly well, and if it is, then you might say, the ball is favouring you. Of course a new pilot is never as good as an old one. All that training fails to fully prepare a young man for the extraordinary experiences of hurling his machine around in the sky to avoid being gunned by enemy aircraft whilst somehow managing to hit them with his bullets.

It's the craziest game ever invented: you're in this device that zips through the air at 300 miles an hour. It will fire shells forward when you press a button, but you cannot aim the guns independently of the plane, so you need to manoeuvre your kite to point where you want the shells to go. And you don't aim directly at the fast-moving enemy craft. You need to fire to a place ahead of that plane - where you think it will be in a few seconds time - just as your ammunition gets there.

Somewhere ahead is one, or several, or hundreds, of foreign machines all trying to knock you out of the sky before you harm them. You, and they, can spin and twist and slice through the air, up and down, left or right, swerving, whipping, looping. Getting used to it makes you better at it. Each time you go up, you are slightly more competent in your range of tasks, able to foresee danger a fraction of a second quicker than you did yesterday. And therefore you can stay up longer and avoid more enemy planes attacking you; instead, execute an attack on them.

Hermann Goering regularly and unfairly criticised his men for a lack of aggression and determination. In July his flyers had commenced pestering shipping in the English Channel. Some of these interferences were challenged by RAF Fighter Command, but not all. Senior British officers did not consider they had the capacity to send out too many of their precious planes each time a Messerschmitt soared across the waves.

The statistics of air incidents make clear the rates of attrition which each side faced. The Germans began with more men and machines but their endeavours hurt them hard. At the time none of the figures were clear. It might take weeks to learn of the demise of a particular plane and pilot. And there were plenty of misunderstandings, miscalculations or manipulation of evidence colouring the score cards.

Through the summer the Luftwaffe believed they were making a severe dent in the capacity of the RAF to continue. Of course the British teams were weakened by their losses, but the nation was churning out more planes and pilots every day of the week to more-or-less compensate (strictly in fighting terms, that is - no replacements for the loss, or permanently damaged life, of a husband, brother, father, son).

News from the front

It was a truth, almost universally acknowledged, that a British airman heading towards enemy planes was in want of a bigger, better gun. Compared with the Luftwaffe, RAF fighter aircraft were generally supplied with poor guns, and pilots were not given much training in working their armaments.

Beaverbrook discovered that 37 different aircraft models were at some stage of development, and so sliced the number down to five. Once based in Whitehall (though often reported to be working from home) his Lordship left day-to-day operations of the Daily Express in the hands of his editorial staff, who took special interest in capturing the evolving nature of aerial activity, the main front page headlines flagging up a succession of extraordinary events.

The month of July alerted readers to the problems, yet indicated that solutions lay ahead:

2nd July	FIRST DAY RAID BEATEN OFF
8th	PLANES: A FINE INCREASE
11th	37 GERMAN RAIDERS SHOT DOWN
12th	AND 22 MORE
13th	R.A.F. MASTER DECOY TRICK
15th	R.A.F. WIN 9 TO 1
19th	INVASION 'SPY' PLANE DOWN
25th	3,000 MORE PLANES A MONTH

We now know that by the end of July Britain had scored 162 'kills' to the Luftwaffe's 71. Of course, a proportion of the deaths on both sides were a result of accidents; not every abruptly-ending flying career concluded with a glorious endeavour against overwhelming enemy forces. But despite the ratio of 'goals' favouring the home side, the Luftwaffe convinced its collective self that only a few more matches would be necessary to defeat those tricky British players.

August commenced with the news that the Express boss was now able to exert more influence on the shaping of the war:

3rd August	BEAVERBROOK JOINS WAR CABINET
9th	53 CHEERS FOR R.A.F.
12th	AGAIN! SIXTY SHOT DOWN

13th   MORE THAN 39 DOWN
14th   BLITZKRIEG – BY THE R.A.F.

Readers could now perceive the war as essentially a numbers game - which side was shooting down the most planes? Of course, only a tiny proportion of readers would have witnessed any of the activity first-hand. People in Kent might peer up to watch the balletic movements of a bunch of noisy machines hurtling around their skies. Others living near south or east coasts could have heard or seen a few aircraft pass overhead; east Londoners would have noticed strange noises along the Thames. But for almost everyone in Britain – as is the case with any news report today – none of what the paper told them was personally familiar. It merely heightened anxiety regarding what might happen next. What could you do? Improve your Anderson shelter, respect the black-out restrictions more vigilantly, send your children on a train to Shropshire, work harder at your munitions factory, volunteer for air warden duties, sign up for military service?

On 15th August the Luftwaffe undertook 1,750 sorties and 77 craft failed to return - merely 4.4%. Bomber Command could only dream of getting their losses down to such modest ratios at this stage in the war. Nevertheless, it was the Luftwaffe's worst day of the month: all that training and experience of flying a military aircraft – gone, plus considerable valuable machinery. Germans later described it as "Black Thursday".

The Express took Air Ministry figures at face value:

16th   UP, UP, UP! 144 DOWN

On the 18th the Luftwaffe lost 67 planes, the RAF 36 – but 26 of our boys survived the demise of their aircraft. We just had ten families to alert to their loss of their sons. In Germany many more parents would be receiving tragic news.

Soon, additional Fleet Street enthusiasm:

19th   AT LEAST 115 MORE!

Then reports of cross-Channel reprisals:

20th   BOULOGNE BOMBED AGAIN
23rd   DOVER BOMBARDED
24th   CALAIS BOMBED AGAIN

This proved a further deadly day for the Luftwaffe: 41 planes lost, compared with 20 from the RAF. However, Goering's boys did succeed in killing 100 people in and around Portsmouth during their efforts to destroy the docks.

Next day, BC forces flew to Berlin to deliver reprisals for the Portsmouth deaths. A handful of bombs were decanted somewhere round the German capital but they didn't eliminate any citizens.

26th   BOMBS AND PARACHUTE FLARES ON LONDON
27th   LONDON HAS 6-HOUR RAIDS
28th   BIGGEST R.A.F. RAID
29th   LONGEST BLITZ NIGHT
30th   HOW WE BOMBED BERLIN
31st   59 DOWN – TEN IN LONDON

The newspaper now profiled an announcement from Lord Beaverbrook:

"Many are they that rise up against us. But the men and women of the aircraft industry of Britain answer the challenge. These brave defenders of the liberties of Britain, ignoring air raids and indifferent to enemy attacks, have provided for the R.A.F. in the last week more fighters and more bombers than ever before in the history of aviation."

There was also a report from an Air Ministry official about recent night raids:

'...it is impossible to believe that the enemy can have had any specific targets in the London area in mind, and certainly no military objectives. The bombers flew mostly at a very great height and dropped their bombs at scattered points with no apparent plan. It can only be assumed that the objective was to terrorise the civil population, and Londoners are best able to judge how completely these attempts failed.'

The official also contrasted the Luftwaffe's 'purposelessness and ineffectiveness' with:

'the methodical and sustained offensive of the R.A.F. against Germany, which is confined to carefully planned attempts on military objectives and is known to be achieving valuable results.'

And so the paper powered forward, never down-hearted, never short of an uplifting story about the capacity of the Brits to battle on.

In a flap

Every military pilot can explain the challenges of staying in the air and taking effective action under fire. Many admirable books profile the anecdotes of airmen, recalling moments of courage and/or terror in the skies while endeavouring to fruitfully engage with the enemy. But one aspect of the difficulties and dangers is seldom mentioned - the state of the plane's tyres.

Today we think of tyres as those heavy, cleverly-treaded devices that sit firmly and strongly below our cars, revolving at an enormous rate; designed to withstand hundreds of miles of fast journeys along motorways as well as the occasional severe bump against a kerb or pot-hole. Back in 1940, pneumatic tyres had not reached anything like such a degree of sophistication. Their construction was crude - the surface of rubber forming the loop and its walls very thin and not always uniform. So it is no exaggeration to say that the most vulnerable element of a flying fighter aircraft was not the pilot or the fuel tank but the tyres - a fragile balloon wrapped round a metal wheel.

In flight, the wheels were generally folded inside the craft's frame, but should a sharp projectile – a bullet or shrapnel – pierce the exterior sheath, the tyre was a goner. Suddenly, where there had been a vital element of the landing equipment, are now just billowing fragments of useless rubber. Unfortunately, the individual at the controls doesn't know this yet. Yes, he will sense his craft was hit, but if that was merely a momentary engagement with enemy fire, then the consequences may not be apparent.

If the plane continues to perform in the air, that's a good sign - no obvious malfunction to the major mechanisms. But when the time comes – as we hope it does – that the aircraft returns to its field, and the pilot lowers the undercarriage (assuming the struts lock down as the cockpit manual indicates they should) the airman will be hoping he has functioning wheels beneath him. He cannot see if that is the case. He cannot feel if there is something amiss. No pulling over on to the hard shoulder to examine the wheels, then calling out the RAC if necessary. Either he has a set of good-to-land pressurised tyres ready for touch-down, or he hasn't. And the time he discovers which is the case is that instant when he tries to bring both front wheels into contact with the ground.

Two wheels – good; one wheel – very bad indeed. The pressured tyre contacts first and immediately the airman detects if the second tyre is also there, or if this wheel is devoid of its pneumatic band and is about to carve into the concrete and so flick the aircraft across the strip in a brutal way. This caused the abrupt demise of many pilots and planes. Their bodies and their fuel tanks would seldom survive those shocking forces.

Good fight
The RAF only challenged a proportion of Luftwaffe attacks on ports and navy facilities along the south coast in August. However, towards the end of the month the Germans targeted English airfields. An assault on Biggin Hill killed almost 40 ground staff; after one brutal raid, Manston personnel refused to leave their bunkers. Brave Hurricane and Spitfire pilots resisted these intrusions with a high attrition rate on both sides, though the Luftwaffe suffered more. Nevertheless the battles resulted in the RAF losing four out of every five of its Squadron Commanders during the month.

British pilots were occasionally given a degree of reprieve from front line duties, whereas Luftwaffe airmen were not rotated; they had to get on with it. UK operational training had been taking six months, but as the RAF ran short of pilots, this preparation period dropped right down to a few weeks. Elderly veterans recall spending merely a few hours of familiarisation in the cockpit of a new-to-them aircraft before being asked to fly it into combat.

You needed extraordinary nerve and luck to be a successful and long-living fighter pilot. What you wanted to do was to spot the enemy before they spotted you. Best way of doing this was to get up high. But the higher you go, the thinner the air gets, and the more sluggish the machine becomes, because there is less air for traction and lift. And you become more dependent on oxygen, so you need to wear a mask which reduces your visibility.

If the sun is shining, head for that, because other pilots have great difficulty spotting aircraft close to the sun. They will blind themselves if they look in that direction.

Dropping down towards the enemy using gravity in addition to engine power increases speed, and the faster you approach the enemy, the less time he has to react. You have just seconds to make these critical decisions – life or death decisions - and there's so much that can go wrong: one or both of you misjudge the flight path, so you crash into each other, or into another nearby aircraft that you failed to notice. Or your plane won't function according to plan: it stalls due to the pressure you've put on its systems, or a hole that's appeared in the fuel line. Maybe a dent – due to a bullet – will have bent a linkage, which stops some flying control working as it should.

Perhaps the guns jam. Or one wing gun jams, which yaws the craft. Suddenly, while your thumb's pressed down on the tit, the aircraft skews left or right depending on which gun has jammed. This might take you straight into the line of sight of the enemy, or throw you way off beam, so you're now vulnerable to him coming at you from another angle. Dare you try pressing the trigger again, or had you best make your escape, if that's possible?

Audacious fighter pilots had a manoeuvre that could, in a few vital seconds, pull them out of problems and instead position them at a distinct advantage over their opponent - looping the plane through a vertical circle. But there were some snags. First, you might black out from the G-forces. Second, there was a fair chance you would vomit. And thirdly, grit on the cockpit floor - or anything else down there - would, at the worst inverted moment in the loop, drop, due to gravity, from the base of your mobile office and land in your face and your eyes.

But was it wise to constantly hurl your plane around with maximum vigour; to withstand severe yaws which - as long as you don't pass out - meant you minimised the opportunities for one of those pesky Huns to make mincemeat of you? Your craft is a machine, built in a factory from metal and wooden parts with lots of critical joints, bolts and welding. It has been designed to be wieldy in the skies, but that does not mean you can shove your controls in any direction and assume the craft will fully respond, and so whip you off at an acute tangent away from enemy shells.

There are limits on the severity of thrusts that the aircraft can handle. Read the manual. Ask others. There's stuff it will not do. In the midst of attempting an extreme twist, the craft may reveal that you have foolishly ignored its parameters of performance. A wing will snap off. Crack, snap, gone. And you're a goner too. No longer controlling a flying machine, you are now trapped in a spinning projectile that is plummeting to earth. No time to extract yourself from the cockpit. You're in a tiny metal cage that's about to impact with the ground in some horrible way. These are your last few seconds of life. And no means to convey to your peers what to avoid when they're next flying one of these things in challenging conditions. Bang.

Study the board
A photograph of the plotting room at Biggin Hill appears in most books about the Battle of Britain. We see a big crude map of south east England on a large table. It is surrounded by women in uniform wielding long poles to manipulate little blocks of wood with coded letters and numbers stuck on them. Each coloured block represented a cluster of aircraft currently over England. Some were Our Boys, others Luftwaffe; unidentified planes were labelled 'Doubtful'. Of course, the blocks were always in the wrong place, because there was a time gap between the location of a particular flight being verified and the transfer of the relevant information to the plotting room.

Every observer, radar reader, squadron leader and air field commander had phone communication to and from this vital hub. The map provided a valuable picture of what was happening logistics-wise out in the skies. It looked very school-boyish, like a big kids' board game, but it worked incredibly well. From a gallery above, senior officers contemplated the moving graphics in order to determine where and when to assign their limited numbers of planes with limited fuel capacity. The system enabled the RAF to move aircraft in and out of contention, to envisage the best deployment of forces across many counties, or to husband assets for further likely ingressions into British air space.

Photographs of the table and its coded blocks were top secret. If Luftwaffe personnel had been able to see this scene, they would have understood the defenders' techniques. But the Germans had very poor behind-enemy-lines UK intelligence. Before the war they had undertaken lots of low-key research, so knew where armament factories were situated, where airfields lay, but they did not have the means to monitor the attrition or replacement capacities of the English Air Force. As the encounters proceeded, German airmen knew they had disabled plenty of enemy planes. They saw flames flaring from fuselages, craft careering towards the ground or sea - the Luftwaffe was surely winning? In fact, several separate pilots might report that they had been responsible for the demise of a specific "Tommy" machine; so one engine fire could go into German records as three planes shot down. The troubled RAF craft might have managed to land; the pilot simply suffering a bump on the head for a great story to tell of events at work that day. Hence Luftwaffe reports erected an erroneous picture of the state of their opponents.

The balance of aerial combat fatalities remained roughly the same through September, but new targets complicated the picture, and provided the Daily Express with huge opportunities for dramatic headlines:

2nd Sept   WE'RE WINNING IN THE AIR
3rd   NIGHT FIGHTERS HUNT LONDON RAIDERS

On the 4th, Bomber Command headed off to Berlin to try to do some more damage there.

5th   HITLER SCREAMS THREATS - BIG RAID BEATEN

Hitler demanded revenge in the form of bombs on London – which he got, starting on 7th September. On this night, 400 Londoners died from German bombing and nearly 2,000 were badly injured. Across the next two nights, there were similar numbers of civilian casualties.

The newspaper was permitted to acknowledge the problems:

9th   BLITZ BOMBING OF LONDON GOES ON ALL NIGHT
10th   47 SHOT DOWN – THEN BLITZ BOMBING No 3
11th   5 ALARMS – THEN ANOTHER NIGHT OF IT

But resistance was being mounted:

12th   TERRIFIC LONDON BARRAGE MEETS GREATEST RAID
13th   WARSHIPS IN THE THAMES ARE DEFENDING LONDON
14th   DIVE BOMBERS TRY TO KILL THE KING AND QUEEN

The small print reveals that one of a 'few dive bombers' releasing ordnance towards 'conspicuous buildings' dropped five bombs on and around Buckingham Palace. An Express columnist considered:

'If either the King or Queen had been killed or injured, the effect would have been to lift the entire Empire to its feet as a single man with one last unquenchable vow to kill Adolf Hitler in revenge.'

The final shot

Fighter pilots were trained to fire at an enemy aircraft in the hope of disabling it and its human cargo. That was their daily function. Achieving the status of Pilot meant you would enjoy a certain number of privileges. You could expect to be treated with respect, to be saluted quite a lot on your home air field. If you were an officer, you might occupy better quarters, eat better meals. And your pay would be higher than most.

But the quality of life for young RAF airmen was no match for their contemporaries in the Luftwaffe. Visitors to German air stations described premises as reminiscent of high class hotels. British boys often had to get by in draughty huts full of rickety beds with small lockers in which each airman could keep his personal possessions. Of course, most of the early users of these facilities had only recently emerged from public schools, so they were not unfamiliar with communal catering and barrack-style bunks.

Each pilot was a big investment for his nation. He was well educated and displayed suitable characteristics for being trained to handle an expensive, sophisticated machine which could enable him to head towards and challenge enemy planes. Every day through the summer and autumn of 1940 courageous young men died prosecuting the war in the air on behalf of their country. There was often an atmosphere of hollow heartiness in and around the station messes: chaps endeavouring to be cheery in the face of the loss of friends and colleagues in recent months and days. They bore a sombre awareness that they might never see their current associates and pals again. Who was to know?

Some pilots managed to function fruitfully for months on end. Others might make an error of judgement that put them in mortal danger. If they could not return to base, they looked for somewhere below reasonably flat; aware that an undercarriage fault could mean a belly landing with the prop snapping off and slicing through the windscreen.

If devoid of functioning landing gear, the lone airman needed to exit the craft while still in the sky. Clambering from a cramped cockpit was more or less impossible in an emergency. Best option: at 500 feet up, detach yourself from cables and straps, punch away the Perspex canopy, then flick the craft over on its back and drop out, letting gravity initiate and maintain your descent.

Some pilots carried a personal pistol in the cockpit in preparation for what they feared most: their aircraft catching fire and the fellow being unable to extract himself. Rather than suffer the horrors of burning, they anticipated it would be better to die quickly with a shot to the head.

Battling Britain

Churchill's declarations of respect for Fighter endeavours are oft repeated and rightly so, but the PM also acknowledged the vital work of the other Commands. In his magnificent speech to the House of Commons on 20th August, following that glorious line about "so much owed by so many to so few", he went on to say:

> "We must never forget that all the time, night after night, month after month, Bomber Squadrons travel far into Germany, find their targets in the darkness by the highest navigational skill, aim their attacks, often under the heaviest fire, often at heavy losses, with deliberate careful precision, and inflict shattering blows upon the whole of the technical and war-making structure of Nazi power."

We now know that this reflected ambition rather than actuality. On 3rd September, he presented the War Cabinet with an assessment:

> 'The Navy can lose us the war, but only the Air Force can win it. Therefore our supreme effort must be to gain overwhelming mastery in the air. The Fighters are our salvation, but the Bombers alone provide the means of victory. We must therefore develop the power to carry an ever-increasing volume of explosives to Germany, so as to pulverise the entire industry and scientific structure on which the war effort and economic life of the enemy depend, while holding him at arm's length from our Island.'

Contrast this forthright statement of intent with Professor Richard Overy's forensic evaluation 63 years later:

> 'Bombing in Europe was never a war-winning strategy and the other services (Army, Navy) knew it.'

The Germans had started assaulting port facilities, munitions factories and military targets in urban areas initially in daylight, then in the dark. Their prime target was dockland, in order to damage Britain's capacity to feed and arm itself. But after a single raid they might move on to another destination, not realising that what looked like devastation from the air might merely be cosmetic damage, from which the victims could quickly recover.

The south east was not the only target for Luftwaffe ordnance. With their radio beam guidance system and some big fuel tanks, German bombers could range right across the UK. On Sunday 25th August, 150 German planes reached Liverpool to inflict almost 500 casualties.

Three weeks later, one audacious Luftwaffe airman bound for London fixed a flame thrower on to the side of his plane as a novel way of blasting RAF defenders. But when the contraption reached high altitude the ignition system would not function and, instead of propelling flames, the machine just squirted out black oil - some of which plastered fighter pilot Ray Holmes's windshield.

The German was killed by his experiment, while Holmes flew on to face a pilotless Dornier bomber heading north over the Thames, abandoned by its crew and flying on automatic. Holmes was out of ammunition so he aimed his plane at the Dornier, and baled out seconds before impact, which caused both aircraft, including the Dornier's bomb load, to fall near Buckingham Palace. Some subsequent accounts of this incident portray Holmes as heroic; others question the wisdom of action which caused the contents of a bomber to pepper Mayfair when it might have come down relatively harmlessly on Hampstead Heath.

Holmes parachuted on to a street in Chelsea, while the pilot of the Dornier drifted into the Oval cricket ground. From the air, this big rectangle of neat grass must have seemed a fortuitous destination. However the locals were in no mood to welcome the alien visitor. He was captured and beaten up by an angry mob. A squad of British soldiers rescued the German aviator, but he soon died from his wounds.

On this day 59 Luftwaffe fighters were destroyed and fourteen RAF fighters tumbled down, while 62 Londoners were killed by German ordnance. But Monday's Express, like other newspapers, headlined exaggerated reports on UK achievements:

16th   175 SHOT DOWN

Next day, acknowledgement of domestic vulnerability:

17th   NIGHT RAIDERS BOMB WEST END

Followed by:

18th   BARRAGE GETS 4 RAIDERS

German bombers killed 240 British civilians this night, and left 500 badly injured. Next:

19th   NEW SHELTERS FOR TUBE-SQUATTERS
20th   NEW NAZI FIRE BOMB FAILS IN BIGGEST RAID
21st   LONDON WILL SEE IT THROUGH

Bomber Command hit back at Berlin on the 23rd. But the task of reaching the German capital from Britain was in a different league to assaulting London from the French coast. Yet:

26th   BIG FIRES RAGING IN BERLIN

And soon:

30th   NAZI BASES CRIPPLED

You will note, defeat was not forecast.

Taking what we call the Battle of Britain as a whole, the encounters resulted in the loss of nearly 2,000 German aircraft and 1,000 RAF machines. Around 3,000 RAF airmen took part in the Battle; 80% were British, the rest were vital and vibrant contingents from Poland, New Zealand, Canada, Czechoslovakia and Belgium. Of the ten most successful aerial fighters, five were British; along with two New Zealanders, an Australian, a Pole and a Czech. The top Allied Ace in the combat was a Czech, who shot down 17 Germans before he was killed.

2,000 Luftwaffe air crew died compared with 1,485 RAF men. However, almost 6,000 British civilians were killed by enemy bombing.

Take a look at the magnificent memorial sculpture on the Embankment near Parliament Square which elegantly captures the spirit of the extraordinary responsibilities of the fighters.

Nearby, at Westminster Abbey, RAF Battle of Britain fatalities are recorded in the Memorial Chapel: alongside the 537 Fighter boys, you will see the sacrifice of 718 Bomber and 230 Coastal Command crew.

Barging about

There was never much enthusiasm within the German military hierarchy for Hitler's proposal to invade Britain that summer. Most senior officers thought it was far too difficult; needing much more time and greater resources than were currently available. Troops were depleted and drained from the vigorous advances to the French coast. Materiel needed replacement and renewal. And how were they to get personnel and tanks across the Channel? There were no special vessels; there had been no trials, never mind training, for launching, then landing boats full of soldiers into and out of the sea, along with enough heavy weaponry to allow them to drive inland from the English coast. But you could only diplomatically point out possible pitfalls to the Fuhrer, whose reputation for demanding more than was practical from his armed forces was now becoming better comprehended. So the Generals liaised with the Admirals and discussed ways and means of getting thousands of men and their machinery across the sea lane.

Senior German sailors knew it would be impossible to muster enough warships to undertake mass transit, so they commandeered merchant vessels and unpowered barges from the continent's inland waterway network and clustered them within the occupied ports facing England.

RAF Coastal patrols soon spotted these movements, so Bomber Command was assigned to disrupt the invasion transport. But, of course, each time a fleet of bombers approached those temporary havens the enemy would fire from the harbour sides and scramble fighter craft to intercept. Nevertheless BC assaults on the barges contributed to looming reasons for the Fuhrer to consider that the invasion of England should be delayed. The plan was secretly put on hold for the winter. However the Luftwaffe was ordered to continue harassing Britain by bombing its cities.

Some speculation: What would have happened if Hitler had launched his forces towards the beaches, say, between Folkestone and Brighton? The RAF and the Royal Navy would have made their crossing a misery, whilst every resource from the UK, the Commonwealth and the USA would surely have been hurled at creating a barrier against the Wehrmacht within Kent and Sussex. An insuperable cordon could have been swiftly established along what is now the south side of the M25, and, if necessary, British warships would have hugged the Thames

58

estuary north of Kent to shell inland at advancing regiments of intruders, whatever the collateral damage to Canterbury and other towns.

Let it be registered that Bomber Command's mucking up of the barges helped inhibit the notion of floating the Nazis onward - for which we remain most grateful.

Figure it out

Churchill's recollections throw vivid light on the significance of the Luftwaffe's change of tactics from 7th September:

> 'It was with a sense of relief that Fighter Command felt the German attack turn on to London. Goering should certainly have persevered against the airfields, on whose organisation and combination the whole fighting power of our Air Force at this moment depended. By departing from the classic principles of war, as well as from the hitherto accepted dictates of humanity, he made a foolish mistake.'

After acknowledging the initial errors of the statistical reports, the ex-PM concluded:

> 'The Royal Air Force, far from being destroyed, was triumphant.
> 'At the summit the stamina and valour of our fighter pilots remained unconquerable and supreme. Thus Britain was saved.'

The compilation of data regarding the fortunes or misfortunes of every individual air force craft and its personnel sometimes took months to accumulate. Like the RAF, the Luftwaffe assembled records, but in 1945 they chose to destroy most of these as the Allies advanced across western Europe and were about to reach particular air fields or office complexes. So there is no definitive record of the fate of German air crew and their planes.

After an air battle, survivors who made it back to base were debriefed on their perceptions as to what had happened to which plane. Some had clear memories of individual incidents; others were hazy about the last known circumstances of their colleagues. They had briefly passed them at some point and perhaps saw some smoke emerging from a fuselage or engine. The Messerschmitt Daimler-Benz power unit hissed out a puff of black smoke when accelerating which could easily be mistaken for mechanical damage.

Station officers wanted to harvest information that indicated success. So they were inclined to accept crew claims at face value and not find fault with heated descriptions. Hence the figures gathered for achievement could very easily expand beyond the truth. For public relations purposes it was often better to leave to one side tragic tales of the decimation of any of our forces. Hence, throughout the war, servicemen, their families, senior officers and the enemy had to interpret all data supplied to the public domain with a degree of scepticism.

In the autumn Bomber Command were charged with attacking oil plants and munitions factories, almost all of which were surrounded by the houses of the relevant workforce. But Churchill was soon complaining to the Chief of Air Staff that 'the discharge of bombs on Germany is pitifully small.'

For Express readers, October promised plenty of retaliation and some respite:

1st	WE CAN HOPE TO STOP NIGHT RAIDS – OFFICIAL
2nd	BERLIN FAMILIES FLEE FROM RAID
11th	36 LONDON DISTRICTS HIT LAST NIGHT
15th	SOON WE MAY BOMB BERLIN BY DAY, TOO
22nd	200 TONS OF BOMBS DROP ON BERLIN
28th	BRITAIN'S HEAVIEST BOMBS ROCK BERLIN
31st	26,000 U.S. PLANES COMING TO BRITAIN

The prospect of additional American armaments (albeit, to be paid for) was always something to appreciate. November provided the editors with opportunities to advance the agenda. Initially, fresh evidence of British capacity to repel raiders:

2nd Nov   5 NAZI BOMBERS DOWN THIS MORNING

Soon, new achievements in the RAF's fight back – specifically at the giant munitions complex in the Ruhr:

9th   KRUPPS ALIGHT FROM END TO END

Then confirmation of the ultimate revenge prospect:

11th   'HITLER IS A MILITARY OBJECTIVE'

At last, clarity on the definitive goal of all Allied endeavour. Adolf had spelt out his bizarre and dreadful ambitions in Mein Kampf. Now the

Express was able to quote a senior Whitehall source: if we can get rid of the Fuhrer, then everything could turn out fine. Here was a worthwhile message not just for fireside suburbia, but for every member of the Armed Forces and munitions industries; perhaps the RAF in particular: keep hurling explosives at Germany and the rat who triggered all this mayhem might be squashed in his sewer.

The cruel sea

Most aerial combat had been taking place above English countryside, but sometimes a damaged aircraft came down over the sea, perhaps with its pilot still aboard, sometimes with fellows floating down gently on a parachute. If air crew reached the water in one piece, what were their chances of making it to land?

Assuming they were lucky enough to be wearing a life-jacket, that might keep them going for a few hours, but sooner or later they'd become swamped, exhausted, cold, listless, lifeless and then they'd drown. There was no system or operational procedure to scan the waves for people bobbing about. Being spotted was a matter of luck; being reached by a vessel that could pull you aboard was rare indeed. Most pilots splashing into the sea drowned.

German air crews were issued with dinghies plus canisters of dye to colour the water which would mark their positions. The men wore yellow skull caps to make them more visible. From the start the Luftwaffe deployed a fleet of rescue aircraft to pick up survivors. These were sea-planes, able to come down on their floats on to the Channel surface. The craft were painted white and displayed prominent red crosses to make clear their mission was mercy. However the British War Cabinet decided it was foolish to permit a German pilot shot down to return to the Luftwaffe in order to harass the UK again. Instructions were issued to the Air Ministry to attack enemy rescue planes in the air and on the water. This policy was pursued half-heartedly. Some RAF personnel chose to respect their opponents' rescue endeavours and gave them a wide berth, though others shared the Prime Minister's view that any dead German pilot was one less problem for Britain. In response, the Luftwaffe seaplanes were re-painted with camouflage and armed with machine guns.

Meanwhile it was known for UK pilots to drown within sight of the white cliffs of Dover. The Royal Navy commenced patrols around the coastline looking for downed aircrew - whatever their nationality - in August 1940, but resources for the task were very limited. From May 1941 Fighter Command began to provide pilots with a tiny one-man dinghy which few considered sea-worthy.

Throughout the war many Bomber Command crew drowned in the North Sea - an alarmingly broad expanse of rough, cold water, frequently whipped with strong winds and waves. The bombers conveyed a cardboard box holding a carrier pigeon. In the event the craft pancaked on to the water the boys could, in theory, scribble a note of their last known location and hope the bird would fly back to base and so alert colleagues to their plight.

If the crew decanted themselves into their miserable dinghy they needed to paddle through waters which Coastal Command could have mined. If they reached a beach, they might stand on sand stuffed with more mines between big screens of barbed wire. The wet survivors would try to give a friendly wave to any Home Guard pointing his rifle at them, hoping the amateur soldier was one of those not yet issued with ammunition.

German trawlers sometimes rescued downed RAF men. Before becoming prisoners-of-war, these guys might suffer a few days of sickly sailing and the imposed handling of heavy nets and wet fish.

Perhaps the RAF's worst experience with water had been in June 1940, following the failed attempts to impede the German invasion of Norway, when unscathed air men hurriedly stowed their aircraft aboard HMS Glorious to escape back to Britain. In the middle of the North Sea the heavily loaded ship encountered two German battlecruisers which shelled and torpedoed the Royal Navy vessel, sinking it, and so taking the squadron's planes and eighteen of its air men to the bottom.

Right in the middle

Living and working in London, Churchill was sorely aware of Luftwaffe raids and their resultant damage. But what could he do? In September he explained to his Home Secretary how citizens might better drain their Anderson shelters:

> 'Bricks on edge placed loosely together without mortar, covered with a piece of linoleum, would be quite good, but there must be a drain and a sump.'

Through the autumn, drainage issues remained a worry:

> '...in October the main sewage outfall was destroyed and we had to let all our sewage flow into the Thames, which stank, first of sewage and afterwards of the floods of chemicals we poured into it. But all was mastered.'

Lack of glass for window replacement plagued the PM, but he was assured the glaziers held sufficient supplies. Churchill pressed the Minister of Transport to make tube stations available as air raid shelters.

No 10 also questioned whether Ministry personnel should to be allowed to head for shelters at the sound of any siren: too many work hours were being lost. But a new menace now appeared: delayed-action bombs, which would cause long-term disruption of transport and factories as efforts were made to defuse the devices.

Churchill was highly aware of the alarming state of the capital:

> '... night after night ten or twenty thousand people were made homeless, and when nothing but the ceaseless vigil of the citizens as Fire Guards on the roofs prevented uncontrollable conflagrations; when hospitals, filled with mutilated men and women, were themselves struck by the enemy's bombs; when hundreds of thousands of weary people crowded together in unsafe and insanitary shelters; when communications by road and rail were ceaselessly broken down; when drains were smashed and light, power and gas paralysed; and when nevertheless the whole fighting, toiling life of London had to go forward, and nearly a million people be moved in and out for their work every night and morning. We did not know how long it would last. We had no reason to suppose it would not go on getting worse.'

An analogy:

> 'London was like some huge prehistoric animal... mangled and bleeding from many wounds, and yet preserving its life and movement.'

Might the hurt beast expire?

> 'London could take it. They took all they got, and could have taken more. Indeed, at this time we saw no end but the demolition of the whole Metropolis. Still, as I pointed out to the House of Commons, the law of diminishing returns operates in the case of the demolition of large cities. Soon many of the bombs would only fall upon houses already ruined and only make the rubble jump. Over large areas there would be nothing more to burn or destroy, and yet human beings might make their homes here and there, and carry on their work with infinite resource and fortitude.'

His reinforced personal quarters were provided with a viewing platform so he could 'watch the fireworks.' His weekly audience with the King now took the form of a buffet lunch sometimes served in the Buckingham Palace air raid shelter.

On 12th November senior Russian officials visited Berlin to discuss prospects for mutual progress with Germany. British sympathisers learned of the arrival of the Moscow delegation and alerted London. Churchill ordered an immediate bombing raid on the German capital. So when Hitler was telling his visitors that the UK was more or less a spent force and of no further consequence in Europe, the RAF arrived overhead and the Russian diplomats were hurried down to bombproof shelters.

Churchill was now concerned about the high percentage of Bomber Command losses. He recommended sending over fewer aircraft, which should not come 'down too low in the face of heavily prepared batteries and be content with somewhat less accuracy', and 'by picking out soft spots where there is not too much organised protection', to sustain the rate of bomb delivery:

> 'There must be unexpecting towns in Germany where very little has been done in Air Raid Precaution and yet where there are military objectives of a minor order.'

14th November

The Luftwaffe's nifty beam guidance system took 449 bomber aircraft to Coventry on this evening, making quite a mess with 1,200 tons of high explosives and 40,000 incendiaries. The raid killed 568 people, seriously injured 900, and left 7,000 houses destroyed or uninhabitable; 30,000 dwellings damaged. Many schools, shops and civic buildings were affected, 35 factories suffered disruption.

Why was Coventry attacked? It was the home of COW, the Coventry Ordnance Works, one of Britain's biggest concentrations of arms and aircraft production, all nestled around the heart of the small city. The Cathedral was never a target; that fine building was merely an element of the inevitably arbitrary destruction caused when hundreds of aircraft try to drop bombs on a huge cluster of munitions plants.

Accuracy was aided by the German's use of flares which were decanted by the leading planes above the designated targets so that following pilots could use them as markers. The Luftwaffe was aiming at manufacturing capacity. Retrieved maps of flight plans show factory buildings highlighted. The crews were not seeking to kill innocent people that night. If they had only wanted to achieve that, there were many locations far more accessible.

However being accurate with bomb delivery was never easy. And well intentioned plans could readily go awry. A moment's impetuousness or hesitation could see ordnance descend hundreds of metres from where it was meant to go, and in Coventry almost every war-effort factory was right next to civilian housing. Of course, amongst the German air crews, there would be a few mavericks, not dutifully following orders precisely. Instead they might aggressively or mindlessly decant their load somewhere different, somewhere handy. They could relish blasting a few English households, particularly if they had relatives back home who had been on the receiving end of RAF bombing.

Coventry's defence measures included the lighting of decoy fires in nearby rural areas in the hope that at least a proportion of the incoming night raiders might drop their payload on to harmless flames, thinking these were targets already attacked. The city's anti-aircraft guns (AA) discharged nearly 7,000 shells into the dark sky, but not one brought down an enemy plane. The barrage balloons proved a mixed blessing.

One German plane clipped a cable and was damaged. To sustain his flight, the pilot immediately jettisoned his cargo, which landed on the unlucky residents of Wallace Road, not near any arms factory. The Cathedral received no more than a sprinkle of incendiaries that evening, but the few people available to snuff them out were overwhelmed, and water supply was reduced because of breaks in the mains. Only gradually did the amateur fire-fighters manning St Michael's find the spread of flames too much to overcome.

A conspiratorial tale later emerged suggesting that British intelligence had decoded German signals which identified the planned target for that night, but chose to suppress the data so as not to reveal to the enemy that they were being secretly monitored. In fact Fighter Command undertook more than a hundred sorties on the 14th, but in the dark no pilot managed to spot, or close in on, an enemy plane in a way that allowed him to shoot one down. Across the subsequent weeks the sore people of Coventry frequently questioned the capacity of the RAF to deal with foreign night bombers.

The impact of the attack was so severe that Whitehall decided to make the urban destruction widely known, so the world would learn the extremes of German action. One Luftwaffe pilot subsequently expressed dismay at the damage to civilian areas caused by their endeavours. Hermann Goering, under interrogation after the war, declared he was very proud of the effectiveness of his Air Force on this occasion – it was a triumph for German planes, pilots, navigation techniques and bombing ability.

Local historian David McGrory records the efficient re-deployment of medical personnel and facilities alongside the calm re-location of patients when Coventry Hospital was struck several times on the night of 14th November 1940.

Through the war there were more than forty bombing raids on Coventry. The final victims of aerial attack were three people killed in July 1942. There were no more bombs after August that year. In all, 55,000 Coventry homes were hit and 2,000 retail premises were damaged. Deaths from the bombing amounted to 1,252; nearly 2,000 people were badly injured.

What a year!

On 19th March 1940, Bomber Command had sent 50 aircraft to raid a German seaplane base off the Danish peninsula. 41 of the returning crews claimed to have successfully bombed the target, but subsequent photo-reconnaissance could find little evidence of any damage.

In April, Hitler battered Yugoslavia by dispatching 700 planes to bomb Belgrade, which killed several thousand citizens. Above Clacton, an AA crew managed to hit a German bomber, which crashed on a house killing the occupants, Mr and Mrs Gill - the first English citizens to die in the war.

In May, three-quarters of the British planes sent to support France were wiped out in less than a week. However the Luftwaffe lost 2,800 aircraft in their charge westward. RAF attempts to attack German-held airfields in Norway resulted in the loss of 30 craft.

On the technology front, the Germans had now perfected their anti-aircraft radar gear and so managed to shoot down a British plane without even seeing it. UK efforts with similar devices lay someway behind, but British factories were now building 300 new aircraft each month.

The vital achievement of Fighter Command - its pilots, tactics, officers and planes - in those alarming Battle of Britain months was that they had kept going; did not fail. RAF and Royal Navy airmen responded formidably, courageously and effectively to the early assaults by the Luftwaffe. However, once the Germans changed to night bombing, the UK had no realistic means of defending its skies, and the intruders proceeded to scatter bombs across urban areas right through the winter and on until June 1941, when they turned their attention to Russia. After the war, captured German generals were interrogated over their perceptions of the thrust of armed endeavours. Many referred to Hitler's attempted invasion of Russia as the point when the Third Reich first over-reached itself and became doomed to eventual and bloody defeat. But some senior officers saw the inability of the Luftwaffe to eliminate RAF fighters along Britain's south coast as critical indication that the Third Reich military machine might not be invincible.

Churchill first referred to the extraordinary air skirmishes as "the Battle of Britain" in August 1940. Next month, he visited the operational control room on Sunday the 15th which proved another dreadfully taxing day for the RAF and citizens underneath. But following the sorties on that date, the inaccurate collation of clashes produced a distinctive blip in the seeming success rate of RAF airmen. The exaggerated figures were reported to the press and soon reached American newspapers where sub-editors sculpted the flimsy evidence into firm triumphs. The 15th was made to seem like a special victory.

A few months later, His Majesty's Stationary Office published 'The Battle of Britain – the Great Days from 8th August – 31st October 1940':

> 'As the days wore on the Londoner, always confident in the ability of the Royal Air Force to protect him in the hours of daylight, began to take that protection for granted... There can be no better tribute to the men of the Fighter Squadrons.'

The booklet further elevated 15th September:

> 'It was one of "the great days" as they have come to be called, and the actions then fought were described by the Prime Minister in the House of Commons as "the most brilliant and fruitful of any fought upon a large scale up to that date by the fighters of the Royal Air Force."
> In the entire day we lost twenty-five aircraft, but fourteen pilots were saved. Such was a typical day's fighting in a battle which lasted for nearly three months over the South of England.'

The Air Ministry acknowledged the capabilities of the Luftwaffe:

> 'Certainly the German pilots showed qualities of courage and tenacity; but these were of little avail against the better quality and still higher courage of the British pilots.
> 'The facts are eloquent. They had only to see the enemy to engage him immediately. Odds were of no account and were cheerfully accepted. Only a very high degree of confidence in their training, in their aircraft and in their leaders could have enabled them to maintain the spirit of aggressive courage which they invariably displayed. That confidence they possessed in the full.'

The booklet reported that 375 RAF pilots had been killed; explaining that the battle 'died gradually away; but the British victory was none the less certain and complete'. The authors carefully separated day from night:

> 'Bitter experience had at last taught the enemy the cost of daylight attacks. He took to the cover of night.'

'The heavy casualties occurred during the hours when darkness prevented the enemy from being met and turned back as he was in daylight. They provide striking, if ominous, proof of the efficiency and devotion of the fighters of the Royal Air Force.'

'To what height would these figures have risen had there been no Hurricanes and Spitfires – resolute, ruthless, triumphant - on the alert from dawn to dusk engaging the enemy wherever he appeared?'

Those three months of aerial aggression had resulted in the deaths of 2,500 Germans; 15,000 British citizens.

The PR proponents noted that their figures for enemy aircraft losses took:

'...no account of those lost at night or those, seen by thousands, staggering back to their French bases, wings and fuselages full of holes, ailerons shot away, engines smoking, undercarriages dangling – the retreating remnants of a shattered and disordered Armada. This melancholy procession of the defeated was to be observed not once but many times during those summer and autumn days of 1940.'

Seemingly the Ministry had yet to consider how those 'remnants' managed to pull together sufficient resources to mount Blitz raids across Britain through the rest of the autumn, then the winter and spring.

Across the first full calendar year of war, losses on BC Operations mounted to 921, whilst non-ops rose to 150. Proportionately, that was an improvement on 1939: only 14% lost in training. For the remainder of the war, the number of training fatalities hovered around 200 per annum, while the operational losses grew and grew as more missions were tackled each year.

Bomber Command sometimes struggled with navigation issues, but one outing would be relished: on Saturday 9th November it was party night in Munich. The National Socialist Party was due to commemorate the anniversary of the creation of the Nazi movement and the head man was going to deliver a triumphant speech. The RAF decided to gate-crash from above. Though their endeavours were somewhat misplaced, this nevertheless meant the Fuhrer needed to stay offstage, huddling in a nearby super-strong German shelter. After the British planes left the arena, the celebrations continued, but without the headline act. The 'Tommies' had stained the occasion. Hitler was so annoyed he demanded a retaliatory raid, which was powerfully delivered on 14th November.

In the mysterious east, the Japanese attacked Burma two days before Christmas. RAF crews aided by American volunteers - the Flying Tigers - attempted to defend Rangoon. The invaders deployed a hundred craft from Thailand, killing several thousand Burmese people by strafing and bombing.

Was there continuous, severe, out-and-out hatred and contempt between the European protagonists after more than a year of fighting? Up to a point. The Germans love Christmas. Wouldn't it be nice to have a proper one again? Without disturbance and danger. In early December representatives of the Third Reich, via their Embassy in Washington, put out diplomatic feelers to the British Government proposing a few days' truce for Christmas and Boxing Day. Whitehall decided that some relief from hostilities would indeed be a desirable change and so a temporary cessation was agreed – secretly. It was never publicly announced, so no-one in Britain - apart from the top brass in London - could look forward to the precious patch of calm that lay ahead. People simply noted that no bombs or gunfire were heard for forty eight hours. Many probably prayed to God for that relief, but in fact it was the enemy they should have thanked. As soon as the truce ended the Germans launched several big attacks. They were surely refreshed by that precious time off and so re-entered the fray with additional vigour. A few days later journalists learned of the truce but bureaucrats on both sides denied any deal had been done.

Perhaps that combat break had been a mistake for the Brits. But consider this: as Adolf buttoned up his master-race jimjams at midnight on New Year's Eve, he must have had a thought or three about the irritating RAF. A year previously, the world had seemed his oyster. First six months of 1940 went like a dream. He'd marched round Paris, then peered across the English Channel at those white cliffs. But like a swarm of wasps the RAF flyers had kept buzzing about, breaking his magnificent German planes. Then the RAF started spoiling all those invasion barges in the occupied ports. The RAF had messed up parts of handsome Heligoland; they had extinguished hundreds of German airmen; had entered domestic Reich airspace and annoyed folk living near factories. Worst of all, they had denied him that so-well-deserved pat on the back from his fans at the Munich fascist-fest.

It was so unfair. *The English Air Force – Schwein!*

1941

WHAT WILL STOP THIS?

"Invasion must be regarded as a standing dish on the Hitler menu."

...declared an RAF spokesman on the front page of the Daily Mirror on 1st January 1941. However he went on to assure readers that:

"R.A.F. striking power in men and machines will grow like a rolling snowball."

Next to these observations the newspaper allocated space to reports from a Nazi news agency telling of four RAF planes that had recently entered German airspace: two were shot down by anti-aircraft crews, the other two 'dropped their bombs in fields'.

At home, the weather was easing matters a little:

AIR WAR LULL

'The Luftwaffe was quiet again up to a late hour last night – grounded on the other side of cloud and fog in the Channel. For several hours after darkness fell there were no raids in any part of Britain. Activity during the day was confined to a few isolated attacks by single aircraft in Kent and Essex. One raider, after dropping nine small calibre high explosives on an East Anglian town, flew low and machine-gunned the streets. There were no casualties.'

Elsewhere on the front page, news that the UK government would make fire-watching compulsory for all business premises. Inside, coverage of Hitler's New Year edict to his armed forces, featuring an assessment of the British Prime Minister:

"At the desire of the democratic war agitators and their Jewish capitalist wire-pullers this war must be continued. For three and a half months this criminal has been ordering German cities to be bombed by night, incendiary leaves to be scattered over German farms, and – as the inhabitants of Berlin know – has been assigning hospitals as special targets."

So, despite the Blitz campaign continuing to dismay Britain, our boys were managing to aggravate Adolf.

Were things about to get better or worse? We can track the trajectory via Mirror front page headlines. On the 13th, revelations of Luftwaffe-delivered misery in the capital:
BOMBED SUBWAY
Next day, news of retaliation:
RAF NOW TAKES OFFENSIVE IN EUROPE
But a few days later, we must:
ENDURE HARDER BLOWS YET
This heralded a sombre Churchill speech:
"Before us lie many months of having to endure bombardment of our cities and industrial areas without the power to make equal reply."

However, a week later, more proof of British capacity to take the aggression to enemy shores - in this case, Italian-controlled Libya:
29th   RAF PILOTS 'ELIMINATE' A BASE
The week after that, a sortie to the French coast:
6th February   RAF DAY RAID ON AIR BASE
Soon a pointer to the global implications of the conflict with reports from the Pacific:
20th   WE MASS PLANES IN EAST

And soon news of mighty support from across the Atlantic:
13th March   £513,000,000 ON U.S. PLANES FOR US
Then proof that the RAF is still valiantly tackling its agenda:
14th   13 BOMBERS ARE BAGGED IN 2 NIGHTS
Next day, the chaps went back to Berlin:
15th   RAF'S SCORE MOUNTS
But it was patently not all one-sided:
20th   4 HOSPITALS IN LONDON ARE HIT

How could this have happened?

A hole in the net?

We are regularly reminded that in September 1940 Hitler recognised opposing forces were too strong and numerous for an immediate invasion of England to be pursued: the Spitfires scared off the Nazis. But the broader picture is full of holes regarding the representation of the days and nights that followed, not least an absence of explanation of what the RAF was up to on the defensive front during the miserable months of the Blitz. This had begun in September, but the bulk of the relentless night-bombing took place from October 1940 to May 1941.

For dozens of successive nights the Luftwaffe sent squadrons of bombers to pummel London docks, factories and the city centre. Occasionally there would be raids on other ports, and sometimes even inland sorties. Each German aircraft did not carry much in the way of ordnance, but a lot of that explosive damaged somewhere or other.

Much of the resulting destruction and death was censored at the time - so the Germans would not get a sense of their success rate. Suppression of the turmoil was also designed to limit dismay and fear amongst the domestic population. But the regularity and spread of the Luftwaffe's disgorging of weaponry could not be ignored so newspapers and radio were permitted to report on a degree of the damage, whilst minimising numbers of fatalities as well as concealing the locations.

Why was London on the receiving end of so much of the bombing? It was big and dense, with lots of docks and infra-structure, holding many government agencies. But most critically for the Germans, it was handy. They were working out of airfields away from home, generally near the French, Belgian and Dutch coasts. From these improvised facilities a few hundred aircraft would head off at dusk to try to drop some bombs on Britain.

The capital was patently a convenient destination - easy to locate up the Thames estuary, but the goal was always an installation of military or political significance. What was the point of wasting a weapon on a house? You might kill a few family members, but that was not going to bring about victory - far better to damage structures relevant to the machinery of the state and its commissioning bodies or war service industries. Naturally, over time, a few of those explosives would land on or near significant public buildings: St Paul's Cathedral,

Buckingham Palace, the Houses of Parliament. Indeed, each of these iconic structures suffered a degree of damage over the months ahead, but there was no concerted effort to destroy those institutions or their occupants.

If the Luftwaffe had been determined to mutilate London, how come they never severed a bridge over the Thames? That would have been a big statement of intent and capacity - a shocking image of crippling impact on the capital's normality. Did they try and fail? According to captured German airmen, and post-war interrogation, such structures were never on their target list. They were always attempting to hit something that had a direct bearing on Britain's ability to continue to prosecute the war – docks, factories, barracks, headquarters, stores – but, of course, not always succeeding.

Nevertheless London's nightly subjection to German aircraft disgorging ordnance was an unpleasant and costly trial. And a massive nuisance - for which the UK had no immediate, viable answers. Yes, there were clusters of barrage balloons to discourage foreign flyers from coming in low, a few weak searchlight beams scanning the skies mingled with intermittent gun emplacements shelling in the general direction of the alien craft, but the Royal Air Force did not have the means to identify the flight paths of the incoming planes, in order to head towards them with their own armed craft and so start shooting at those bombers before they reached built-up areas in the dark.

The Blitz is presented these days as a concerted attack on London, and to a lesser degree on other towns and cities. Look at the location of those other urban areas. Almost all were on the coast. i.e. easy to find from the sea. Clockwise, the targets lay in Portsmouth, Southampton, Plymouth, Bristol, Cardiff, Swansea, Liverpool, Manchester (in a bit from the Mersey estuary, up the ship canal), Belfast (on a bit from the Isle of Man), Glasgow, Edinburgh, Tyneside, Teesside, Hull.

During November and December 1940 the Luftwaffe undertook 9,000 bombing sorties against the UK. The RAF managed to shoot down six of those flights. In January 1941 the Luftwaffe made 2,000 bombing attempts on Britain. Anti-aircraft gun crews reckoned they shot down a dozen foreign planes. The RAF claimed three. Next month the Luftwaffe, facing bad weather, conducted 1,600 UK sorties. The RAF announced four German craft downed, while acknowledging four of their own were lost in those challenges.

There were only a few inland locations for major Blitz endeavour: in particular, Coventry, Birmingham, and Sheffield. How did the Luftwaffe find those places at night? They had an electronic guidance system in operation, which projected beams from two different directions. Aircraft were equipped with signal readers, so they could follow the line of one beam and when the other beam crossed it, they were at the required address. Once British scientists registered the beams, work started on distorting the signals, and eventually they devised a means of skewing the invisible lattice. By May 1941 the boffins also came up with kit to enable British crew to identify enemy planes electronically and so head toward them in the hope of intercepting.

What was anti-aircraft gunnery achieving? Not much. Statistically 6,000 shells needed to be fired to bring down one German aircraft. However, between June 1940 and March 1941, the Luftwaffe lost more than 2,000 aircraft on missions to Britain, mostly due to accidents during take-off, mid-flight mechanical problems or piloting errors.

In total the Luftwaffe dropped around 45,000 tons of bombs on Britain, killing 41,000 people in the process. Proportionally, consider that in merely one month in 1943 Bomber Command would unload over Hamburg enough ordnance to kill a similar number of Germans.

When the Battle of Britain is publicly commemorated, there is seldom any mention of what our boys were unable to do for the next seven months as the Blitz continued. It wasn't really a hole in the net. There was no net.

Where are we?

A good navigator must be armed with good charts and a good compass: essential tools for successfully finding your way from A to B in the air. You know where you started from, what direction you are going in and how fast the plane is flying, so it's just a matter of drawing a line on the chart that follows the route of your craft; then you can work out how far it will have travelled at any point in time. This is called Dead Reckoning (DR), which had worked well on ships for centuries; though down there you had the advantage of not travelling too swiftly, which gave you plenty of time to do your calculations. Up in a plane, you needed to work fast.

But many of the shortcomings of DR applied whether on water or in the sky. Your pencil is never sharp enough. That line of lead across the sheet is representing a corridor perhaps several dozen metres wide. How accurate are your aircraft's gauges? What about the wind? Is it blowing you to one side of your projected path? As an aircraft climbs, wind parameters can change - more complicated calculations. Just think how difficult things are going to become when you leave the UK and cross the North Sea hoping to arrive at some recognisable point on the Belgian, Dutch, French or German coast. And, of course, all of the above refers to efforts taking place in daylight. Imagine trying to do any of that in the dark.

Crossing the sea, one way of sizing wind drift was to drop a series of flaming floats on to the waves, then get the rear gunner to evaluate how far off that line the plane was now flying. Once above enemy territory recognisable landmarks were vital. Big rivers flowing towards the sea are intermittently sandwiched with built-up areas that are well-known towns or cities, with a distinctive shape which the map-makers should have reproduced.

A decent railway line can be a big help - assuming it's on your chart. When it was clear that Hitler and co. were menacing the nations on their borders, it would surely have been advantageous to get hold of at least one copy of every map ever published covering any part of Germany plus all other countries that a plane might be required to fly over. Unfortunately British officials failed to acquire a comprehensive collection of maps from Europe prior to September 1939. Time and again, as the top brass contemplated options for flights and targets, the lack of appropriate tourist publications would bug them.

In the early years of night bombing raids, by judicious use of the available geography field trip aids, navigators reckoned they had done well to get within 20 miles of their intended destinations. What chance of finding and destroying some specific factory along the Rhine?

Fiddly

'Before the war, public men of importance in Sheffield, on occasions such as dinners of the Aeronautical Inspection Department, had said openly that if one air raid could blot out certain streets in Sheffield, there would be no more steel supply for a year. Those speeches were reported in the Sheffield papers in the hopes that the Government might be induced to set up alternative steel-production plants elsewhere.'

So noted Charles Grey in his book, 'Bomber', published in 1941. What the authorities did see fit to do was supply Sheffield with balloons – of a barrage nature. These would be filled with lighter-than-air gas and attached to a very long steel cable, so the metal rope could be lifted by the balloon up into the sky and there act as a deterrent for enemy planes flying past that point. Or, better still, provide a hell of a shock should the visitor impinge on a cable at night.

What do we know about these seemingly impressive temporary structures? The first ones were adaptations of the observation balloons that had been deployed above the trenches in the Great War. For the second war against Germany it was decided that dedicated teams of personnel should be ready to fill up, then winch up, balloons around the edge of London and other major cities. The precise quantity of hydrogen per balloon was critical; unless it was correct, the balloon might float tail up or down and so fail to resemble a static, bloated plane. The fiddly things were very vulnerable to bad weather. A storm over Bristol unleashed flashes of lightening amongst a bunch of balloons, setting them on fire, and causing the freed cables to whip to the ground.

Were the inflated suspensions effective? Certainly no pilot in his right mind would fly near those things. If you saw them ahead, you'd give them a wide berth. Go round them or above them. Yes, minor nuisance factor. However they did indicate that something lay beyond them that was probably worth bombing. In fact, they acted as a useful pointer as to where you could fruitfully drop a load of weaponry if you had any spare and weren't sure what to do with it. Secret was to keep well above the balloons and try to release your load beyond the barrier.

Of course, unlike anti-aircraft batteries, barrage balloons cannot distinguish between friend or foe: you hit the cable, you're in trouble.

Ironically, Coventry's barrage first snagged a RAF training flight. The plane clipped a cable and was seriously damaged. Some of the crew baled out but died in their fall. The pilot landed his craft on a cricket pitch where it caught fire before he could escape. A few months later, one afternoon a Hurricane hit another of the thick vertical wires, killing the pilot.

There were three types of consequence if you flew into a suspended fence. A wing might be sliced off and the rest of your craft would abruptly drop, no time for parachutes. Or the aircraft could pivot on the cable, losing speed by perhaps 100 mph, which would destroy the plane's trajectory, causing it to fall fast. A third prospect was that the impact wrenched free a length of the cable from the winding truck and/or the balloon, so the plane now has an extra element to its weight, chronically unbalancing the thrust. On a few occasions aircraft later landed with lengths of barrage balloon cable still strung around a wing.

Sheffield was a major location for armament production, not least the manufacture of components for RAF planes. The city was supplied with around 70 balloons, which could be raised to a maximum height of a mile. Sheffield experienced sixteen visits from Luftwaffe crews, the first a single craft on 18th August 1940 which dropped one canister of explosive. The final fly-over came on 28th July 1942, but the intensive bombing took place over two nights in December 1940, and was preceded by German airmen shooting down a couple of balloons to clear a route for their colleagues. Most of the ordnance fell in the city centre. Some people consider this had always been the intention; others contend it was the consequence of beam bending by British boffins, or that German pathfinder pilots mistook tram lines for railway lines and so commenced their flare drops in the wrong place.

The balloons may have done something to give the good folk of Sheffield a sense of safety in their beds at night, but the pre-Christmas bombardment was patently not inhibited by those slender stalks of steel in the sky. 300 German planes from occupied Belgian airfields crossed the North Sea and decanted explosives, killing nearly 700 people, and leaving thousands injured, with tens of thousands of properties damaged.

Pressure on air defence personnel soon forced the authorities to consider whether women could man balloon squads. Trials were undertaken in Sheffield in 1941 which concluded that female teams could do it all just fine, so the city became a centre for training women to join barrage units.

Elsewhere in England, someone thought it might be a good idea to fix a mechanism on aircraft wings that would cut through German balloon cables in the event an RAF pilot failed to spot and/or avoid one. A compact contraption was fixed to a number of bombers: a formidable wire cutter incorporated into the leading edge of the wing. The cable would hopefully catch in a slot where an explosive trigger could cut it with a bladed bolt so allowing the aircraft to pass on its way. It was an ambitious theory which seldom worked in practice. Hundreds of fiendish cable cutters were fitted to aircraft wings and one of the armament crews' regular tasks was to check the state of each cutter and, if necessary, re-load the explosive bolt. The devices were awkward and unpredictable. Dozens of ground crew lost fingers or thumbs whilst trying to manipulate those vicious mechanisms into or out of primed position. Far too fiddly.

It's cold up here

The higher you fly, the colder it gets. Everyone knew this, and so, before the war, planes stayed low. Why rise into that thin air when it made you so uncomfortable? But once you are trying to fly over foreign territory yet not be spotted by enemy planes, there is a lot to be said for travelling as far above the surface of the earth as possible.

Each model of aircraft has a ceiling of performance – a height above which the machine will not stay stable because the air has become so thin. Patently the load aboard the plane affects the effective ceiling: the more you are carrying, the less high you can travel. The build-up of ice on mechanical surfaces will also affect performance and, unlike ships steaming beyond the Arctic circle, you can't send someone outside to try to hack chunks off.

Most of the aircraft available to the RAF in 1939 were not designed to keep the crew warm. Few had anything in the way of heating systems. But young men accepted that the conditions aboard a high flying craft would be chilly at times, and so dressed to keep the cold out. Of course there were limits to how many layers you could wear without turning into a giant useless ball of wool. You needed to function aboard the plane, move about when required, and handle instruments or machinery as necessary. You might wear several pairs of gloves, which you could remove if trying to manipulate a pesky item, such as a tiny switch or a big chart.

Through the winter months, thermal underwear and additional layers on top counted for very little. Exposed skin became sore, then numb. Hands would be in agony. Frostbite started to set in. Fingers would stick to any metal surface they encountered. Your body and brain began to freeze up.

When those back at base learnt of the failure of crews to operate effectively under such conditions, engineers explored ways of keeping the boys defrosted. Strange heated suits were supplied with electric filaments sewn through them connected to a cable leading to a socket. But anyone required to move through the fuselage had to unplug and thus discover just how debilitating the cold air would be. Structural modifications were made to feed heat off engines into the plane but for many bomber aircrews operating above 20,000 feet, work was extremely unpleasant.

If an aircraft was shot at, causing some part of the cockpit canopy to be broken away, pilots had to try to head home whilst exposed to the ambient temperature and could easily lose fingers to frostbite on the way. Their flying days would be over. Not impossible that some might perceive this as a bit of good fortune.

Flaking hell
Firing shells up at intruding aircraft was essential. Sooner or later you might hit an enemy plane and do it serious damage. The smarter shells were designed to explode when they reached the same height as the craft: to violently propel a shower of sharp shards in all directions. These would make holes in the plane and possibly the systems and people inside.

So anti-aircraft guns could – if utilised sufficiently well and in quantity – reduce the number of menacing enemy aircraft in your vicinity. Occasionally those crashing planes hit houses, shops, factories, schools, hospitals, but this was rationalised as a necessary repercussion of eliminating the aggressor.

However, the odds of a shell, or series of shells, hitting or exploding near an enemy aircraft were extremely low, because the goal was very difficult to achieve. The plane is flying at 200 mph, perhaps 10,000 feet high. You can hear and hopefully see it coming. Your gun barrel needs to be aimed at some point in the sky where you anticipate that aircraft may reach in the next ten seconds. The direction and moment of fire are absolutely critical to give the shell half a chance of arriving in the required location. Most will miss, many by a mile.

Flak was primarily a deterrent rather than a killer. Any sensible pilot would endeavour to keep his craft distant from such hazards. Clusters of AA tended to cause aircraft to veer away from that area; unless there was no alternative (e.g. orders) but to head through the menace. But the principle of batteries of anti-aircraft guns around important installations remained universal: it put pilots off.

Gun emplacement teams were always eager to blast shells upward, with some sites always busier than others. You'd be warned that an enemy squadron was heading your way. Now you were the front line of defence: all that training and technique to be deployed in the hope you and your crew could down one of those approaching monsters.

Chances of success were tiny, but the principle of loud, vigorous efforts alarmed the airmen and it lifted the spirits of those living nearby. People cowering in their shelters wanted to hear those batteries booming, and would complain if the guns became silent while there was still the sound of foreign planes above.

Military commanders became concerned at the waste of ammunition, wear and tear on gun barrels, the menace of falling shells - exploded or otherwise - dropping on suburbia, but the demand for constant challenge to the infiltrating aircraft remained. Dozens of civilians were killed or seriously injured by shells crashing down, sometimes detonating.

In one month a quarter of a million shells were hurled up in the general direction of Luftwaffe planes around London. The British Anti-Aircraft Command accumulated a staff complement of 400,000; overall UK Civil Defence amounted to 700,000 full time personnel, aided by 1.5 million part-timers, all of which contributed towards another vital statistic: the average German bomber crew survived just 17 missions to Britain.

A mangle of metal

When it became apparent that planes would arbitrarily drop out of the sky and crash in a field or street or even on top of a building, both British and German authorities realised they needed systems in place to effectively clear up such messes and to some degree remedy the situation. It didn't really matter if the plane was one of your own or one of theirs, you didn't want it left where it was.

First folk on the scene were generally concerned for any crew member who might still be aboard the craft. Chances were the airmen had died, or had been badly injured. Most survivors were treated with sympathy; some were considered evil mass murderers. Kids would try to steal souvenirs from the craft, and from the uniforms and pockets of dead airmen. In England BMW engine badges were particularly popular.

Experts would want to examine any foreign plane for information or equipment that might be news to the boffins. If it was one of your own side's craft then recovery personnel might extract parts that could be used again. But the whole of an enemy plane could be taken to scrap yards, though a few examples of downed foreign craft were put on display in public places to act as an incentive for passers-by to make contributions towards fighting funds.

Britain established the Civilian Repair Organisation which kept many people busy until the summer of 1941, after which its work load declined as far fewer German machines appeared over British skies.

War artist Paul Nash, who had hauntingly represented First World War trenches, became intrigued by the sights of crashed German planes across the English countryside and painted many in situ; more at a dump near the Morris factory in Cowley where they were scavenged for aluminium. He proposed to the War Office that prints of his pictures, with an overlapping image of Hitler, could be put on leaflets for sprinkling over German citizens.

As the war continued, more and more British and, later, American aircraft came down on Third Reich territory, where forced labour had to clear up the mangled metal, make good the immediate landscape and shift wrecks to furnaces for enriching domestic munitions output.

Your 'War' weekly

'It must be to aircraft that we must look for striking at the enemy and wearing down his will. It must be to aircraft that we must look for protecting our bases in Britain and overseas.'

Several publishers produced magazines presenting latest developments on the battle fronts. 'The War' dominated the market, selling for 3d in the early years, 6d by 1945. Taking one edition, published on 28th March 1941, what sort of snapshot do we find of the broad-ranging belligerence, especially in the air? The week's front cover is an artist's drawing of the Empire's re-taking of British Somaliland from the Italians. The text explains that Indian, Somali and Aden Arab troops surrounded the town of Berbera under the cover of naval guns and R.A.F. planes: 'The resistance of the Italian rear guard was speedily destroyed.' That could only cheer readers.

Page 2 brings news of the R.A.F. fruitfully supporting British forces approaching the capital of Eritrea, and attacking Italian concentrations at Tripoli in Libya. Page 3 examines aerial transport logistics and the flow of supplies from 'the immense industrial organisations of America to the outposts of freedom in these islands.'

The next page alerts readers to the capacity of the Luftwaffe to direct Atlantic U-boat crews to find and attack Allied shipping convoys, especially first thing in the morning when Coastal Command patrols had not reached the full extent of their ranges. This is adjacent to photographs showing the wreckage of one of nine enemy aircraft shot down 'while raiding this country' on the night of 12th March 'by our fighters, A.A. guns and "other devices".' Another picture is of captured German airmen at a London station on their way to internment camps. They look like cheerful teenagers on an outing. A news article explains the challenges:

'Coastal cities and London were again made the object of heavy German air attacks as the air war intensified towards the end of March. Meanwhile the R.A.F. hit back with its newly-found strength. German ports and especially those where submarines are built, repaired or maintained, were made the object of vigorous assaults in many of which the new and heavier British bombers were in action.'

Next a commendation from beyond the eastern perimeter of the Germanic empire:

'In a broadcast last week Moscow Radio paid an unexpected tribute to the R.A.F.: "They have made a big effort to bring it up to considerable strength and to improve greatly the quality of their machines and their operations. The systematic bombings of German aerodromes in France, Belgium, Holland, and in North-West Germany, and especially in the raids on Berlin, Bremen and Hamburg, have definitely demonstrated these achievements."'

Two pages on, bad news, and pictures to prove it:

'Buckingham Palace has again been attacked in a recent raid on London. It will be recalled that in September last no fewer than three attacks were made on the Palace, in the course of which the private chapel of the Royal Family and some stables were damaged. The latest attack was also deliberate. Several flares were first dropped to illuminate the whole area brilliantly. Then came a shower of incendiary bombs. They blazed fiercely, but were quickly extinguished by fire-watchers. Next came five high explosive bombs. Two fell in the Green Park, near the Palace gates, two fell in the Palace forecourt; the fifth bomb hit the North Lodge. A policeman on duty at the back of the lodge was killed.'

Alongside photographs of damaged Royal property, recollections of a Flight Lieutenant:

"I saw the Nazi a mile and a half away. It looked just a little black spot silhouetted against the haze. Coming up behind him I gave one burst, and something fell off the bomber. I was immediately covered by a blinding cloud of smoke. When I flew out of it Jerry was already on his way towards the sea, well alight. I found myself perspiring as if I had been in a Turkish bath, although it was a very cold night."

Next, reports on the Luftwaffe's recent visit to Clydeside, and an announcement from The Lord Provost of Glasgow:

"After watching the police, firemen, ambulance staff and A.R.P units during our first experience of an intense raid, I have to give them an unqualified testimonial for their brilliant work and unflinching heroism. Their reckless indifference to their own safety was something at which to marvel. They are ready if necessary for another dose tonight."

While down in London:

"The wall at the end of the dance hall suddenly caved in with a roar and the roof fell in. Lumps of brick and plaster fell on the band and the dancers. Some people were trapped and killed. As I rushed to the entrance another bomb came down. It landed almost underneath a bus which was just pulling away from the pavement. The next moment there was a dreadful roar as the bus started to burn. People were screaming and shouting for help. Men and girls from the dance hall, many of them injured, ran to the rescue. Some of the people in the bus, women among them, were already dead."

Next page, stuff to cheer us up again: illustrations showing how the Germans will need to increase armour plating on their planes which will slow them down, and reduce both their bomb carrying capacity and flying range. The text adds that British bomber design and construction 'can withstand the effect of cannon fire far better than anything the Germans possess'.

There were also welcome reports of help on its way:

'More than 3,000 pilots have applied in New York to the committee dealing with applications to join the R.A.F. These men have all come without being asked. American law forbids the soliciting in the United States of recruits for foreign fighting services. Already more than 525 pilots have been accepted since last July. About 400 of them are serving as instructors in Canada. Forty other are "ferrying" bombers to Britain.'

Why shouldn't we win this damned war?

Overseas aid

Books and films often portray Britain as standing alone against the mighty German war machine across the greater part of the Second World War. In fact Britain was the heart of a huge global empire in the 1930s, benefiting from many assets around the world, not least human resources. From the commencement of the war, the armed services were able to call upon foreigners – commonwealth and dominion citizens - to come and help. Recruitment offices and advertising were quickly established within every overseas country that formed part of the British Empire. And from these outposts, the army and navy soon had fresh manpower to enrich their regiments and vessels.

The RAF too could benefit from this massive source of able and eager people. Such volunteers needed to be especially smart to be considered for air training, but there was no shortage of suitable candidates. Many Australians, Canadians, Indians, South Africans and New Zealanders soon swelled the ranks of RAF Commands. They joined Czech, Dutch, French, Greek, Polish and American airmen who had chosen to throw in their lot with the Brits. A UK flying school in the spring embraced students from Portuguese East Africa, Argentina, China, Eire, Bermuda, Portugal and Rhodesia. The British were never alone in the air, and statistics compiled subsequent to the war demonstrated that some of those foreigners were the very best flyers for the RAF, though I have been told that occasionally poor comprehension of the English language resulted in mighty mistakes regarding how to handle certain aircraft or to reach the required destination of particular flights.

For those mean-spirited citizens who feel that, despite being one of the richest countries in the world, Britain spends too much on overseas aid, please note that during the war many nations around the globe also provided generous and vital funds for RAF enhancement. Amongst the nations rustling up money to pay for one or more fighter aircraft were the Indian Province of Punjab, the Persian Gulf, Nigeria, the Belgian Congo and Brazil. The RAF's Natal Squadron was maintained entirely by donations from citizens of Natal in South Africa. People of the occupied Netherlands secretly funded the construction of more than forty Spitfires at around £5,000 a time. In all, 23,000 Spitfires were assembled between 1937 and 1946. Hundreds of the vital craft were paid for by foreigners.

Meanwhile the London Lord Mayor's Air Raid Distress Fund benefited from overseas contributions, including that of five Armenian farmers in Berber whose £122 was dutifully forwarded from the National Bank of Egypt.

To all our friends from overseas: a great big Thank You.

Avoiding the Vatican

The beauty of flying at night was that made it much harder for the enemy to see you. Providing you fixed shields over the engine exhausts and switched off all your lights, it was possible to travel through foreign air space without the opposition being able to identify where you were.

Perched along the perimeter of the belligerents' borders were thousands of listeners, some voluntary, others pressed into service. They were tasked with listening in the dark to try to detect the sound of approaching planes. Initially they used their ears; then they were given enormous horns to concentrate incoming sound waves. Later, they received directional microphones and headsets.

Behind the listeners, protecting assets, were gunners who could – before searchlights - only guess at a machine's aerial whereabouts based on engine sounds. Meanwhile, the pilot in a defending aircraft is boxed in with noise, with no means of detecting alien audio.

So night flying was safer for bombing campaigns. If it wasn't cloudy or raining, you could peer below and hopefully spot some landmarks that would indicate your whereabouts. Big conurbations found it hugely difficult to achieve utter darkness along their streets. Once the first few bombs had blasted on to whatever was below, fires would inevitably start which made it nice and easy for your colleagues behind to see where they needed to add to that conflagration.

On 16th April the Luftwaffe conducted yet another night raid on London. Next night, the RAF sent squadrons to Rome, and the following morning Downing Street provided the world with an explanation:

'In view of the German threats to bomb Athens and Cairo, His Majesty's Government wish it to be understood that if either of these cities is molested they will commence a systematic bombing of Rome. It is part of a regular policy adopted by the R.A.F., under instructions from the Government, of the bombing of objectives in the two guilty countries, which are most likely to weaken their military or industrial capacity. This policy will be continued till the end of the war, it is hoped on an ever-increasing scale, irrespective of whether any attacks are made on the British Islands or not. The greatest care will be taken not to bomb the Vatican City, and the strictest orders to that effect have been issued.'

BC crews generally preferred the long haul to Italy, because they were far less likely to encounter much opposition in the skies or on the ground, and everyone enjoyed the views over the Alps on the way back.

Round the bend

The evening of 10th May saw hundreds of German bombers approaching London. 300 miles north, a lone long-range Messerschmitt entered Scottish airspace from the North Sea. At the controls was Rudolf Hess, Hitler's deputy, who aspired to initiate negotiations with the British that might terminate hostilities between the two nations. Rudolf had been planning his secret flight for months. He'd got fed up with the man with whom he had once shared a prison cell, wherein they had drafted some of the maniacal narrative that became Mein Kampf.

Hess had enthusiastically helped build the Nazi Party and had been rewarded with senior positions in the Third Reich government. Now he reckoned he could pull off a neat deal with the Brits to wind down the war in the west. It was just a matter of a commencing a quiet chat, pilot-to-pilot, with the Duke of Hamilton, a distinguished Scottish airman based at Dungavel House near Glasgow.

Unable to spot the relevant premises, or somewhere flat to land, Rudolph decided the safest course of action was to parachute down. Meanwhile London was being pounded by German bombs in what would be the most intensive night of aerial assault on the capital.

Hess hurt his leg from the parachute jump. A farmer found the intruder, who pretended to be a civilian and requested to be taken to Dungavel for an important meeting. Instead the farmer called up the Home Guard who conveyed the prisoner to an army barracks in Glasgow.

Around London, Fighter Command sent up hundreds of planes to defend the capital. Anti-aircraft guns fired off nearly 5,000 shells, but the Luftwaffe only lost twelve aircraft that night, as they released 700 tons of high explosive and 80,000 incendiaries, which initiated more than 2,000 fires.

RAF Wing Commander Hamilton reached Glasgow the next day, and Hess fessed as to his real identify. The would-be Nazi mediator spoke and understood English but he couldn't decipher the Duke's heavy Scottish accent, so he demanded an interpreter. A foreign affairs expert from London was send up to interview the curious captive. Rudolph claimed he could pull off a peace treaty that would allow the Brits to exit the war at this point, leaving Germany to expand eastward into Russia. The civil servant reported back but Ministers were distracted by the fact that 1,400 Londoners had just been killed, 1,800 seriously injured, and 150 unexploded bombs lay around the city, making many streets impassable.

The lone infiltrator now complained about his medical treatment and accused his captors of trying to poison him, which did nothing to win him credibility. Hess was a hypochondriac – always anxious about what he ate. He had a soft spot for alternative medicine and carried homeopathic remedies on his journeys. Unfortunately he had left his current complement of concoctions aboard his plane.

Back in Berlin, the absconder had left a letter for Adolf revealing that he aimed to organise a truce with the UK. Surprise, surprise, the Fuhrer was furious, and announced that Rudolph was round the bend. Hitler reckoned his old side-kick had lost his marbles due to dependency on dodgy quacks and cranky potions, so he ordered the rounding up and execution of lots of faith healers, back-street medicine men and fortune tellers (who, surely, should have seen this coming).

Hess was moved to a secure location for further interrogation but failed to convince anyone that he had a viable role in achieving an acceptable peace in Europe. Was his mission given the green light by some part of the German High Command looking to get the Brits off their backs before Operation Barbarossa, or just a crazy endeavour by a mad Nazi? The prisoner kept complaining about various ailments and insisted he swap suppers with his guards to ensure he wasn't poisoned. Physicians noted that he was now suffering from - or possibly faking - amnesia. Five weeks after his ignominious landing on British soil, Rudolph tried to commit suicide by jumping off the balcony of a staircase, but all he did was break a leg. This got him moved to a guarded hospital in Wales where he spent the rest of the war in relative comfort.

The costs of damage to London from the raid on the 10th May amounted to £20 million. It was a brutal, dramatic flourish from the Luftwaffe designed to distract attention from their sneaky shift to eastern Germany.

The wizard war

Winston Churchill's fascinating 'The Second World War' history has a chapter entitled 'The Wizard War'. To what was the great man referring? Secret apparatus invented by unconventional scientists that had the capacity to wrong-foot the enemy. The PM detected particular promise in the use of radio waves for aerial communication, but he acknowledged that the Germans were already well along that path before the war began:

> 'With their logical minds and deliberate large-scale planning, the German High Air Command staked their fortunes in this sphere on a device which... they thought would do us in. Therefore they did not bother to train the ordinary bomber pilots... in the difficult art of navigation. A far simpler and surer method, lending itself to drill and large numbers, producing results wholesale by irresistible science, attracted alike their minds and their nature. The German pilots followed the beam as the German people followed the Fuhrer. They had nothing else to follow.'

Churchill reckoned that deflecting or jamming beams caused around a fifth of German ordnance to fall in fields. Not a solution, but a degree of relief. Luftwaffe pilots who reported back that there might be something amiss with the systems were initially given short shrift, but eventually the Germans realised that some distortions had diminished effectiveness, and so a new wave of radio guidance was developed. Once British boffins unpicked the new German technique they could then forecast a future target several hours in advance, but, as Churchill noted:

> 'Our night-fighters had, alas! at this date neither the numbers nor the equipment to make much use of the information.'

However he claims it was useful for the assignment of Civil Defence personnel and fire-fighting teams. The memoirs explain that Britain's limited endeavours at wavelength counter-measures in the early months of the Blitz were all that the nation had to deploy:

> '... when all other means of defence had either failed or were still in their childhood.'

Winston's love of laboratory alchemy encouraged the development of two defence systems that never made it into operational mode. The

91

capacity to deliver sufficient deadly flak from Ack-Ack guns into the body of an overhead bomber was recognised as extremely poor. Would the mass launch of small armed rockets do the job better? Many months and man-hours were spent on perfecting rocket batteries that could pepper the sky with a mass of projectiles and so dramatically increase the likelihood of at least a few impacting on the body of an approaching plane.

Even more ingenious was the notion of aerial mines suspended on wires from parachutes that could be decanted into the sky ahead of an enemy bomber formation. The approaching fleets would not be able to weave away from this cloud of ordnance and would therefore be obliterated en masse. Churchill placed great store on this wizard concept. Unfortunately it was hugely difficult to achieve in practice.

What came to Britain's rescue ultimately? Hitler withdrawing the bulk of the Luftwaffe from the French coast, so he could deploy his planes against Russia in the summer of 1941.

Churchill remained in awe of the potential of aerial mines and tells his readers he was mystified that the Germans did not develop such a defence weapon against RAF and American bombers later in the war. That would not have been wizard.

Out of the blue

Through the spring of 1941 the Royal Air Force continued to do its best to provide evidence of worthwhile action, and hence positive headlines for the Daily Mirror:

8th April   RAF RAID SOFIA

That was Bulgaria. Next, it's Yugoslavia:

12th   R.A.F. BATTER PANZERS

Less than a week later, a photograph of a dead man, face down alongside a damaged building:

18th   DUTY DONE

'He was a fireman who, in London's greatest air raid yesterday morning, gave his life for his country. He saw his duty clearly and followed it unflinchingly to the end. For him the fire and the fury have passed. He is at peace and none will doubt that the path to duty was the way to glory.'

The action and destruction continued at home and abroad:

10th May   400 PLANES DID THIS TO THE HUN

12th	ABBEY, HOUSES OF PARLIAMENT WERE HIT
17th	R.A.F. IN ACTION AGAINST NAZIS IN SYRIA
21st	HUN GLIDERS LAND 1,500 MEN IN CRETE
22nd	WAVES OF SKYMEN IN CRETE BLITZ
26th	HUN FLEET HIT BY AIR
2nd June	RAF GUARD 15,000 OUT OF CRETE

On 11th June, the Daily Mirror reported Churchill's speech to the House of Commons in which he revealed that the total number of British war dead, excluding civilians, now amounted to 90,000, of whom all but 5,000 were "from the Mother Country". Adding the domestic victims of Luftwaffe bombing raids on Britain would take that total to around 130,000. But was the speech designed to demonstrate that servicemen and their families had at this stage suffered far more than civilians? Might this have been a means of deflecting criticism of the Air Force's recent efforts? What lay round the corner?

14th   RAF TORPEDO BATTLESHIP ON RAID BID

Yes, the Air Force determination to fight back (this time, in Norway) provided a glimmer of hope. Next, Boulogne would receive a rough visit from the British flyers:

18th   200 PLANES BLITZ NAZIS INVASION PORTS BY DAY

This news item also explained about the recent addition to RAF equipment that was starting to make their job fractionally easier: 'radiolocation'. At long last the boys had a means of spotting the Luftwaffe in the sky at night. So were the bloody cross-channel skirmishes to remain the gruesome pattern for the foreseeable future?

A few days later, a game changer: an extraordinary development in the affairs of the globe; a new dimension of earthquake proportions, with the potential to alter the war and peace landscape beyond recognition.

In his book, 'I flew for the Fuhrer', Heinz Knoke documented the start of the momentous mission:

> '0430 hours: all crews report to the squadron operations room for briefing. The Commanding Officer reads out the special order of the day from the Fuhrer: Germany is to attack the Soviet Union.'
> '0500 hours: the squadron takes off and goes into action. I have done considerable bombing practice in recent weeks. It will be a pleasure for

me to drop them on Ivan's dirty feet. We are to carry out a low level attack on one of the Russian headquarters. Everything appears to be asleep. We fly low over the wooden buildings, but there is not a Russian soldier in sight. Swooping at one of the huts, I press the bomb release button on the control stick. I distinctly feel the aircraft lift as it gets rid of the load.'

'Great masses of dirt fountain up into the air, and for a time we are unable to see because of the smoke and the dust. One of the huts is blazing fiercely. The Ivans at last come to life. The scene below is like an over-turned ant-heap, as they scurry about in confusion. Stepsons of Stalin in their underwear flee for cover in the woods.'

Knoke circled several times and machine-gunned any Russians trying to fire back. His squadron returned to their base for re-fuelling and re-arming at 0556 hours, and took off again at 0630 for a second assault on this camp. The pilot recalled the rationale and his instincts:

'We have just fore-stalled the Russian time-table for an all-out attack against Germany for the mastery of Europe.'

'We have dreamed of doing something like this to the Bolshevists. Our feeling is not exactly one of hatred, so much as utter contempt. It is a genuine satisfaction for us to be able to trample them in the mud where they belong.'

The attack by the Germans against the Russians at dawn on 22nd June 1941 was in contravention of a pact between the muscular neighbours. That day would prove to be the most destructive for aircraft losses in history.

Promising planes had been developed in Russia through the 1930s, but the communist criteria for desirable outcomes frequently inhibited the thrust of aeronautical advance. Designers and engineers whose prototypes crashed with a respected test pilot at the controls might be accused of sabotage. The Russian dictator, Joseph Stalin would instigate purges amongst senior personnel in the air force or air industries perceived as not delivering progress.

Evidence of the limits of Soviet military capacity had been exposed when the Red Air Force mounted its assault on Finland in November 1939. The Russians deployed nearly a thousand planes against the Finnish complement of less than one hundred. The Soviets were quickly swamped with local difficulty: machine failures, breakdowns, crashes, all before encountering their opponents, who proved far more proficient in the sky with their small force of reliable and well-handled craft. The Russians had to double the number of planes devoted to fighting the Finns before achieving an armistice five months later. Another wave of purges followed this debacle, monitored by the Germans, who concluded that they had little to fear from Russian flyers.

Prior to the war, Stalin had enjoyed terrific propaganda mileage from his air force; fearless fellows who flew their planes over the Arctic breaking records were heroes of the Soviet Union. Novels were written about their feats, poems penned, films produced. The Red Air Force accounted for merely 9% of national military expenditure, but in a country the size of the Soviet Union, that amounted to a third of a million personnel manipulating many thousands of planes.

Early in 1941 the Luftwaffe undertook hundreds of reconnaissance flights over Russian territory, which Stalin had not challenged for fear of being accused of provocation. So the Germans built up a good picture of where their neighbours' airfields lay, as well as all army units close to the mutual border. They identified rudimentary bases short of camouflage and defence, scattered with aircraft finished in a silvered metal designed to improve their speed, and thus easy to spot from above.

By the time Hitler was ready to mount his surprise attack, Russia had deployed 7,000 aircraft along his western border. At the end of the first day of Operation Barbarossa, the Soviets had lost 1,800 of their machines (most of which had not taken off), whilst the Luftwaffe was short of just 35 planes. By the end of the first week of the invasion, Russia was down to 3,000 planes, whereas the Germans had lost only 150.

Stalin growled that this humiliating devastation was the result of poor command, and so he sacked and had executed a further cross-section of Soviet commanders. Naturally the massive Russian losses meant that even less experienced crew were quickly required for front line duties. Their likelihood of succeeding against the highly prepared and practiced (over Britain) Luftwaffe was even lower than their predecessors.

The desperation of Russian squadrons faced with the ferocious advance and audacity of the Luftwaffe reduced them to try ramming enemy bombers. The Soviet fighter pilot would point his plane at an approaching German craft and aim for impact. This was not a precursor to the later Japanese kamikaze one-way missions. The principle of the Russian endeavours was that the pilot jumped out just before his semi-obsolete plane crashed into the opposing machine. That way the airman might descend gently to Russian soil and so be ready to go up again soon. The tactic was respected and encouraged, and some Russians repeated this scary stunt a dozen times, though it did nothing to swing the battle in the Soviets' favour.

Perhaps Hitler's boasts of defeating the communists within months was not mere fancy? It wasn't long before the Luftwaffe was menacing Leningrad and approaching Moscow. However the Russians had had plenty of time to study how the British and the RAF had defended themselves against the Germans, and Stalin had no intention of allowing the Luftwaffe to pepper his capital the way Churchill had witnessed London being bombarded through that previous winter. Moscow was well prepared, and the calibre of anti-aircraft defence and fighter squadrons charged with protecting the Kremlin came as a considerable surprise to the Germans.

Meanwhile, Stalin had initiated the mass re-location of munitions production to sites further east. He was tooling up for a long game, and learning fast from his mistakes. Once the Russians established fresh factories far away from possible enemy assault, they would build 36,000 formidable Yak fighters. They had already destroyed 30% of German air power within the first month of the invasion.

Back in Britain, the Daily Mirror was swift to challenge any breath of complacency:

23th June   RED BOMBERS HIT BACK AT HUN INVASION

'We begin with a warning – Hitler's attack upon Russia must not for a day, for an hour, for a moment be used as an excuse for weakening air attack upon Hitler. On the contrary, this latest and largest of Nazi war is a signal to us, a call, an incentive to renewed and intensified effort. Through the R.A.F. and with every other means in our power we must continue to smash at Germany in the west.'

And so it was to be.

Our feathered friends

Bomber Command attempted several strange means of taking the war to the Germans. One concept was that by starting fires in forests, wildlife would be driven on to farm land, where the fugitive animals might consume farmers' crops which, in due course, could cause food shortages. However wild a notion, it was tackled by dropping cotton wool primed with phosphorus into acres of trees, a task which most air crews could achieve. But the would-be fire-raisers reported back that the vegetation failed to burn.

Another initiative was the decanting of small celluloid sheets impregnated with a phosphorus syrup. These were to be delivered in the dark, to flutter down on forests where concealed munitions workshops were believed to be sited. No evidence of their arrival, but in the morning, when the sun came up, the litter would ignite, potentially starting troublesome fires. The Germans condemned this unconventional ordnance, pointing out that school-children had collected the intriguing rectangles, and later got burnt. The experiment was soon abandoned.

Of course, in those trees, and everywhere else, were lots of birds. Our feathered friends don't go away even when there's a war on. The flocks have gathering areas, homing patches, migration routes – all normal, natural, wildlife stuff.

So sooner or later you're going to get birds flying in front of planes, which is never good. A pigeon can crack the Perspex window of a cockpit or the dome of a gun turret. A propeller will slice through any fowl in its arc, but a whole bird or bits of one, or more, can easily plop into an engine intake and foul the moving parts, slowing or even stopping the machine.

A single seagull can put a plane out of action; a cluster of starlings can do plenty of damage. Undoubtedly, the demise of some of our sons in those skies was brought about by birds.

One thing is certain

In the autumn of 1941, His Majesty's Stationery Office published a handsome 130-page booklet about the activities of Bomber Command since the start of the war. The content, including 100 photographs and six maps, was carefully calibrated to make a good impression. The text does not deny disasters, but understandably concentrates on the positives. One phrase indicates the tone:

'They accomplished much, they dared all.'

A chapter highlighting RAF efforts at making life difficult for enemy shipping notes that in October 1940 a British mine dropped off the French coast caused a cargo ship carrying livestock to sink. Within a few days those living along the coast discovered 'the corpses of pigs coming ashore'. We don't learn if the locals considered this a nuisance or a welcome addition to their larders.

Another success story was the BC raid on an airfield in France from where German planes had been setting off to harass Allied convoys:

'...it would seem that the morale of the aerodrome personnel was affected. They all took to the woods clad in their night-shirts.'

The dropping of the flammable sheets in German forests was also given a spin befitting of an episode of 'Allo, Allo':

'... some were picked up by souvenir hunters who put them in their trouser pockets where they burst into flames.'

The authors emphasise the significance of the attacks on the assembled German invasion vessels along the English Channel the previous year. Two pages were devoted to a large map of Germany showing the locations of RAF bombing as of 26 July 1941 – in excess of 300 different places:

'As soon as German morale begins to wilt, victory will be in sight.'

Readers were assured that enemy morale had already suffered and would continue to do so, but:

'... that it is fast cracking under the strain is, however, not yet true. What the future holds no one can foretell.'

The new generation of British and American bombers would deliver:

'… an overwhelming onslaught which will bring the enemy to his knees and then lay him prostrate in the dust of his own ruined cities.'

'One thing is certain. Bomber Command will allow no pause, no breathing space. Our attack will go on, fierce because it is relentless, deadly because it is sure.'

Class warfare

Equality of opportunity is a relatively recent principle of aspiration for British society. Prior to the 1940s it was little more than an ambition of socialist politicians. But the war proved to be a mechanism whereby the socio-economic strata could become fractured. As the conflict required more and more men and women to do unconventional stuff, so it was that people from different layers in the social structure would find themselves working alongside others from a distinctly different place in society. This was often disconcerting for all parties. Most obviously, the voices heard would be a spectrum apart: working class regional accents alongside Received Pronunciation exponents.

The higher ranks of the pre-war RAF were the preserve of posh people. One needed to be well-heeled to get close to aircraft, to be able to travel on one, to have a chance to learn to fly. The top brass and airmen were all fine chaps, most of whom had been to public school. Take a look at the war-time feature film 'The First of the Few' starring David Niven as a Spitfire test pilot. He's a terribly decent fellow, patently from the elevated echelons. Fans of 'Reach for the Sky' will recall that every recruit at Cranwell in 1928 turned up wearing a bowler hat, albeit Kenneth More perched his somewhat askew.

One group of pilots were known as "The Millionaires", because their families were immensely rich. They included Lord Beaverbrook's son, who became an RAF skipper, to serve in Britain, then the Mediterranean and finally Coastal Command; reaching the rank of Group Captain before the war ended, when he could join the family newspaper business. Money, of course, could not buy safety and some of those fortunate fellows had very unfortunate experiences in the sky.

Middle class RAF recruits were permitted to handle machinery or undertake office work. Air station layouts provided officers' quarters in one area, with facilities for the rest of the men elsewhere. On the ground it was relatively straightforward to have systems that ensured the class structure remained intact. But once the first waves of officers died in flight, squadrons had to consider allowing a non-commissioned officer (i.e. a Sergeant) to take to the air in some sort of role. It soon became apparent that some NCO men were better at flying than a proportion of the public school intake, so occasions arose when a Sergeant might be at the controls of an aircraft, with an Officer, as navigator, wireless operator or even gunner, answerable to the skipper for flight instructions.

The Luftwaffe buzzing off to bomb Russia was like a huge cloud lifting from the skies over Britain in the summer of 1941. It allowed the RAF to do a bit of recalibrating. Experienced air crew - who had survived so far - were given a bit of leave. They were replaced on the front line by newcomers, tasked with blasting munitions factories or oil production plants on the continent. (Easier said than done, of course; and the novices had no idea how formidable were the German fighter aircraft left to patrol France on the lookout for a lumbering bomber full of green "Tommies".)

When the old hands returned from Rest and Recreation they were assigned to support tasks. Best option was public relations, whereby a couple of flyers would take a train to a bomb-making factory and meet the workers – often young women. The boys would make a speech about how important it was to have lots of great munitions which they looked forward to dropping on enemy facilities. Then there'd be some photography - the airmen in uniform alongside the smiling staff - after which the visitors moved to the management canteen for a slap-up lunch. Who wouldn't want a day out like that?

But most alternative duties were more down to earth, particularly training recruits. This consisted of two parts: the official line on how you were supposed to do everything, and the unofficial, deep-intake-of-breath version, when you indicated - though perhaps did not spell out for fear of being quoted - exactly how difficult things could be as soon as you got a machine up in the air and hoped it would work properly before you spotted any enemy aircraft. You didn't want to put the kids off, but you felt you had a duty to convey the enormity of the tasks they would face, which you had miraculously survived so far. With a bit of luck, further down the line, the newcomers might get to hug pretty bomb builders before tucking into free sausage rolls.

Tragically, of course, it would take enormous luck to survive thirty sorties over Germany. And a massive amount more to see out the second wave of missions which the trainers themselves had yet to undertake.

Off target

The difficulty of delivering ordnance to a specific enemy location haunted Bomber Command from beginning to end. They had practised before the war, and concluded that you needed to hurl lots of bombs in the general direction of the aiming point to have any chance of a few of them landing near the relevant grid reference. The trials had been done over British countryside in good weather with no distractions. When it came to crossing to the continent where anti-aircraft guns blasted shells up at you and fighter aircraft swarmed towards you, the likelihood of decanting your weapons at a precise place, angle and speed which would launch them toward the destination was minuscule.

It's all about physics. You can try it at home, Blue Peter-style, with a set of darts. Open a city A-to-Z on the carpet and draw a circle with a penny coin on a map page to represent, say, the dimensions of a tank factory. Stand upright and hold a dart at arm's length to your side. Swing your hand horizontally to travel above the map and release your weapon. See the difficulty.

The least likely way of having too many bombs go astray was to fly straight and low and steadily towards the target, enemy permitting – always hoping the device will explode if and when it gets there. Unfortunately many of the early weapons did not work properly: there was no big bang as you wrenched the aircraft away from the treacherous vicinity.

But frequently crews failed to find their target and so decanted their deadly load elsewhere. Dropping bombs in fields was patently futile, however hitting suburban streets seemed wrong, so everyone on board was on the look-out for a structure that might be a legitimate target but not full of civilians; the only option often being an empty stretch of canal or railway line.

Initially, RAF and Luftwaffe crews were told to bring back bombs that could not be fruitfully unleashed: munitions were expensive - no point in wasting them. But airmen disliked returning to base carrying explosives. Landing a plane with ordnance aboard was dicey; you might bang down and the whole lot would go up. Best to get rid of the canisters while over the sea.

As the war proceeded, British aircrew sensitivities regarding civilians declined; any town was bound to be full of people who were tolerating if not actively supporting the Nazi regime. Causing discomfort to any of them would surely shorten the war. Hence the boys would just jettison their cargo on any urban landscape and head for home.

Of course, those on the ground who saw a canister dropping towards them naturally assumed the deliverers of that device specifically wished them harm. The Germans considered the RAF were deliberately attacking civilians, because there was no evidence of a concentration of ordnance that might indicate intentions to assault the Wehrmacht.

By the summer of 1941 the UK had mounted modest missions over the continent – a few planes looking for military targets or clearly defined munitions factories – seldom easy to find. But Churchill needed vivid demonstrations that Britain was able to take the battle to the enemy. It was essential to show the Russians and Americans that the UK was doing its bit.

The men returning from missions tried to put a positive slant on their efforts, but subsequent photographs of the sites allegedly devastated showed little evidence of disruption. There were growing levels of suspicion - not least from the Army and Navy - that the RAF was not doing as well with its bombing as it claimed.

Cameras were fitted to aircraft to bring back objective images of what had happened after the payload was discharged. A civil servant, Mr David Butt, studied the pictures for a month and reported an alarming analysis back to his bosses: hardly any bombs had landed anywhere useful; few seemed to have even been in the vicinity of a target. Of the crews that had later claimed to have bombed as required, it turned out only one in three was actually within five miles of the location when they released their explosives. If the Ruhr was the required destination, Butt discovered that only one plane in ten got within five miles. And the worse the weather, even less chance of reaching the right region.

Churchill was horrified by the report, though probably not wholly surprised. It confirmed his fears – that the RAF was doing no more than annoying the Germans. The survey was kept secret, but to improve perceptions, in August the Ministry of Information released a newsreel-style film showing the work of the RAF in damaging German infrastructure. 'Target for Tonight' was a celebration of commitment, equipment, skills and courage – putting sophisticated machines in the air each evening to take a formidable flight to western Germany, there to unload ordnance that would destroy enemy war-prosecution capacity. In that same month more than 100 RAF bombers were lost on their way to, over, or returning from, the Ruhr. In September the figure reached 140, a third of which went astray over England. Next month, a hundred lost again.

The solution was to widen the arena of ordnance deployment. Studies of the effects of the Luftwaffe's bombing of British cities showed that workers whose homes were destroyed tended to be absent from their factories for a few days at least. Building more big bombers to carry a punchier load to the major centres of population in Germany would sooner or later destroy sufficient proportions of the housing stock to make it very difficult for the German work force to continue to produce munitions. That was the theory.

A little private space

If you wanted to reduce a pilot's capacity to concentrate on the job in hand, nothing could have been devised to be more annoying and distracting than the oxygen mask kit. When you are above 10,000 feet you need a source of oxygen other than the air, so cockpits were fitted with cylinders of oxygen piped to face masks that allowed you to breathe as you flew. But the rubber tubing had a habit of dislodging from the cylinder valve or from the mask itself which never fitted well. Mid-flight, the oxygen apparatus might fail to function. Fiddle with it fast and if no improvement could be achieved, you had to get closer to the ground in order to breathe ordinary air again. Otherwise you would pass out.

What if you needed the lavatory mid-mission? Fighter pilots were never in the sky long enough for this to be an issue, but bomber crews had to deal with maybe ten hours of flying, so one or more of the boys might require facilities. Simple chemical toilets were deployed: a tin bucket with a seat and a lid. A layer of disinfectant would cover what was deposited therein.

Occasionally the skipper of a badly damaged aircraft ordered all unnecessary gear to be jettisoned to lighten the craft to aid its return. In theory, it was possible to drop the toilet out of a hatch, but the smelly bucket had a notorious reputation for getting stuck in the chute, then dribbling its contents into the slipstream in a way that often blew the material back inside.

If the aircraft had to undertake severe evasive action the bucket might become dislodged and so flung along the fuselage; the contents cascading out, the hefty canister banging anyone in the way. In many cases noble, exhausted air crew attempted to clean up the mess while heading for home. On other occasions they might just walk away from their landed kite, leaving the ground crew to discover the state of the interior. A minor inconvenience compared with what had gone on in the sky.

Back to the drawing board

'A highly trained and physically fit pilot, who is used to performing aerobatics regularly, can only withstand an acceleration of about 6g without blacking out.

The faster a turn of minimum radius is flown, the higher becomes the acceleration to which pilot and aeroplane is subjected, and there is a limit to what either will stand.'

The Journal of the Royal Aeronautical Society regularly reported on the implications of the advancement of technology. Prototype devices could prove difficult to manage under menacing circumstances - just not ready for action. Constant dialogue between production teams and front line forces was essential.

Tendering competition for factories seeking a slice of Ministry commissioning theoretically delivered advantages in design, build and application. This process - irritating though it could be – generally worked better in Britain than in Germany, where there was often debilitating rivalry between aircraft builders, exacerbated by antagonism between senior Luftwaffe officers. Hermann Goering persistently sowed conflict amongst his managers, triggering endless debates as to what aircraft should be developed, with which specifications and in what numbers. And because Hitler anticipated short wars - as he had so far delivered - there was seldom long-term thinking in the Berlin Air Ministry. Meanwhile, trial models were neurotically examined for performance and capacity; manufacturers might be told to undertake thousands of amendments to a machine before a decision could be made for possible approval.

Within the Luftwaffe constructive criticism was not always well received. One group of flyers were asked for their opinions on existing aircraft and systems, and so diligently drafted notes on possible improvements. Their commander then accused the young men of treachery, warning they would be court-martialled if they ever uttered such mutinous descriptions of the service and its assets again.

The Allies were better at evaluating advice from the front line to achieve upgrades. Some early British aircraft engines had a tendency to catch fire, and the surrounding fabric on the wings and fuselage was flammable. This was remedied by covering the craft with flame-retardant paint - which the RAF had purchased in Germany before the war. First wave Hurricanes were fitted with machine guns that could only handle 300 rounds, giving the pilot just fourteen seconds worth of fire-power. Later models delivered 4,000 rounds. One UK plane maker believed their prototype would be more effective with a wider wing span, but was told to abandon the ambition because such a craft would not fit inside existing hangers. It was discovered that if a Lancaster's engine caught fire the propeller could revolve faster and faster until it spun off, but Rolls Royce soon fixed this.

Testing new planes was always dangerous. A one-off model might suddenly reveal a fault that could not be remedied in the air. Trial crews also faced the peril of their own side's fighters mistaking any curious-looking machine for the enemy. British prototypes were supposed to be painted with yellow marks. One craft took off without the added colour and was swiftly shot down by an RAF crew who thought they had encountered a new German plane.

Trouble in our town

Plymouth dock yards were an intermittent destination for Luftwaffe ordnance. Examining the edition of the Western Evening Herald newspaper for Saturday 15th November 1941, one can perceive the relative importance of national, international and local events. The front page was dominated by coverage of the demise of a ship familiar to many Plymouth citizens:

DRAMATIC FLIGHT TO SAVE ARK ROYAL: 18 MISSING

That tragedy had occurred in the Mediterranean, following a convoy voyage to Malta. Next most prominent headline concerned 'Nazis struggle in Crimea'. Alongside this, readers could contemplate a picture of Sergeant Pilot Maurice Jenkins, RAF, aged 21, of the Ship Inn, Plymouth, reported as missing on air operations over Germany. He had been on the paper's photographic staff. Elsewhere on the front page:

R.A.F. AIRMEN PRISONERS

'Sixty-two British airmen were taken prisoner following the big RAF offensive over Germany during the night of November 7-8, says German radio. This was the occasion when owing to weather conditions 37 British planes failed to return after raids on Berlin, Cologne, Mannheim and other targets.'

Immediately below this, we learn:

NINE DEAD IN DAY RAID ON NORTH-EAST

'When a German raider made a sudden daylight swoop over a North East coast town and dropped bombs nine workmen were killed and there is a number of injured. Certain damage was caused. An enemy bomber was shot down into the sea off the East Coast of England by one of our fighters today. A lone raider passed over another N.E. coast town this morning and dropped bombs. Joseph Hog was taken to hospital suffering from injuries to the leg and detained. He was apparently hurt by falling debris. About six houses were slightly damaged. Bombs were dropped in a South West area last night. They fell near a village, but burst in open country, causing neither casualties nor damage.'

This news received just a few inches on the lower half of the front page. Further down, next to football results:

'British bombs on Sicily. The British Air Force dropped bombs on Derna and Barce, damaging some buildings and causing some casualties among the local population.

'Egypt's Coast Bombed: It was learned in London today that during the night of Wednesday-Thursday enemy aircraft dropped incendiaries and about 30 high explosive bombs near Bagush, which is close to the coast. There were no casualties or damage.'

Any one of those stories could today command swathes of a tabloid. Page 2 of the four-page Herald was devoted to Classified Advertising, the first column of which included ROLL OF HONOUR and DEATHS, and family tributes to half-a dozen men 'killed on war service', one of whom was a Pilot Officer. The final column alerted shoppers that Austin Reed's new Plymouth address was 4 Thornhill Villas, its previous premises having been hit by enemy ordnance.

The next page covered more domestic matters, with one column listing civil defence awards to local people; for example a British Empire Medal (Civil) to Walter Searle, Firewatcher, Post Office:

'During the early part of an air raid Mr Searle, at great personal risk, dealt effectively with a large number of incendiaries, and an outbreak of fire was effectively prevented. Heavy bombing followed and Searle worked throughout the night, showing great courage and devotion to duty in dealing with the many dangerous situations which arose. Later the building was demolished by a direct hit, and Mr Searle was buried for seven hours, two of his fellow firewatchers being killed.'

For such activity, Walter Searle was allocated two column inches halfway down Page 3.

The extraordinary had become ordinary.

A poke in the eye with a sharp stick

Hitler always reckoned it would be handy to have an ally round the back of Russia, so when the day came that Germany was ready to pounce on the peasants, the communists would be torn between facing their foes in Europe, and protecting their backsides. Good theory, but whenever a Japanese delegation turned up in Berlin for talks on mutual interests with the Nazi regime, all that bowing and smiling followed by clumsy translation of curious concepts about ancient aspirations indicated that the visitors saw China and America as their major opponents for power and prestige around the Pacific.

There was a complex history of antagonism that triangulated the Land of the Rising Sun and its neighbours. Most simply, Tokyo's political hierarchy harboured huge imperial ambitions and Hitler egged them on to believe they could pull off something similar to what he claimed he had achieved in Europe. The Fuhrer counselled his oriental associates to forget about China or America and instead muster their armaments for an almighty assault against the Soviet Union. Hence no-one could have been more dismayed than Adolf on learning what the Japanese had done on the morning of Sunday 7th December. They had crept up, so to speak, on the USA, in the dark. At dawn, off the decks of their aircraft carriers, Imperial forces launched an attack on the American bases on the islands of Hawaii.

More than 350 planes strafed, bombed and torpedoed the naval facilities, sinking four battleships and seriously damaging six more big vessels. The Japanese also destroyed nearly 200 US planes, losing only 29 of their own craft in the sorties.

What about American radar? Did this not provide Pearl Harbor with some advance warning? Yes, but a novice crew had been told that an additional complement of US aircraft were due to arrive that morning, so the boys assumed the shapes on the screens indicated the appearance of their new colleagues. A few American planes in the air scouting for enemy shipping urgently reported back their shocking sightings, but these messages were slow to reach those in authority on a seemingly benign Sunday morning.

Wikipedia states:

> 'The defenders were very unprepared. Ammunition lockers were locked, aircraft parked wingtip to wingtip in the open to prevent sabotage, guns unmanned (only four of 31 Army batteries got in action). Despite this low

alert status, many American military personnel responded effectively during the attack.'

2,000 Americans were killed in two hours. Half died when the ammunition store on one ship was hit by one bomb which blew up the whole vessel. Several American planes attempting to engage the intruders were shot down in error by desperate, unfocused gun crews on US ships.

That night, as a result of the news from the Far East, Winston Churchill enjoyed the first decent sleep he had had since entering Downing Street. In the morning, as he anticipated, US President Roosevelt declared war on Japan.

A few days later, Hitler - sensing it was necessary, PR-wise, to be seen to be honouring his pact with the Japanese – announced that Germany would support Japan in waging war against the U.S.

According to Wikipedia:

> '15 Medals of Honor, 51 Navy Crosses, 53 Silver Stars, four Navy and Marine Corps Medals, one Distinguished Flying Cross, four Distinguished Service Crosses, one Distinguished Service Medal, and three Bronze Star Medals were awarded to the American servicemen who distinguished themselves in combat at Pearl Harbor.'

No mention of any gongs pinned on the audacious raiding pilots by their grateful Emperor.

The Japanese now sank two British Navy ships off the coast of Malaya, which rattled our man in No 10:

> "In all the war I never received a more direct shock. As I turned and twisted in bed the full horror of the news sank in upon me... we everywhere were weak and naked."

However, in his heart of hearts, Churchill knew that what he had been praying for, angling for, now had every likelihood of coming off: the Americans would directly help Britain challenge the Germans.

Hitler needed all this like a hole in the head – which, of course, was what he eventually gave himself.

Another bad year

23,000 tons of bombs were dropped on German soil by the RAF during 1941, but that did not really add up to a success story. Through the spring months, of thirty attacks on German oil installations, only one caused any damage.

In January, celebrated aviator Amy Johnson had drowned in the Thames in an accident ferrying a plane. In April, the Luftwaffe gave Hitler a birthday present in the form of a thousand tons of bombs delivered to Plymouth. Because of the heavy losses of Allied shipping to U-boat attacks, Bomber Command was told to concentrate on harassing the German Navy in ports and at sea.

Good news for the Brits was that Germany had commenced dispersing its forces to other fronts, including Yugoslavia and Greece. Nevertheless around 100 RAF aircraft were lost on missions each month. Lord Beaverbrook stopped driving the production quotas: after one too many arguments with men in the Ministries, he parachuted out of his job in April. But Churchill soon gave him another role, keeping him close to future decision-making.

By the time the Blitz petered out, 43,000 Brits had died from aerial bombing, and a couple of thousand had been killed in road accidents caused by the black-out. Meanwhile, over continental Europe RAF bombing had extinguished nearly 1,000 people.

In May, the War Damage Commission opened offices across the country: victims of German bombing or RAF crashes could apply for compensation. A by-election in Birmingham saw three candidates stand: a National Conservative, a Pacifist, and a Retribution Party representative - campaigning for more area bombing of Germany. The Tory, a retired army captain, romped home; the other two lost their deposits.

The RAF undertook 'circus' missions over the continent during the summer months. These were designed to irritate the enemy and also initiate encounters with the Luftwaffe. From June to September, the UK lost more than 200 planes in such sorties, which defeated 130 Luftwaffe challengers.

Coastal Command's attrition rate from attacks on German shipping amounted to 13% in the summer months. On 12th August a big BC assault was attempted on Cologne's power stations. Twelve aircraft were lost (15% of the assigned force); output from the plants was reduced by just 10% for 10 days.

Civilian flying also hit a bad patch. On 10th August a 'transoceanic' plane crashed shortly after taking off from a British airport for a flight across the Atlantic. Passengers included Americans who just ferried vital military aircraft to the UK. All 22 passengers and crew were killed. Four days later, a passenger aeroplane heading for Canada suffered the same fate.

On 7th September, fifteen bombers were lost over Berlin. Through the month, seventy-six RAF planes crashed overseas. On 14th October, a mission to attack Nuremberg accidentally delivered its cargo to a town forty miles away. This month saw the loss of 100 BC planes. On 31st October, forty-eight aircraft set off for Bremen, but just thirteen of the crews reached the right location. Max Hastings notes:

> 'Although specific aiming points were given to every crew, it was thoroughly if tacitly understood that most craft were merely carting explosives to the surrounding city areas.'

On 7th November, 300 RAF bombers flew towards Berlin in terrible weather. Only 73 reached the capital where fourteen houses were damaged and nine people were killed. Almost 10% of the bomber force was destroyed.

On 13th November, Whitehall decided to halt BC endeavours above Germany until some better techniques could be brought to bear on the terrible task. However, more than 40,000 tons of bombing on German ships in port helped keep its navy from active engagement. Forty German vessels were sunk, though at the cost of 130 UK planes and their crews.

By now Bomber Command had logged nearly 7,000 air crew deaths, while killing a similar number of Germans on the ground. Statistically, it took five tons of bombs to eliminate one enemy citizen, while a British aircraft was lost for every 10 tons of bombs dropped.

The Luftwaffe had not completely abandoned Britain. In the month of December they caused air raid casualties of 34 dead and 55 injured. And they spent Christmas installing further formidable defence systems to make the RAF's life hell and short when it next dared to intrude.

1942

WHERE ON EARTH ARE THEY?

'At the beginning of last year we still stood alone, and worse than alone because only half-armed, against the most formidable military power that human malignity has contrived. Now the greater part of the human race is arrayed to vindicate the cause on which we, with Poland and France, staked our existence in 1939.'

... The Times leader article of 1st January 1942. Despite reports of Japanese advances around parts of the Pacific, there is an air of optimism to be detected within this sober journal, but it needs a bit of digging out because, unlike the more popular publications, The Times maintained its traditional layout of allocating the whole front page to classified advertising.

Exploring the internal modest headlines - not ordered or sized to bring spectacular attention to particular items - in this edition, the RAF got a look in, not in Britain but in Burma: on Christmas Day British and American pilots had managed to shoot down 20 Japanese planes over Rangoon. The Governor of Burma wrote to their commanding officer:

'...the wonderful success which your men have achieved against heavy odds will surely rank with the historic Battle of Britain. No words of mine can adequately express the thanks of Burma both to your pilots for their high courage and superb execution and to the ground staff for their devotion and skill. The determined way you set about the enemy is a great inspiration to us all.'

Alas, the Japanese would soon overrun Rangoon, then expel the RAF from the whole of Burma.

The Times announced that a critical new chapter in the 'global slaughter and sacrifice' had been reached:

'The great triumphs of the present hour are being won by our allies in eastern Europe. If the people of the bombed towns of England, with the out-numbered fighter squadrons battling overhead, taught the world to defy power that seemed invincible, it has been left to the Russians to shatter the illusion of invincibility itself.'

The column suggested a new world peace could be designed:

'It is evident that irresistible strength can rest on no other foundation than the permanent association of the British Empire, the Soviet Union and the United States in triple partnership; nor will it have worldwide authority without an enduring harmony with the multitudinous and unconquerable peoples of China.'

It was all just a matter of beating back Axis armed force. The Times saw fit to quote Hitler's New Year message. The dictator was in the dumps:

'What I and the National Socialist movement have been prevented from achieving by this war fills me with deepest sorrow. It is wretched not to be able to stop duffers and lazybones from stealing the valuable time which one wants to devote to cultural, social and economic tasks.'

Yes, it was getting to him. A few days later, the paper presented rumours from Berlin of army generals plotting to challenge the Nazi regime – perhaps a repercussion of Russian success in resisting the advance of German forces towards Moscow.

On Wednesday 7th The Times reported President Roosevelt's promise to produce 60,000 planes this year, 125,000 in 1943. The leader column added:

'The power of the United States as it will develop in the next two years is alone sufficient to make both Germans and Japanese, whatever their momentary advantages, aware that they are confronted by invincible strength, and, in the end, with inevitable doom.'

Another article featured a round-up of 1941 Allied achievements across the globe: from 'Greece to Somaliland, the western desert to Iran', Imperial Air Forces had shot down 2,095 enemy aircraft. However no news of activity from Bomber Command in recent days: the weather in England, over the North Sea, and across the continent, was regrettably keeping the squadrons grounded. But next day:

'Aircraft of Bomber Command carried out widespread operations on Tuesday night. Attacks were made on the docks at Brest and Cherbourg, and on objectives in west and north-west Germany. Coastal Command aircraft bombed enemy convoys off the Dutch coast.'

Our boys were up and at 'em.

Welcome to our squadron

A new airman would reach his designated station aware he was replacing someone who was probably a pal of those around him. People were silently missing their lost colleague, and now this new chap was trying to fit in and be one of the boys; an uncomfortable scenario for both sides. And everyone knew that the newcomer might not be around for long. The novice pilot was most vulnerable to making a flying error. So what was the point in being friendly to this anxious unknown face?

In Fighter Command, a new pilot could arrive in the morning, be assigned a mission that afternoon and never return. He perhaps never even unpacked. There was a subtle act of fellowship undertaken by the occupants of an accommodation block: prior to staff removing a deceased's personal belongings, a colleague would examine the locker and extract any items that might disconcert mourning relatives.

Bomber Command crew were issued with modest flight rations each evening: a few biscuits, an apple or orange, a lump of barley sugar, chewing gum, perhaps some raisins, all in a brown paper bag. They would also take on board their own flask of tea or coffee. But no sense of a cosy picnic in the gun turrets, where the isolated man simply nibbled, hung on and hoped for the best. Failure of power supply or oxygen feed could render the gunner unconscious - others unaware of this for many cold hours, which could be fatal.

Each squadron would aim to send out its complement of 20 or so aircraft for every assigned mission. Many surviving BC air crew recalled that their training had not truly apprised them of the character of a real sortie, which was frequently far more unpleasant than they had anticipated.

If baling out became necessary, everyone relied on the pilot to point the aircraft in a harmless direction before he jumped out as well. Failure to get this right could result in the plane turning in a long, declining circle to power back directly into the path of the descending airmen.

Everyone had a handy escape kit: a small tin box containing flimsy maps of Germany and the Low Countries, water purifying tablets, a mini compass and a tiny pocket knife.

If you made it back to UK airspace, you hoped the wireless operator remembered to switch on the IFF (Identification, Friend or Foe) transmitter. This pinged a signal to Anti-Aircraft crews below to indicate that you were not an enemy to be fired on. It didn't always work.

If you returned with bombs unreleased, you wanted them disarmed so they were less likely to explode from the impact of landing. Commanders often banned such aircraft for fear their runways would be ruined when the undercarriage hit the asphalt. It was known for pilots not to radio ahead that ordnance was aboard to avoid being sent somewhere else to land.

Most of a squadron's planes and men would return, but a few would not. The station might learn of the fate of missing people from others on that mission, or scraps of information could be fed back from the police or hospitals. Those landing far from base were obliged to report in as soon as possible.

The commander had to alert the family of each missing airman to the circumstances as currently known. In parallel, the squadron's strength needed to be topped up straightaway, often with personnel already standing by to adopt vacant roles.

You might think that surviving a hairy sortie would ensure a welcome return, but not always. One crew got their damaged kite down, but overshot the runway and rammed through a fence to skid on to a road, coming to a halt outside a pub. Drinkers emerged to see the boys clamber out of their shot-up fuselage, and be yelled at by their Wing Commander from his car for having failed to operate within Air Ministry guidelines.

What can women do?

In 1939 Gwen Thomas was working as a maid at a big private house in London and had joined the Auxiliary Territorial Service for something to do on her free weekends. As soon as hostilities were declared, she was required to report for duty. She spent the first two years of the war based at Hounslow Barracks in west London, essentially undertaking cookery duties on a vast scale, not least for General Montgomery who was based there, and who, she recalls, did not seem to like women in his vicinity.

Gwen remembers being strafed by a German plane while carrying a cooking pot across the parade ground. A spray of bullets rattled in her direction as she dived for cover. A month later, she was on leave one night when her Hounslow bus was halted by a Blitz fire crew. She stared at flaming, broken buildings and thought: "I wish I had a gun".

A few days later she saw a notice about training for anti-aircraft gun crews and "jumped at the chance". She found aircraft identification easy and quickly learnt to operate the Predictor machine that registered height, direction and speed of an approaching bomber, and generated readings to be applied to the gun.

Gwen was assigned to an Ack-Ack battery on Hayling Island and worked shifts to defend Portsmouth docks. One night she was responsible for the Predictor functions when a Dornier bomber appeared from the English Channel. She called out the numbers to the gun crew who fired off a shell, and a few seconds later the Dornier caught fire. As the craft shuddered overhead, someone clambered out and jumped away. His parachute opened, but "he was on fire" and he descended in a ball of flames into the sea.

Gwen and her colleagues were "jumping with joy" at their success: "Then we stopped. That's a man." A sobering moment, but she continued with this work through the rest of the war, she recalled to me proudly, in her nineties, at her home in Kidderminster (see our website).

During just one week in the spring of 1941, four women had been awarded British Empire Medals for formidably dealing with Luftwaffe intrusions:

> Mrs Ida Hacker, Rest Centre Service Organiser: 'gallantry when the Centre was damaged in a raid'.
> Miss Biddy Harris: 'rescuing trapped people over 12 hours in a heavy raid'.

Mrs Mary Fitzgerald: 'carrying on under heavy bombardment after her ambulance had been wrecked'.

Miss Joan Hobson, Auxiliary Fire Service: 'improvising a fire pump and hosing a blazing building'.

The recognition of the ability of women to do work traditionally associated with men grew through the war years. In Britain females became essential in the steel industry and munitions factories. If they had limitations on their capacity to lift and manipulate heavy metal objects, they were unbeatable at delicately filling shells with high explosive - a constantly dangerous activity, which had long-term health repercussions from toxic chemicals.

The Women's Auxiliary Air Force had been established in 1939, the recruitment advertising specifying the parameters:

'The W.A.A.F. wants women keen to help in the great work of the flying men of the R.A.F. If you have had experience as Secretary, Typist, Shop Assistant, or Cook, you can be readily trained for important duties.'

They would soon demand to do more. Consider WAAF medical orderly Joan Pearson, woken in the night by a plane crashing at her airfield. She ran outside and recognised the burning bomber, clambered inside to extract the injured pilot, and laid him on the ground. Then one of the bombs exploded, so she lay across his body to protect him from the blast.

In January 1942 single British women, including widows, born before 1921 became eligible for National Service. By the end of the year there were 180,000 WAAFs, undertaking a wide range of roles, including transport, parachute packing and radio operating. Many worked as engineers and armourers. In planning and intelligence, women had vital roles but almost all subservient to men. "Very clever girls" with science degrees were routed to radar design and testing.

German women were initially discouraged from entering the workplace or the forces, but official statements recommended other options:

'Pure blooded German girls have a duty that is not concerned with wedlock. This duty is to become a mother by a soldier off the front. A young girl who has avoided her highest duty is a traitress as foul as a soldier who deserts the colours. Men, show that your honour is not solely to give the country your lives, but also to present the country with new life before you go to death.'

Only later in the war did the Third Reich seek females in factories, where male managers then complained they did not take 9-to-5 commitments seriously.

Radically different values in the Soviet Union, where hundreds of women trained as pilots, many taking on combat roles. They could fight alongside the men, but that was not enough. They wanted their own squadrons, with their own planes, their own (female) ground crew and engineers. And they got them. Much of the advocacy for female military flight had been undertaken by a scientist whose father had been an opera singer: Marina Raskova persuaded Stalin that women warranted their own aerial commands. Russian women undertook thousands of sorties and killed hundreds of Germans in the air and thousands on the ground. The Luftwaffe described them as 'Night Witches'. Marina was killed in a bad landing near Stalingrad. This Hero of the Soviet Union was given a state funeral.

Before the war British newspapers had relished tales of triumph by golden girls of the skies, but there was no appetite for females flying into danger to cause harm. With considerable reluctance, some women were allowed to ferry new aircraft from factories to airfields. The female pilots relished this role, which was not without hazards. They had no radio to contact the control tower; they were simply given a time window for permission to land. If outside that slot they might be fired on by Ack-Ack crews. The women were not trained to use many of the cockpit instruments, so were supposed to land before it got dark.

But could a female in uniform be taken seriously in the face of advertising's capacity to stereotype gender roles? In newspapers, adjacent to articles proclaiming the daring-do of male pilots, readers might find a sketch of a pretty WAAF with a fancy hairstyle in front of a fleet of Spitfires, alongside:

'How is it that some women are able to preserve their beauty and femininity no matter how strenuous and arduous the duties they have to perform? The answer is that they have discovered the true secret of beauty and charm, without which no woman can ever be really attractive. They have achieved an air of freshness and daintiness which clings to them so intimately that it seems almost to be part of their personality.

Vinolia Soap gives a woman that air. Vinolia imparts a clean agreeable fragrance which does not cloy. 6d - a large tablet.'

Groups of women, not least nurses, frequently raised sufficient funds to provide the RAF with new aircraft. The Women's Division of the New Zealand Farmers' Union donated a Spitfire to Fighter Command's squadron of New Zealand-born air crew.

After the war, Churchill recalled one young woman who had made a big impression on him in 1940:

"...successive raids from the 19th to the 22nd November inflicted much destruction and loss of life. Nearly eight hundred people were killed and over two thousand injured; but the life and spirit of Birmingham survived this ordeal. When I visited the city a day or two later to inspect its factories, to see for myself what had happened, an incident, to me charming, occurred. It was the dinner-hour, and a very pretty young girl ran up to the car and threw a box of cigars in it. The gift must have cost her two or three pounds. She said: "I won the prize this week for the highest output. I only heard you were coming an hour ago."

I was very glad (in my official capacity) to give her a kiss. I then went on to see the long mass grave in which so many citizens and their children had been newly buried. The spirit of Birmingham shone brightly, and its million inhabitants, highly organised, conscious and comprehending, rode high above their physical suffering."

Finally, let us acknowledge Rachel Workman, an American who met and married a Scottish baronet, Sir Alexander MacRobert. They had three sons, all of whom took up flying. The eldest died in an air accident in 1938, the other two joined the RAF but both were killed in action in 1941. Lady MacRobert chose to pay tribute to her boys by funding the cost of a Stirling bomber and three Hurricanes. The fighter aircraft were named after her sons, and the widow requested that the bomber be named 'MacRobert's Reply'. She did her bit.

Nothing straightforward

Turrets were buggers: a giant, fragile bubble fixed to a bomber fuselage from where a man could fire at enemy planes in any direction. The appendage needed an access gap so the gunner could squeeze in and out, and it had to be engineered to revolve quickly for the operator to face attackers; the guns mounted to dip up and down.

The turret was cased with translucent plastic - Perspex - which the fellow could see through, but, unfortunately, also be easily shot through. He needed a tiny seat and a drive mechanism to turn the platform, but not swing so far to accidently shoot his own tail plane, wing or, worst of all, his pilot's cockpit. The guns had to be fed with a long belt of decent shells. The quantity per gun grew to 2,000. After they had been fired, there was nothing more that the occupant could do. Ideally he would have audio contact with the pilot, and be kept warm at high altitudes.

Some turrets, when turned in the air, caused the aircraft to skew. A retractable version slowed one plane down by 15 mph, putting weird pressures on the air flow which the skipper had to counter.

Water-wary gunners wore their flotation jacket throughout the flight, but a chance jerk could trigger the inflator and so trap the man. He might release himself with a knife, but now had no buoyancy aid when he hit the sea.

The rear gunner's turret was a brittle blister at the back of a big machine. If one plane bumped into another in the sky – which happened quite often – the bit most vulnerable to breaking up and falling off was that tail compartment, the rest of the crew perhaps unaware it had gone. If power supply failed, the turret had to be manually winched to its central position for the fellow to extract himself. What odds of achieving that with the plane on fire?

The Air Ministry was never satisfied with the turrets available. In January 1942 they asked one factory to deliver eighteen new prototypes by October: two fresh versions of fidgety domes per month. They were a bugger.

Up or down?

The Times admirably documented the major issues of the day across eight pages, sandwiched by classified ads. Its scatter of headlines for the first fortnight of February 1942 reveals the vastness of the British Empire, and thus how much was exposed to assault from the Japanese; all while Europe and north Africa were battle-grounds, and the UK remained vulnerable to Luftwaffe strikes, which had caused 112 deaths in January. This is how the landscape looked from Monday 2nd February:

COAST TOWNS RAIDED Three killed in East Anglia
LEADING FIGHTER PILOT A PRISONER OF WAR
ATTACK ON AXIS SHIPS Hits with torpedoes by naval aircraft
FRENCH DOCKS BOMBED Five British aircraft missing
SEIGE OF SINGAPORE

3rd TWO VICTORIES FOR RAF FIGHTERS New Dornier shot down
AIR DEFENCE OF RANGOON
ENEMY AIRCRAFT OVER SOLOMON ISLANDS (Indonesia)
SINGAPORE PREPARES FOR ALL OUT ATTACK
TRIPLE ATTACK IN LUZON (Marshall Islands/US Pacific fleet)
SHARP THRUST BY ROMMEL (Libya)
RUSSIANS THRUST TOWARDS DNIEPER (Ukraine)

4th JAPANESE AIR OFFENSIVE SPREADS (Indonesia)
GRIM FIGHT IN DESERT (North Africa)
RAID ON INVASION FLEET (Borneo)

5th TWO BOMBERS HIT OVER MALTA
EVACUATION OF DERNA (Libya)
TWO DIVE BOMBERS DESTROYED (Atlantic)

6th NORTH SCOTTISH ISLANDS BOMBED
BATTLE OF SINGAPORE
MORE RAIDS ON SURABAYA (Java)
FLYING BOATS RAID PORT MORESBY (New Guinea)
BOMBS IN N.E. ENGLAND
MORE INTENSIVE RAIDS ON MALTA

7th RAF HIT HARD IN LIBYA
BOMB EXPLOSION ON TANGIER QUAY (North Africa)
BOMBING ON EAST COAST

What a week! Churchill had just returned from meetings with the American President. He was brought back by a US flying boat; a journey that took 16 hours: quite a ride for a man of 68, with so much on his plate. In his absence, in London, there was a growing sense of national vulnerability: politicians and pundits were hinting that perhaps one man was carrying too big a burden; the PM could do with a deputy to share the load. Parliament expected a report, but with the military circumstances so complicated that was a substantial task.

No respite through the second week of February:

9th   THREE ATTACKS ON CONVOYS FAIL (Atlantic)
            AIR OFFENSIVE IN NORTH SEA
            BOMBS IN S.W. ENGLAND
            ROMMEL'S FORCES HARRIED
            MANILA PORTS BOMBARDED (Indonesia)
            ENEMY BOMBER DOWN (North Sea)
10th   BESEIGED LENINGRAD
            BASES IN GREECE BOMBED
            FIRST RAID ON BATAVIA (Borneo)
            INTENSIFIED RAIDS ON MALTA
            AIR RAIDS ON ALEXANDRIA (Egypt)
            SINGAPORE INVADED
11th   GERMAN THREATS TO EIRE (Ireland)
            TWO GERMAN BOMBERS DOWN (North Sea)
            GRIM BATTLE IN SINGAPORE
            ENEMY LANDING NEAR MACASSAR (Indonesia)
            OFFENSIVE SWEEPS BY FIGHTERS (North Africa)
            AXIS CONVOYS ATTACKED (Mediterranean)
            ENGAGEMENT NORTH OF MARTABAN (Burma)
            ENEMY LOSSES IN RUSSIA
12th   LEYTONSTONE AEROPLANE CRASH
            (RAF debris hits school)
            INCENDIARY BOMBS AT PRETORIA (South Africa)
            BOMB EXPLOSIONS IN PARIS
            BOLD RED ARMY TACTICS (Russia)
            JAPANESE AIRCRAFT OVER PAPUA (Indonesia)
            THREE MALTA RAIDERS HIT

And now Friday the 13th, when, if all of the above wasn't bad enough, readers learnt that British forces failed to overcome an audacious enemy naval operation on their doorstep: German battleships steamed out of Brest harbour on the French coast and up to Wilhelmshaven - right through the English Channel. 600 RAF planes attempted to intervene; to bomb, torpedo or strafe the convoy, but none made any discernible impact on its progress, which benefited from relays of Luftwaffe fighters looping out from occupied airfields in France to keep the British at bay. The Times first mentioned the humiliation on page 4:

SEA AND AIR BATTLE IN THE STRAITS OF DOVER

The Royal Navy was Britain's mighty Empire protector; how come it failed to destroy those German ships in the Channel? Why hadn't the RAF bombed Brest enough to knock them out in the first place? How could slow boats pass Portsmouth docks and the airfields of Kent without being effectively intercepted by Britain's defence forces?

In parallel, we had lost an Empire pawn: our troops in Singapore had suddenly surrendered to the Japanese.

Churchill decided to speak to the nation via BBC radio, and spent the weekend preparing his words, asking the fundamental question: 'Are we up or down?' He pointed out it was nearly six months since his previous broadcast:

'In those days the Germans seemed to be tearing the Russian army to pieces, and striding on with growing momentum to Leningrad and Moscow... Our British resources were stretched to the utmost. We had already been for more than a whole year absolutely alone in the struggle with Hitler and Mussolini. We had to be ready to meet a German invasion of our own island. We had to defend Egypt and the Suez Canal. Above all we had to bring food, raw materials and finished munitions across the Atlantic in the teeth of German and Italian U-boats and aircraft without which we could not live; without which we could not wage war. We have to do all this still.'

We were further weakened by our responsibilities to our ally in eastern Europe:

'It seemed our duty in those August days to do everything in our power to help the Russian people to meet the prodigious onslaught which had been launched against them. It is little enough that we have done for Russia considering all she has done to beat Hitler and for the common cause.'

Pessimism based on recent set-backs was understandable, but he asked listeners to consider the bigger picture:

'Taking it all in all, are our chances of survival better or worse than in August 1941? How is it with the British Empire or Commonwealth of Nations? Are we up or down?'

Timely acknowledgement of the capacities of our substantial allies:

'The US is now unitedly and wholeheartedly in the war with us – comrades standing shoulder to shoulder in a battle for dear life... That is what I have dreamed of, aimed at, and worked for, and now it has come to pass. The Russian armies have not been defeated... they are advancing victoriously. More than that, they have broken the Hitler legend – two tremendous fundamental facts which will in the end dominate the world situation and make victory possible in a form never possible before.'

A reminder of how stretched we were:

'Not a ship, not an aeroplane, not a tank, not an anti-tank gun or anti-aircraft gun has stood idle. Everything we have has been deployed either against the enemy or awaiting his attack.'

No wonder a few German ships could sail through the Straits unscathed. And remember our responsibilities on the far side of the Mediterranean:

'We are struggling hard in the Libyan desert. We have to provide for the safety and order of liberated Abyssinia, of conquered Eritrea, of Palestine, of liberated Syria and redeemed Iraq, and of our new ally Persia. A ceaseless stream of ships, men and materials has flowed from this country for a year and a half in order to build up and sustain our armies in the Middle East.'

Of course there would be weaknesses in our armoury, not least due to those who had caused us delays:

'Tonight the Japanese are triumphant. We suffer. We are taken aback...

We were exposed to the assault of a warrior race of nearly 80 million with a large outfit of modern weapons... while our good people were prating about perpetual peace and cutting down each other's navies in order to set a good example.'

Of course it's tough:

'You know I have never prophesied to you or promised smooth or easy things, and now all I have to offer is hard adverse war for many months ahead.'

But that does not mean we cannot succeed:

> '... the same qualities which brought us through the awful jeopardy of the summer of 1940 and its long autumn and winter bombardments from the air will bring us through this other new ordeal, though it may be more costly and will certainly be longer.'

> 'One fault, one crime – and one crime only can rob the united nations and the British people, upon whose constancy this grand alliance came into being, of the victory upon which their lives and honour depends. A weakening in our purpose and therefore in our unity – that is the mortal crime.'

For which a summary punishment, perhaps characteristic of our foes, is warranted:

> 'Whoever is guilty of that crime or of bringing it about in others – of him let it be said that it were better that a millstone were hanged about his neck and he were cast into the sea.'

You can feel Churchill's anguish through the text. He has given his all, struggled on, and now sees hope in the fact that two giant powers have also been assaulted by the belligerents and so are now mounting far more formidable force than Britain could ever have mustered. But we can set an example:

> 'This ... is one of those moments when the British race and nation can show its quality and its genius.... This is one of those moments when it can draw from the heart of misfortune the vital impulse of victory. Three-quarters of the human race are now moving with us. The whole future of mankind may depend on our action and upon our conduct.'

We have merely experienced a few set-backs:

> 'So far we have not failed. Let us move forward steadfastly together into the storm and through the storm.'

Magnificent advocacy: summarising achievements, acknowledging the challenges, anticipating the conclusion - if we valiantly hang on in there. Drafting this across Saturday and Sunday was surely one of Churchill's most constructive weekends; delivering it to a microphone, one of his finest hours.

Damage

The withdrawal of most of the Luftwaffe to eastern Europe allowed the UK to contemplate how the nation had fared from the previous winter's aerial assaults. Sociologists wanted to identify possible long-term effects on children who had been in the proximity of bombing. If family members, especially parents, had been injured or killed, then the consequences would be severe, but alarming events in a neighbourhood did not necessarily disturb a youngster living nearby. Children might have seen someone covered in blood; they often witnessed relatives, neighbours or school teachers burst into tears on learning of the loss of a loved one; kids could be told that a school classmate would never return, but none of these moments seemed to cause much distress.

Those allowed to play near bomb sites collected souvenirs of the raids: fragments of Perspex, lumps of shrapnel. A dented foreign canister was irresistible. Dozens of boys were badly burnt trying to open incendiary devices. Three lads who discovered an unexploded bomb attempted to haul it home by rope, but it blew up and killed them.

People allocated a temporary home would write their new address in large letters on the front of their old dwelling so others could track them down. Youngsters whose homes had been bombed often made furtive returns to extract toys and other belongings from the rubble. Rescued furniture from a ruined building could be treacherously impregnated with slivers of window glass.

Households which had suffered from bombing could apply to the new regional offices of the War Damage Commission for compensation. You just had to fill in a form:

'State briefly what, in your opinion, was the cause of the war damage, for example, high explosive, incendiary bomb dropped by enemy aircraft, anti-aircraft shell, enemy bombardment from land or sea.

Extent of damage. If possible, answer Yes or No.

a) Buildings. Do you consider the damaged property:

A) totally destroyed

B) so badly damaged that it is not worth repairing

C) seriously damaged but worth repairing, or

D) slightly damaged.

b) Land, apart from buildings. Describe the damage briefly.'

Vast contingents of clerks assessed the claims; swarms of surveyors, architects and builders were assigned to examine and price the required work. The Commission struggled to be consistent with criteria: some households received full compensation, other families fought for a contribution towards their damaged dwelling. If someone was paying a mortgage on a destroyed property, the building society usually demanded that they continue the monthly payments.

Lawyers unearthed a valuable seam of work handling fraud cases for or against the civil servants wherein some party alleged to have claimed too much and/or had not spent the awarded sum as agreed.

As well as repairing shops, offices and factories, the Commission endeavoured to re-build churches, schools and bank branches. Perhaps its most popular award was to the Manchester United ground at Trafford Park: £4,800 for the removal of debris from Luftwaffe damage to the stands, then £17,478 assigned for their re-construction.

By 1947 the Commission had paid out £470 million for re-building and repairs, and estimated that the compensation for structures totally destroyed would drive the spend towards £1.5 billion.

Taking on Tokyo

The United Kingdom and much of Europe were immensely fortunate that the USA saw fit to brace up to the Nazi empire after Pearl Harbor. The Americans could have decided to singularly concentrate their military endeavours against Japan. Not that the US President ever considered the humiliation at Hawaii could be left on the back burner. Roosevelt had immediately asked his generals how they could achieve some dramatic revenge for those shocking insults.

It would not be easy. The islands of Japan were patrolled by massive warships and aircraft carriers capable of launching their weaponry far out to the east and south. Could an American aircraft drop ordnance on Tokyo? The US had some long range planes designed for rising off substantial runways in California to scan the Pacific. Might these machines be adapted to fly from a carrier? Could that ship get close enough to Japan for the planes to convey ordnance to the enemy mainland unscathed? Where could they land? Not back on the tiny, rocking boat. China had air strips not that far from Japan. A bit of furtive work on extending and strengthening the Chinese facilities and they should be capable of accepting a fleet of bombers veering over from Tokyo.

So lots of diplomacy and aeronautical engineering: the bombers would need extra fuel tanks for the escape to China, which meant stripping out non-essential weight, including some guns. Ex-test pilot Jimmy Doolittle was assigned commander of the operation, and volunteers were sought from the American Army Air Force to fly the special planes. After intensive preparations the aircraft were discreetly loaded on to the reinforced carrier in California along with 80 airmen. It would take sixteen days to steam far enough across the Pacific to be within aerial reach of Japan, with sufficient fuel for flying on to the Chinese airfields.

Spirits were high, determination rock solid, when a Japanese patrol ship spotted the carrier and its escorts in the middle of the Pacific - a long way short of the planned launch location. What the hell to do? The guys realised the Japanese skipper would radio back to HQ that a carrier over-loaded with big planes was heading their way. Rather than abort, Doolittle decided to launch immediately before the Japanese could mount a response. So the crews took off and made for Tokyo and other conurbations, encountering little resistance; most of the 16 planes dropping their cargo in relevant vicinities on 18th April 1942.

But the aircraft were short of juice for the rest of their journeys. Almost all crash-landed on the edge of the Chinese mainland. A few fell into the sea, and one came down inside the Soviet Union. Most crews parachuted out and were sooner or later in the presence of peasants who reported them to the authorities.

The Japanese invaded the Chinese coastline to inhibit further missions and track down any of Doolittle's men who had yet to be extracted. Eight were captured and two were put on trial, then shot, for having allegedly strafed streets full of Tokyo citizens. 10,000 Chinese people accused of collaborating with the Americans were executed by Japanese soldiers.

Doolittle considered his undertaking a disaster, but most Americans saw the raid less than six months after Pearl Harbor as a terrific achievement. Doolittle could do no wrong. He had raised morale with audacity and courage, setting a standard to which many would now aspire.

A year later, American appetite for revenge was further satisfied when their Air Force discovered that Pearl Harbor strategist Admiral Yamamoto was due to fly to a meeting on the Pacific coast. Several US fighters intercepted the Admiral's flight and peppered it with gunfire. Yamamoto was shot in the head before his craft crashed in jungle. The Americans were delighted. The Japanese government kept the incident under wraps for more than a year.

Making a fist of it

Once the Japanese had smashed their way into the picture, much of the globe had potential to become an arena of combat. Planes could reach distant locations fast; anywhere, any time, explosives might be unleashed upon civilians. Critical aerial activity ranged from Iceland to Australia. The UK Air Ministry constantly struggled to achieve fruitful deployment of resources; maps and graphs of priorities always shifting. RAF units were assigned to all regions, though never in sufficient numbers for the local commanders.

A small island in the middle of the Mediterranean Sea became a focus for concern: Malta, 50 miles south of Italy, 200 north of Libya. Its port of Valetta had been vital to the Royal Navy for centuries and now this modest element of the British Empire would play a pivotal role in the fortunes of the Allies south of Europe. From here planes could fly to and from Gibraltar and Greece, and all along the north African coast.

Britain was using Malta as an aerial reconnaissance base, to acquire intelligence on the movement of troops through the desert, and on shipping activity across the whole of the Med. But the Italian Fascist dictator, Benito Mussolini, told his pal Adolf he would soon put a stop to that by taking over the island. It was simple - Malta was just twenty miles long, nine wide - Axis Air Forces had blitzkrieged far tougher territory. Benito reckoned his aerial Aces could make mincemeat of Malta within weeks; they would blast the docks on the north shoreline, plus the small airfields to their south. The Italian flyers did not have far to come - plenty of bases on Sicily, and the English only had a few planes on the island - such was their Ministry's laughable allocation.

The Italians' first sorties to Malta were in June 1940 when they killed or injured 70 people, which triggered serious effort to improve defence. Malta would be critical to the British prosecution of the desert war, but needed a steady supply by sea of food, fuel and machinery. Were the island to become an Axis outpost, this might aid Rommel's attempts to overcome Montgomery. The tiny RAF contingent used their old fighters with skill and daring, whilst Navy and civilian crews manned anti-aircraft positions around the harbour and aerodromes with relentless courage.

Soon Benito had to confess that his Aces were not achieving the promised result, so Hitler allocated German planes, ships and submarines to intercept shipping bound for Malta, which reduced the RAF to just a few days' worth of fuel and ammunition, and starved the inhabitants.

The Royal Navy tried to escort convoys from Gibraltar or Egypt to sustain the battle and the resistance capacity of the population, but every Allied vessel was assaulted, some vital cargos sinking just metres from Valetta harbour; those reaching the docks being unloaded under bombardment from the air.

Half the total tonnage of enemy ordnance that descended on Malta hit in April 1942, mostly on the port. 10,000 buildings were damaged and 300 locals were killed. The RAF had, at times, just half a dozen planes to challenge the intruders. 100 enemy craft were shot down by AA, the teams deploying final reserves of shells with immense care. Then an American aircraft carrier brought a fleet of Spitfires within flying range of the island. These were immediately attacked by Axis raiders, but ground crews re-fuelled and re-armed most new arrivals, enabling the Spits to repel further assaults.

In May, HMS Welshman managed to reach Valetta with a pivotal cargo - massive smoke generators which blanketed the whole harbour, and so stopped enemy planes seeing targets. Fresh ammunition was distributed, and the Spitfires mounted a formidable defence, then challenged the Axis forces. In the first ten days of July, another 100 German craft were shot down, while the RAF lost twenty.

Some defeated Luftwaffe pilots were taken to Maltese hospitals, where a group of gracious British flyers called in to see their opponents. One UK crew met a German who had lost an arm in his aerial spat. They were dismayed to learn he had been a violinist before the war.

By the end of the year, 14,000 tons of bombs had been dropped on Malta, killing nearly 1,500 citizens. Over the next couple of years, the islanders would face enemy aerial raids on more than 3,000 occasions; but 1,000 Italian or German planes would be shot down, while the defenders lost 560 aircraft. Malta battled on, and Hitler eventually concluded that the pesky little place was absorbing too many resources when he had given himself so many other taxing engagements across the northern hemisphere.

Malta's Air-Sea Rescue squads pulled 123 RAF boys from the drink, as well as 34 Germans and 21 Italians. The Axis also undertook its share of saving airmen from drowning. One RAF plane splashed down in the Adriatic. The crew's dinghy was spotted by an Italian seaplane which picked them up and flew them to a small island for a meal and beds for the night. In the morning everyone got back on the seaplane for a flight to the Italian mainland, and hence a marvellous photo-opportunity for Benito. But the RAF chaps hijacked the plane mid-flight and took it towards Malta, where Spitfire patrols almost brought it down, despite the escapees waving their white vests out of the cockpit window. The Italian craft reached the water and was towed into Valetta, its original crew becoming prisoners of war; the hijackers heroes.

Failing to overcome Malta needled the Roman tyrant. Only shred of comfort was that the Berlin military maestro couldn't crack it either. Mussolini hated those unyielding islanders, and remained aggrieved about that irritating clump of rock until his dying day – which, as luck would have it, lay just three years on, when partisans caught him, shot him and hung him upside down on a meat-hook.

Can Harris change the landscape?

Arthur Harris became Chief of Bomber Command in February 1942. His objective, according to the Air Ministry, was to target 'the morale of the enemy civil population and in particular the industrial workers' - but he inherited fewer than 400 aircraft for the task. Much of Harris's first year was spent lobbying for more kit - challenging the Army and Navy for a bigger share of the munitions pie; however, the land and sea men made it clear to anyone who would listen that aerial bombing could not on its own defeat Germany.

The new Commander's first endeavour was a 200 plane raid on Essen and its Krupps armaments plant. Not one bomb hit the huge complex. Some houses were destroyed, killing ten occupants, but 90% of the RAF's ordnance landed more than five miles away.

In March he despatched 200 bombers to the Renault factory near Paris, and achieved better accuracy thanks to new electronics aboard a group of planes out in front which dropped flares over the targets. Half the factory and 2,000 vehicles were damaged, but 300 French people were killed. This was rationalised in official reports:

> '...to attack the areas in which workers living under the domination of Germany carry out their tasks is distasteful. No one realises this better than the crews of Bomber Command. That they carry it out unflinchingly is proof of their high sense of duty, even when that duty may entail death or injury to citizens of friendly but enslaved powers.'

The Command pursued 26 operations on French factories in the spring of '42, of which five were 'marked successes', while others saw the loss of up to 10% of the planes. BC claimed their locally broadcast warnings, if heeded, could have allowed the enslaved workers to stay away from the relevant premises.

Harris was convinced the destruction of German cities would shorten the war and so save the lives of many Allied soldiers. On 28th March he sent 230 craft to Lubeck, a lovely old town full of fine, timber-framed buildings on narrow streets. 40 planes broke down or went astray; the rest ruined the heart of the place, killing 320 citizens. 12 craft were shot down by German defences, which Harris considered tolerable. Hitler proclaimed the assault a "Terrorangriffin" – terror attack, but the RAF explained:

'Great quantities of stores accumulated during the winter for use in the Russian campaign were destroyed.'

... which would surely have played well in Moscow.

On 30th May, Harris mustered 1,000 planes to devastate Cologne, third biggest city in Germany with a population of 800,000. He had a message for the flyers: if successful:

"...the most shattering and devastating blow will have been delivered against the very vitals of the enemy. Let him have it – right on the chin."

This enormous fleet, though shored up with some "half-trained crews in clapped out aircraft", managed to kill 500 citizens and make 60,000 homeless. This was a psychological victory for the British high command: big numbers, big results, acceptable losses on paper at least. The Times reported that the Command received the immediate congratulations of the PM, 'who speaks of it as the herald of what Germany will receive city by city from now on'. Their editorial added:

'Now that the striking power is passing from the Luftwaffe to the R.A.F., Germany will begin to realise the folly she committed in entrusting her destinies to Hitler and his comrades in crime.'

The Cologne mission inspired a further publication from HMSO: a compact booklet packed with justification. 'Bomber Command Continues' profiled 'excellent' factory workers and 'expert' ground crew. Through the winter the Command had 'faced heavy assaults from its ever-lurking foe – bad weather'. Explaining the German's Channel dash of 12th February, the authors pointed out the weather was 'vile'; 15 bombers were lost, 'some very probably owing to collisions in the murk'. BC had previously attacked those big boats 34 times in Brest, and their exit would now allow staff to concentrate resources against other locations. The force took pride in its leafleting campaigns, now amounting to 250 million sheets, including sheaves delivered to Holland featuring pictures of the Dutch Royal Family, which were 'collected and treasured by its gallant inhabitants':

'Since the beginning of the war Bomber Command has been a hammer in the hands of this country, which is using it to batter the walls of Germany.'

Statistics showed that many ports had been raided 80 times, several Ruhr cities received 100 visits from BC squadrons; Cologne on 80 occasions. All this effort – using aircraft designed and built in Great Britain – was keeping German arms along their western border, and therefore not supporting the Russian front. Perhaps the booklet's prime purpose was to provide evidence to Stalin that we were doing our best?

Cologne's suffering did not end there. In the summer of 1943, the city received a raid that killed 4,000, injured 10,000, and left quarter of a million homeless.

Meanwhile, the attrition of air crew troubled the Air Ministry. It had always been policy to have a spare pilot on board a bomber so that, if the man at the controls was hit, injured, sick or scared rigid, a second fellow could slip into his seat to continue the mission and/or bring the plane and the boys back home asap. But crews reported it was almost impossible to manoeuvre an injured chap from the driving seat and shove in a replacement without soaring the craft all over the sky. So, defying Harris's wishes, Whitehall made a masterful decision: why stick two highly trained fellows in one plane when in practice they can't hand over, and on most occasions there is no need for a swop. Fact is, if you've got two pilots on a machine that's in trouble, chances are you will lose two valuable human resources on that sortie. Better, on balance, to lose one pilot (along, obviously, with the plane itself and the rest of the crew) than a pair, because we need all the skippers we can get and it takes ages to train each of them.

Harris relished charts that showed how his capacity to diminish the enemy was growing. He came up with a convenient way of assessing success: the weight of bombs dropped for crew lives lost. He liked the new Lancaster because, within this formula, its capacity was unbeatable: only nine airmen would die during the decanting of 100 tons. The Lanc could also survive more missions than other craft - calculations revealing that each machine should, in its short lifetime, deliver 68 tons. Patently Harris needed more Lancs to continue bruising Germany and, hopefully, Hitler's ego.

Distractions

A big factory making munitions in an urban area would inevitably be liable to aerial assault. So it made sense to establish another secret location elsewhere for the necessary production to safely continue day and night. Britain developed a matrix of shadow factories before the war. A large complex was created within the sandstone hills of Kinver in south Staffordshire: broad passageways cut and lit to house an equivalent to the huge Austin production site at Longbridge in Birmingham, now turning out tanks and plane parts.

To skew enemy night raids, compounds full of flammable material were constructed in rural areas, ready to be ignited if foreign planes approached. The fire would look like a current bombing site, inclining the intruders to dump their load in that vicinity.

The Third Reich always feared it might become subject to bomber attacks from Russia, and so had efficiently commenced the re-location of industrial processes away from its eastern border. But the regime had never expected British planes to fly over the Fatherland. When the Germans recognised the 'Tommies' were improving delivery accuracy, they devised decoy targets that looked - from the sky at night - like factories or military depots, but lay a safe distance from the real thing.

An early theatre of deception was with Navy-like vessels built from old boats: mock-up hulls moored in unoccupied estuaries alongside fake buildings; luckless prisoners assigned to searchlight and flak duty adding to the impression of their importance. Inland, false factories were constructed; even the representation of a whole town erected, to draw enemy aircraft away from the genuine article. Meanwhile vast smoke screens billowed upward to conceal key facilities.

Air crews valued rivers which were impossible to disguise; however static stretches of water could be concealed with netting to deny night navigators a reference point. One big German lake was packed with barges covered in metal sheeting, which hid a landmark and generated mystifying signals on radar scans.

Because BC crews often struggled to locate targets it was decided to give them expert guidance: the best pilots and navigators formed a special squadron whose job was to indicate the way toward the destination. Pathfinder planes would fly ahead and decant coloured flares as instructions for the pilots behind: a route to the target, then the approach height, then the bomb release point. The first pathfinder outing was towards a U-boat factory by the Baltic Sea, but teething troubles meant the systems didn't quite work and the guiding crews positioned their coloured blazes above the wrong estuary. Next attempt proved over-ambitious: 300 aircraft followed the pathfinders, but the Luftwaffe intercepted and shot down 30. An outing to Nuremberg saw the demise of 13% of the dispatched force. The German defenders then began to replicate those flares - to launch versions at an angle ahead of the intruders, and so divert whole fleets to farmers' fields.

When Allied bombing began to disrupt western Germany, factory work was radically dispersed - fragmented and quadrupled - so attacks on an individual plant would not halt the supply chain. Cavernous workspaces were constructed below thick layers of concrete and steel; the tops surfaced with grass, trees, crops and livestock: ingenious, elaborate and effective.

However one theatrical Nazi mega-structure failed to fool our boys: an RAF daytime photo reconnaissance mission near the German border discovered a new military airfield complete with planes - but something was not quite right. Further flights revealed the air station clock always showed the same time, and it was realised the whole installation was like a 3-D film set made from pine and cardboard. So a BC crew sculpted a big wooden bomb shaped like a dart and took a detour from their next sortie to drop the dummy weapon on the bogus airfield.

Shift work

Temperamental engines on test were dangerous beasts. One could roar, yet fail to turn its propeller; then, upon close examination, it might abruptly release, the blades slicing into staff.

On every airfield, all sorts of challenging tasks were undertaking by ground crew to prepare each plane for its next outing. Returning airmen would alert team leaders to malfunctions in the controls or damage to airframe, but the engineers would swarm over the whole craft to determine exactly what was required. If a turret had taken a serious spray of enemy rounds then, after the gunner's body was removed, someone would have to wash out the chamber.

Dedicated fitters - male and female - could re-build most of the mechanisms for each model, but some planes required specialist attention off-site; the Air Ministry contracted dozens of firms to fix or salvage badly damaged machines.

There was permanent pressure to supply the required complement of craft for the next mission; but no point in sending up a plane that was not fully airworthy. Of course, Sod's Law could be relied on to throw in some human error. On one occasion an armament mechanic was manually checking settings for an aircraft's bomb release switches when finger fumble caused the cargo to fall off. But nothing went bang and the ordnance was warily loaded back up.

Each skipper was obliged to sign a form prior to take-off to acknowledge he considered the plane fit for purpose, but how could he be sure? Every bomber had hundreds of moving parts which sometimes failed to function as required at a critical moment.

An aircraft full of ordnance could be revving up for take-off, when someone would spot an engine on fire. People might try to unload the weapons from a burning craft, but a bomb could explode during unhitching and obliterate the plane, air crew, fire crew and anyone else nearby.

The Halifax suffered rickety fuel feeds that could see an engine stop mid-flight. Its cockpit had a disconcerting configuration of switches which rattled some skippers: bomb door buttons adjacent to wing flap toggles: hit the wrong one and you're dropping instead of the ordnance. The average Halifax undertook just ten missions before becoming unstuck in some way.

When BC craft were over their target, weapons might fail to uncouple from the claws in their bay. Now the crew could try to manually release the ordnance, coming off oxygen and quickly feeling sluggish or dizzy. Alternatively, the boys could just fly back to base keeping their fingers crossed that the damned things didn't explode on the way.

Flares that failed to release often had barometric fuses: if the aircraft descended the device would ignite. Such blighters had to be shifted, whatever the trials in that breezy cavity below the fuselage. But this was all in a night's work for BC fellows.

Many people had high hopes for the new Lancaster bomber. Its maiden operation was a trip to Augsburg on 17th April 1942, seeking the MAN submarine engine factory (Yes, those big lorries with MAN on their engine grill are offspring of the power units that sank British shipping). A dozen Lancs were sent in daylight to undertake the raid but only five returned. The rest were shot down by flak or fighters. 17 bombs descended towards the factory though only 12 exploded. Not a great start.

14,000 bombers were damaged on missions through the war, another 4,000 in non-operational accidents. Ground crew admired and respected the airmen for their capability and courage; the airmen praised the blokes and girls on the station for their diligence.

A drop in the ocean
Coastal Command was always the poor relation in the RAF. CC began the war with a second-rate bunch of planes and struggled to argue the case for re-equipping with better. What was their job? To fly over sea and sight the enemy. Straightforward in theory, but plagued with problems. Have you ever tried spotting a ship from a plane? You can go for hours without seeing a single boat.

In the early days, all the boys had to do was report back to base where they had identified an enemy vessel (or one that might be). But defining locations from the air and accurately explaining destinations on charts was a challenge, so it was decided Coastal crews should do their own attacking. However the old planes were not effective, nor were the weapons. Len Deighton explains about early torpedoes exploding the moment they hit the water, and blasting the underside of the aircraft. First consignments of depth charges were from stock used by the navy – not configured to be dropped from the air.

Upgrades to kit were slow in coming, and the Command was issued with several types of unsatisfactory planes as a result of hasty deals with manufacturers who had some spare capacity and promised to deliver a marvellous new model.

A high proportion of CC machines suffered performance problems, but the saving grace of some was that, unlike those in the other Commands, these were craft designed to descend on to water: sea planes and flying boats, which, if in trouble over the ocean, might be brought down carefully and not sink.

At the start of the war the Germans peppered the North Sea with mines designed to explode when the magnetic field of a ship encountered them. How could these pesky weapons be neutralised? The boffins concluded the job was best achieved from the air. A pulsing magnetic coil could be bolted to the underside of a plane, to pass over a mine and activate it well away from the nearest boat. Teams fiddled with prototypes and concluded the coil needed to be bigger, the plane had to get closer to the water. They settled on an enormous coil with a diameter the length of the fuselage, the sides of the giant hula-hoop reaching far along the wings. These adapted planes were difficult to manipulate on the ground and in the air, but eventually some were ready to scan the sea and throb out an electrical wave to trigger floating explosives. The power for the cunning ring came from a big fume-emitting engine inside the plane, which choked the nervous crew who had no idea when the flux might set off a mine right in front of the craft's low flight path. Mercifully this technique was soon replaced by devices aboard dedicated minesweeping ships.

It was only when the German U-boat menace grew that the War Cabinet acknowledged the need to beef up CC in order to lessen the loss of shipping to enemy torpedo attacks from beneath the waves. The force was slowly issued with better craft and kit, which they then had to learn to use. Through no lack of courage or determination, the boys achieved their first successful strike in July 1942: hitting and sinking an enemy vessel from the air - almost three years into the war.

They disabled a dozen more by Christmas, but elsewhere on the water the dreaded U-boats sank a thousand merchant ships in this year, destroying five million tons of food or munitions as well as drowning hundreds of sailors. The following July, CC succeeded in sinking a dozen U-boats in that month alone: a mighty leap forward.

Some of the Command's frustrations stemmed from Bletchley Park's inability to comprehend U-boat fleet communication. The secret signals kept the brainy ones stumped for months, and when they did start to understand the messages they discovered the Germans had been long intercepting and deciphering British naval codes.

In August 1942 a CC flying boat hit a big rock off the coast of Scotland. Among the fatalities was Prince George, the Duke of Kent, the only member of the British Royal Family to be killed during the war.

Hitler had aimed to completely deny the United Kingdom access by sea. Every month many Allied ships were sinking to the bottom of the oceans; men, equipment and provisions tragically lost. But the sly subs were being spotted and attacked with increasing regularity and success, so the Germans started sending out fighter planes to deter aerial depth-charging. This saw off dozens of CC aircraft, each with a crew of twelve, all unlikely to be rescued from somewhere in the middle of the Atlantic.

Laughing over Lille

How do you deliver a whole new air force to a different country and prepare it for combat? With a massive amount of effort and a huge level of care - especially if you are operating in a democracy wherein journalists and politicians have the right to examine your progress and comment on the outcomes.

When the USA agreed to bring planes and men to help Britain challenge Hitler, the logistics would inevitably be enormous. Most of the airfields in East Anglia were required to accommodate the Yanks and their gear. They would also need hubs closer to Scotland and Liverpool where incoming equipment could be sorted and stored. To do the anticipated job the United States American Army Airforce (USAAF) estimated a requirement for 150 bases. The United Kingdom got them to settle for 127. Personnel and gear would arrive by ship to Merseyside, but the bomber aircraft were never designed to fit in boxes; they had to be flown to Britain: a tough, cold route, hopping to Greenland, then Iceland, then Scotland. Some planes never completed that journey; they came unstuck above the Arctic Circle. Ice inhibited flight functions and craft crashed on bleak rock around the Greenland coast. The men were rescued, the machines written off.

In East Anglia the newcomers needed longer, stronger runways for their heavy machines: concrete covered in tarmac, with wide dispersal of ancillary kit in case the Luftwaffe tried to attack. Vast civil engineering projects shaped up sites to accommodate the bombers. The first of the B17s and B24s reached their British bases in July 1942. Both had great names: Boeing's 'Flying Fortress' and Ford's 'Liberator', emerging from factories which knew a thing or two about effective mass production.

The officers running the American Eighth Air Force were primarily fresh recruits from industry; not seasoned military personnel. Many had a business mind-set regarding organisation and procedures. They appreciated plans and objectives, and recognised that initial efforts would be an experiment, from which everyone would learn. They needed space and time to develop an appropriate working formula. The British climate proved problematic for some of the aircraft systems, dampness affecting moving parts: taking a plane upwards froze moisture in the joints, fouling whole mechanisms above 20,000 feet. The Americans planned to bomb Germany from a great height, so reliable oxygen supply and crew heating were critical. Test flights kept revealing issues for technical amendments before any serious mission could be contemplated.

Soon there was muttering in the newspapers that the guys from across the pond ought to be getting up and out there to give Hitler and his henchmen a taste of American aggression. Sod's law saw a B17 get lost on a training flight in Wales and so crunch into a hill, killing all aboard. But a week later, the Eighth was ready for its first trip across the Channel to drop ordnance on French rail yards. With an escort of RAF Spitfires, a dozen Fortresses headed off one August morning. Most reached the required destination and decanted their loads, then returned to base - an encouraging start, though some RAF bystanders pointed out that the gun-heavy US planes could not match the quantity of ordnance the Lancaster was now conveying. And if one of those fancy American machines came down, ten men were lost to the cause, rather than just seven aboard the British craft. The new arrivals countered that they were going to be far more accurate with their payloads, so didn't need the weights that BC hauled towards the enemy. And those extra guys aboard the US planes were producing more fire-power, so better protecting that huge asset and its contents.

By mid-1942 the Luftwaffe had a thousand fighters to defend daytime Reich skies. Their factories were turning out more planes every day, but these had to be shared between the various theatres, especially the eastern front. The German leadership tried to play down the potential problems of the USA coming over to Europe to help Britain bomb the

Ruhr. Hermann Goering amused his entourage by declaring: "The Americans can only manufacture refrigerators and razor blades."

With an eye for marketing criteria, the USAAF issued target objectives: submarine yards, transportation systems, electric power supply, oil production, aluminium and rubber manufacture, aircraft industries - nice and clear, circled on a map, tabled into priorities; each goal to be ticked off the list sooner or later. They began tentative operations into occupied territory and quickly learnt more about practicalities: some planes would not reach the heights promised by the manufacturers when loaded with explosives and fuel. Crews found the heady atmosphere debilitating. Half of them were suffering from freshly acquired English colds. Elaborate electrically-heated boots failed, causing airmen to lose toes to frost-bite. Jettisoning heavy shell cartridge cases wasn't a good idea when others planes from supporting squadrons were travelling directly below.

Training flights never adequately prepared a pilot for the aggressive behaviour of experienced enemy fighters. The first encounters over France saw American flyers manoeuvring according to good practice, but this was predictable stuff that allowed the Luftwaffe to anticipate their opponents next turn or dive.

A couple of B17s soon crashed in France, enabling the Germans to examine the impressive wrecks. So much for Goering's flying fridge: these monsters could go incredibly fast at very high altitudes. They had substantial armour, and stacks of big guns. It was like one of those wild west... yes, fortresses... that could fly. And, according to The Times, thousands would be coming over soon. Not good.

On 9th October 1942, the Eighth was ready to tackle a French munitions factory: 108 US bombers headed for Lille, with an escort of British fighter planes. 39 bombers turned back with function problems, leaving 69 intruders to face the Luftwaffe. The American gunners blasted away but their aim was terrible. One German craft was damaged, wounding a crewman. The pilot told him to bale out and the fellow jumped, but his parachute didn't open so he plunged to his death: the only Luftwaffe fatality from the battle of Lille, which had also seen the shooting down of four American planes.

But when the guys got back to East Anglia they were hyped up over how well they had hammered the Huns. All in all, the gunners were confident they had shot down at least 56 German planes. This was reported to Washington where President Roosevelt announced the results with pride in his next radio broadcast. Oh, did the Luftwaffe laugh: those Americans - with their fantasies from cowboy films. Perhaps our boss was right all along? There is nothing to fear from fridges with wings.

The Americans realised they needed to interrogate the claims of returning airmen. The courageous gunners were firing their weapons through wild arcs while casting around for the next incoming assault, logging almost every shell discharge against a Luftwaffe machine as a fatal blow. Rigorous post-op analysis was required: ground staff cross-checking claims, seeking specific times and places to reduce overlaps, multiple perceptions, quantities of confirmed 'kills'.

The Eighth pressed on with their assaults, getting a better grip on the capacities of their machines, as well as the outlines of the English and continental coasts - so they less often mistook what country they were above. They became proficient at recognising British planes and not treating them as German fighters. They reduced the discharge of their weapons into fellow airmen's workplaces.

They got better at all of this, while the Germans got better at challenging them, concluding that the most vulnerable bit of a US bomber was the front. Approach it head on, squirt off some cannon fire into the cockpit and you could disable the pilot so the whole thing dropped out of contention.

American forward planning had not anticipated the attrition rates by enemy forces or mechanical breakdown. Lots of planes were grounded until extra parts could be shipped in and new crews became available; which did nothing to sustain morale on the bases when there were empty tables in the canteens. This was something the RAF had learned: have more men ready to take the place of those lost, otherwise the survivors feel vulnerable, numbered.

The hearty East Anglian contingents were getting all the elements of their campaign in good order when the powers-that-be assigned a big chunk of them to move to Morocco to participate in Operation Torch, the invasion of North Africa.

By the end of 1942, the Americans had barely made any direct impact on the European war. All that was still to come.

Sand

If you've got to cross a desert, there's a lot to be said for a camel. Sand doesn't bother it, and the animal can go for ages without any fuel (food or water). Different story with machines: vehicles struggle to get a grip over sand, and the gritty stuff is always inclined to trickle into the moving parts, which does them no good at all.

Aircraft don't flourish in the desert either. Take-off and landing always throws up puffs which can enter orifices and foul an engine or clog a mechanism. So in an ideal world you'd keep your planes away from deserts.

After the British Empire had acquired the French-excavated trough that formed the Suez Canal, there was immense vested interest in keeping that nautical artery operational and protected from troublesome foreigners. The Egyptian channel trimmed weeks off sailing times from Britain to India. It was no longer necessary to slog around South Africa. However every inch of the man-made corridor needed to be guarded with troops on the banks; plus ships patrolling the entrances, planes scanning the horizons.

The United Kingdom built substantial air bases in Egypt. The locals got used to the Royal Air Force, Middle East. There were compensations for accommodating the flyers: the Brits and their pals expected all sorts of support services and Egypt had a thriving service economy – plenty of people able to undertake hard graft in the heat for very modest pay. Cairo was full of small workshops capable of engineering parts for planes. The governing regime permitted the foreigners to take over the caverns cut from the excavation of stone to build the pyramids. These huge holes were fitted out to become shelters for aircraft and equipment. The radar wizards were even allowed to stick a contraption on top of a pyramid to alert them to possible aerial danger while Winston Churchill was visiting.

However, the huge leg of Italian coastline thrusting south in the Sea enabled Axis powers to dominate the Mediterranean; and the British were forced to once again sail around the whole of Africa to re-supply their Egyptian outpost. Unsurprisingly, Hitler had his beady eyes on the Canal. Wouldn't it be convenient if he could grasp that civil engineering facility and so gain a swift passageway to Middle East oil reserves? Dismayed by Mussolini's blunders in the region, Adolf realised he had to ship military resources to Libya, then have a mighty German army advance eastward to Cairo. It would be easier without all that sand, of course, but his engineers could adapt their vehicles to minimise the inevitable ingression of grit, surely. The British army had the same problem − keeping lorries, tanks, motor-bikes and guns operating amidst dust, gravel, rocks.

The desert war across north Africa was primarily a land battle, but planes played a critical role; some would say, they proved the decisive factor. Only good thing about the terrain was that it was more or less impossible to get lost. Flying over the Atlantic or continental Europe, there were plenty of opportunities for failing to understand where you were. Along the southern edge of the Mediterranean, it was easy: if the water was off your left you were heading to Egypt, if the water was to starboard, you must be going towards Morocco.

Down below, miles of sand. Tiny tracks marked crude thoroughfares east and west; along some stretches were railway lines, nice and clear, weaving around mounds and depressions. A fighter aircraft was light enough to land on sand. Whether it could take off again hinged on the hardness of the stuff, assuming not too much had entered the engine intakes. You didn't really want to try this. Best wait for ground units to identify a possible temporary airstrip and prepare it. Clear it of brush and big rocks, bulldoze away disconcerting dunes, fill in holes and crevices.

So the scene is set for planes to support troops on the perimeters of their spheres of influence. Both camps relied on the delivery of more men, machines, food, fuel, spares and ammunition from Europe; and sufficient quantities could not come by plane. The Third Reich was able to send vessels directly across the Med from French, Italian and Greek ports, the UK had to ship goods to Morocco for a long, dusty drive eastward, or steam the kit round Africa to reach Egypt from the Indian Ocean.

The balance of back-up would prove pivotal. Germany mustered impressive forces to commence their assault on Allied lines: sufficient to knock the Imperial troops (including a proportion of the one million Indians now supporting the cause) back to El Alamein, inside the Egyptian border. It was imperative to inhibit the Reich from reenforcing across the Med, and this was what RAF Middle East set about. They flew towards German shipping to strafe, torpedo and bomb it, setting fire to and sinking thousands of tons of further supplies. Many of the Egypt-based airmen were South Africans who, along with big contingents from Rhodesia, Canada, Australia and the USA, menaced the Med and blasted enemy troops edging along the north African coast. These aviators kept walloping enemy supply lines, often under-defended because of the transient nature of north Saharan manoeuvres. They raided temporary German airfields in Libya, eliminating swathes of Luftwaffe fleets. Army bases were easy to detect and assault, while trains carrying fuel to the front made for great targets. Because of the lack of defence, Allied pilots could approach such prospects at far lower altitudes than in Europe, which made their strike rate better.

Of course, plenty of planes crashed in the desert. Able crewmen clambered out and walked towards the coast, looking for water and help. RAF recovery squads scoured the desolate landscape for downed craft. They craned remains on to low loaders and edged them back to Cairo, to have the machines rebuilt within those back street workshops.

The opposing armies battled ferociously across the north of Africa through most of 1942, but slowly the Allies gained the advantage of superior supply lines; the Germans finally forced to retreat, thousands becoming prisoners of war. The campaign was a belated triumph for Hugh Trenchard, who had always insisted the Suez Canal be provided with major aerial defence.

After the war, hundreds of broken German aircraft, tanks and trucks remained scattered across the desert. As you would expect, they eventually became covered in sand.

Could there be a horizon ahead?

In January 1942, Liverpool suffered yet another Luftwaffe raid and more fatalities. By now nearly 4,000 people on Merseyside had died from German bombing; 350 of them children under the age of five. After London, this was the city most subjected to Luftwaffe attacks because it was the prime entry point for American supplies. No-one knew this at the time, but there would be no more deadly aerial assaults on the port after this month. However only very slowly would the atmosphere of anxiety start to ease; there was no announcement to declare the ordeal was over. Photographs show whole streets of exoskeletons of devastated buildings - Britain's most severe concentration of destruction, matching what would eventually be the bleak vista of many German conurbations.

At the end of January, a Japanese military plane shot down a Quantas passenger aircraft just north of Australia, killing eleven aboard when it crashed into the sea. A few survivors managed to swim through shark-infested water to an island estuary crowded with crocodiles – a James Bond-style escape.

Many Russian planes could operate on either wheels or skis, designed so the undercarriage swop was swift. Once heavy snow was blanketing airfields across the eastern front and Luftwaffe aircraft were stuck in drifts, this capacity proved invaluable. Meanwhile one of Hitler's closest aides died in a flying accident. Was this fate or had Adolf got fed up with him? A few days later, a senior Luftwaffe officer was on his way to the funeral when his plane crashed - the third General to die this way in just a few months.

The Japanese took a leaf out of the RAF's book and sprinkled leaflets over Singapore for the benefit of British soldiers, asking: 'Why do you submit to the intolerable torture of malarial mosquitos merely to pamper the British aristocracy?' Hugh Trenchard made his presence felt in the House of Lords, and in the letters columns of The Times, not least by pointing out he had said all along that Singapore needed more aircraft.

In March, Commander Harris decided to hammer the Heinkel airframe factory in Rostock. 500 bombers were sent there across four nights, killing many residents and damaging historic buildings; but subsequent reports revealed the mission had done little to destroy the plant, which returned to normal levels of production within weeks.

However, Hitler wanted revenge for Rostock and demanded the Luftwaffe assault "cultural" conurbations in England, such as Bath and Canterbury. In April and May this brought about the deaths of 1,637 British citizens, some of whose families would in due course become beneficiaries of the Lord Mayor of London's National Air Raid Distress Fund.

In hit-and-run raids across the Channel from March to June, the RAF lost 300 planes to 90 Luftwaffe craft. June brought BC losses of 5% or more over Essen and Bremen.

The Americans tried to damage Romanian oil fields from Egypt, subsequently landing their B24s in Iraq, but more than half the force went astray. Better news from the Pacific: de-coding of Japanese naval plans gave the US advance warning of an attack on the island of Midway. So the Americans were prepared - even though many of their torpedoes failed to function – and went on to sink several enemy ships; eliminating 3,000 Japanese sailors, though losing many of their own aircrews and planes in the process.

And now a diary entry that can only exist with hindsight: on 22nd July 1942 Europe was halfway through its war. In just another 1,052 days it would come to an end. Would that foresight have cheered or dismayed?

At the end of July, 100 British aircraft were dispatched to Dusseldorf with losses en route in excess of 10%. August saw the USAAF bring down a Luftwaffe plane for the first time: a lieutenant ferrying his fighter to Britain spotted a German reconnaissance patrol off Iceland and gave it a blast with his brand new guns. Then a RAF pathfinder raid on the Saar coalfields ended up accidently targeting the wrong town, thirteen miles away. On 23rd August the Luftwaffe commenced the Battle of Stalingrad by assigning 1,000 planes to drop 1,000 tons of incendiaries to destroy the main residential areas. In response, the Soviet air force had a go at bombing Berlin with 100 planes, but almost all were shot down.

Bomber Command contributed to mine-laying through the milder months, resulting in 160 German-controlled vessels being sunk; though the same number of British planes were lost seeding those seas. In direct attacks on ships, the RAF sank 50 vessels but wrote off hundreds of planes in the process - nevertheless a big improvement on those frustrating days back in 1939 when hitting any ship had proved so difficult.

By now the RAF had lost 14,000 personnel. To mark the third anniversary of the start of the war, the British Air Ministry issued a score chart of aircraft losses showing that the Axis powers had suffered 8,985 planes destroyed on their western perimeter, against 6,231 British craft.

In October, the pathfinder system was still being bedded in when the boys tried to bash the German settlement of Aachen and accidentally decanted tons of bombs on a Dutch town twenty miles away. Later that month, BC attempted to smash the Schneider aircraft engine factory in France and achieved better accuracy, though some tonnage descended on a workers' housing estate.

Here's a tip: flying a bomber, never wave to chums at the controls of civilian airliners. One military pilot did this over California and veered, causing his props to cut through the passenger plane's tail, killing all twelve aboard. More advice: if you and your pal have had a few beers, don't offer him a lift in the confined cockpit of your Spitfire. This very unwise practice eliminated two RAF chaps in a prang that would never stack up as heroic.

In November Harris allocated more squadrons to take payloads to Italy – missions which promised better odds of getting back unscathed than the rotten Ruhr or bloody Berlin. Mussolini was now making cartoon strip appearances in the British Beano comic: tales featuring variations on "You gotta me in da mess again!"

December saw BC off to Eindhoven in Holland, home of the Philips electronics factory. 93 bombers went there one night; 14 were shot down, 53 limped home damaged. German radar production was put back by six months, but nearly 150 Dutch workers were killed.

Stalin's birthday fell on the 22nd December and perhaps his spirits were lifted this year by a telegram from the Chairman of the London County Council:

'On behalf of the people of London, who are full of admiration for the brave and unwearied resistance of the Russian people, I send hearty greetings and good wishes. The cause of civilisation and the better world which the allied peoples mean to achieve owes a heavy debt to your brilliant and inspiring leadership.'

The Times reported that fragments of the stone from the bomb damaged sections of the Houses of Parliament were being sold as seasonal presents; and on Christmas Day church bells would be allowed to chime celebration peels for the first time in four years. The paper's leader focused on a new initiative from the Imperial War Graves Commission:

> 'It is not only fighting men who lie in the war graves of our time; there is need also for a national memorial to those who are struck down in their homes, or in the performance of their civil defences, by the blind fury of aerial bombardment.'

Bomber Command flew over 35,000 sorties through this year, mostly at night, unloading 37,000 tons of ordnance on to German soil. In good weather, about a third of this arrived within three miles of its intended destination. Nearly 5,000 Germans died as a result, but the RAF lost 1,716 aircraft; around 34 each week. Additionally 1,000 British planes were destroyed in accidents. But the aircraft factories could more or less match this number with new machines coming off the production line.

The lost crews? They all had to be replaced with novices. The Air Ministry launched a new advertising message:

> 'BOOK YOUR SEAT FOR BERLIN
> Not bombs alone. Not 'planes alone. Not guns alone will win this war – but Men!
> Men – under 33. Determined men. Men who know that they have a great cause to fight for. Men who know that team-work is the hardest work of all.
> Thousands of them are training to fly with the R.A.F. Thousands more are needed – to be ready for training when required.
> Now is the time to reserve your place in Britain's Air Crew teams of the future.'

1943

ACROSS THE NORTH SEA AGAIN AND AGAIN

'Adolf Hitler, this is the fourth New Year in your war against civilisation. Slaughter, suffering, starvation and savagery – the Four Horsemen of your Apocalypse – have followed the Crooked Cross of Nazidom from one end of Europe to the other.

Til now, every First of January brought its boast of fresh conquests. More bloodstained earth had been added to your evil empire. Farther and farther stretched your greedy grip into countries which had never challenged or molested you, strangling freedom of body and soul, seizing plunder, crushing to a cruel death all who dared resist you. But in 1943 you face a different situation. Where formally you were advancing, this New Year finds you on the retreat.'

Stirring stuff from the Daily Mail's feature writer G. Ward Price. The newspaper was soon able to report on a new plan from Churchill and Roosevelt: the RAF and USAAF were to:

'...achieve the progressive destruction and dislocation of the German military, industrial and economic systems, and the undermining of the morale of the German people, to a point where their capacity for armed resistance is fatally weakened.'

Secretly, Bomber Command missions would soon be greatly aided by H2S, a hefty but mobile navigation device. Once installed in bombers, this radar system would enable them to accurately cross the North Sea, then take a vector into Germany directly towards a target. It was ready to roll in January 1943 but one of the first planes carrying the kit crash-landed in Holland, allowing German technicians to examine it and deduce a way of distorting H2S signals, which the Brits were a long time in recognising.

Targets not requiring sophisticated navigation were the U-boat pens on the French coast, tucked beneath reinforced concrete built to be impervious to bomb attacks. BC undertook many raids on these structures at the start of the year, but none made any impact on naval facilities; instead just mucked up nearby seaside towns.

Arthur Harris dispatched a couple of hundred planes to Berlin in January, however the distance, winter weather conditions and defences confirmed the painful nature of such challenges: nearly 12% of the force failed to return. What was the answer? The Command decided to prioritise hammering the Ruhr, hence diminishing Germany's capacity to produce steel and munitions. In theory every explosion could damage something to fractionally inhibit enemy weapon-making: a factory, bridge, road, lorry, train, town hall, house, human being. From February 1943 a series of substantial missions were directed to these valleys, but did not seem to make much impact; while the squadrons lost many planes and crews. By Easter, Air Ministry statisticians were able announce that the RAF had now decanted 100,000 tons of bombs on Germany. Stiffening resolve to battle on were the deaths of several hundred Londoners on a tube station staircase one night, crushed when someone tripped on their way down to their shelter - patently Hitler's fault! On 14th April, an attack on Stuttgart encountered hefty defences causing Bomber Command its largest loss on a single night so far: 54 aircraft destroyed - a miserable new number to add to the charts.

On 16th April, 329 BC crews set out to hit the Skoda armaments factory in Pilsen. Most missed and instead destroyed a lunatic asylum some ten miles away. 36 aircraft were lost on the mission: 252 airmen, 11% of the assigned personnel.

Four days later, RAF bombing killed 600 people in the town of Stettin. This impact drove the Third Reich to withdraw some big guns from the east to better protect Ruhr populations. Allied missions were starting to make a difference: the Germans needed to treat the air above them as a new war front, thus taking a degree of pressure off the Russians.

On 4th May, a dozen British bombers tried to attack a power plant in Holland but only one returned. Next night 600 planes set off for Dortmund and 40 failed to survive. On 29th May, 720 bombers were sent to the Ruhr. 62 turned back early with "technical problems", while six were damaged by incendiaries falling from same-side aircraft higher in the sky, whose crews had either been unaware of colleagues below under cloud, or had not allowed for winds that could blow light ordnance astray.

Returning crews never knew what damage their cargo might have achieved. Some airmen could be wounded - most likely rear gunners who had caught a blast of enemy fire - but a proportion would go up again within a few weeks. BC sent hundreds of craft to major industrial areas every time the weather promised a viable window, but there was almost always heavy cloud over the Ruhr - a combination of prevailing meteorology and the dense smoke emerging from chimneys. Creep-back was a frequent irritation: the BC pathfinders released their markers, generally close to the required destination, but first wave bombers in the stream often estimated their unloading point a little too early in the approach flight, so these weapons fell a bit short of the target. Second wave crews saw the fires started by their predecessors and they too decanted their load moments too soon, starting fires even further from the target, which in turn became the prospective strike point for the next wave of bomb aimers. The drift could end up delivering ordnance ten miles short of a designated factory.

In the first half of 1943, BC unleashed more bombs than the Luftwaffe had used in the whole of the British Blitz. Average missions now numbered 700 aircraft, but 30 might fail to return. Proportions far above this caused questions to be asked about those squadrons: their capabilities, the weather, the route. A string of results in excess of 5% could indicate problems in persevering with that target.

Between March and July, thirty-one raids were made on the Ruhr, which cost Bomber Command more than a thousand aircraft and more than five thousand crew, while killing 15,000 people down below. BC boys had a one-in-three chance of surviving these sorties. For a vivid sense of the terrible activity, let me hand over to Simon Read's 'The Killing Skies':

'The red glow of fire climbed skyward on billowing clouds of black smoke and mists of dust and debris. A crimson dome rose from the city centre like a massive molten bubble, expanding upwards and outwards. From the inferno stretched beams of blue and white light, groping in the darkness for the bombers passing overhead. Burning incendiaries glistened like stars, while high explosives detonated in vibrant white flashes. Everything was bathed in a violent spectrum of colour. Tracers rocketed skyward in luminescent blurs of red and green. Black clouds of flak hung heavy in the glare of searchlights. British bombers burned in lurid shades of red and orange. One fell in a long, shallow dive and disintegrated in a ball of flame.'

Is it a boat, is it a plane?

The Sunderland flying boat is a magnificent looking machine - an adaptation of a pre-war passenger plane designed to deliver mail and people to faraway parts. Imperial Airways used them and Quantas had a fleet for servicing Australasia: much easier to find a stretch of calm water somewhere rather than construct an expensive runway.

A huge hull allows the vessel to float. The fuselage looks whale-like, whilst its nose is reminiscent of the profile of a duck. Maintenance crews motored small boats out to the sides of the Sunderland to work on structures and engines. An armaments launch would bring depth charges alongside, the crew standing in the wobbly tender to engage the brackets on the underside of the wings.

Coastal Command (CC) Sunderlands had an air crew of twelve, who appreciated plenty of space compared with the cramped conditions on other aircraft. There was an upstairs and downstairs, with a galley bigger than many modern kitchens, and bunks for the relief crews to rest during 14 hour patrols. The flying boats weighed 12 tons and could travel at 210 mph. Fuel tanks holding 2,500 gallons allowed them to cover 3,000 miles across the Atlantic looking for U-boats menacing convoys.

One squadron was based on a big lake in Northern Ireland. Often the most feared part of missions was getting from the lake to the ocean because a Sunderland can't land on land. It needs water at the end of its descent. And not any old water; benign conditions were essential. Try bringing down a Sunderland on choppy sea and there's a high likelihood the wings will catch a wave and the whole craft will break up. At night there was the added difficulty of unlit waves: the pilot could not accurately determine how close he was to the water. The secret was to fly at 200 feet per minute and gently edge downward. Sooner or later, the underside would get wet.

The machine was invaluable for rescue missions. In the first month of the war a Sunderland came down near the Scilly Isles to pick up sailors from a ship that had been sunk by German torpedoes. Off the shores of Greece, a Sunderland lifted 90 sailors and soldiers to safety, all in one load. One patrol successfully depth charged a U-boat in the Bay of Biscay, then saw desperate German sailors from the stricken submarine bobbing amidst the resulting oil slick. The Coastal chaps took pity on them and dropped out a dinghy.

The Germans referred to the well-armed aircraft as the "flying porcupine". Unfortunately the Sunderland had a soft spot – its underbelly; an expanse of delicate aluminium with no armour or weaponry to protect it, making it vulnerable to Luftwaffe attacks from below. The answer? The Sunderland pilot would fly very close to the surface of the sea so no enemy plane could get beneath him.

Forty Sunderlands were brought down by enemy fighters during the war. They would have made a big splash and not all the crews were able to escape in those dinghies. One plane suffered a disastrous return to its base off the Scottish island of Islay on the evening of 24th January 1943. To enable the craft to come down in the dark, small boats were sent offshore to show a row of flashing lamps and so provide the pilot with an appropriate trajectory. In heavy winds the Sunderland circled a number of times then clipped the top of a hill on the island. It stayed aloft then attempted an approach towards the water, but the descent was misjudged and the plane pranged against the edge of the beach. Eleven of the crew climbed out despite injuries, but realised their rear gunner was not amongst them - so most went back to extract their colleague, but the plane's depth charges now blew up killing the eight rescuers and their trapped gunner. The explosion was heard right across the island, some locals thinking it was the start of an invasion by the Germans.

May 1943 was the pinnacle of Allied success against U-boats: 41 were sunk, each with a crew of 60 sailors. This attrition caused the Germans to withdraw their subs to the Bay of Biscay to instead menace coastal shipping and the approaches to the Mediterranean. This allowed CC to concentrate its efforts: May to July 1943 became known as the Battle of the Bay, when the Command sank 20 U-boats, though lost 28 aircraft; incidents which resulted in the deaths of 1,200 Allied or Axis personnel.

In 1944, CC kept U-boats at bay before, during and after the D-Day landings. But the Allies then faced a new challenge: a big pipe poking from the top of a U-boat which allowed air to circulate while the vessel remained below the surface. This meant the captain could run his diesel motor to re-charge the batteries for powering the electric engines and not expose his vessel to enemy surveillance aircraft. Mercifully the snorkel did not get a chance to be universally fitted and deployed before the end of the war.

The Atlantic consists of ten million square miles of surface water. Let us never forget that, through the war, 10,871 men died – mostly from drowning - while serving in Coastal Command.

Not in the brochure
Second World War planes were designed to fly to attack enemies in the air or on the ground; then to return to where they set off from, there to re-fuel and re-arm before heading off to do it all again. A fighter needed to be light and manoeuvrable. These days, people find the Spitfire adorable, but current enthusiasts did not serve as ground crew in the war, and so were never called upon to perch on the tail plane or the wing whilst the craft was manoeuvring across the airfield, sometimes at considerable speed.

This disconcerting task was necessary because the celebrated machine had a couple of nasty characteristics. One was that it was impossible for the pilot to see what was ahead while on the ground. The position of the cockpit behind the high point of the nose meant the driver had no idea if his way forward was clear. Out on the runway, he would assume he was good to go, and so power forward hoping for the best. If trying to perambulate across the field then it sometimes paid to get a member of the ground crew to squat on a wing and signal to you where to steer.

Additionally, Spitfires on their wheels did not deal well with bumpy bits of ground. The balance of weight behind the fulcrum of the two main wheels was marginal. One lump on the grass could cause the craft to tip forward, thus carving the prop into the earth, maybe breaking off a blade, which could chop someone. Solution? A by-stander would be ordered to perch on the tail plane to help keep the machine stable as it moved across any rough patches. Sometimes these helpers had to stay on the tail until the plane commenced take off. It was just a matter of jumping clear before the machine picked up speed. But on more than one occasion a ground crew man or woman hung on too long. They surely shouted to the pilot to bring them back to earth, but it was unlikely the fellow in the cockpit would be able to hear their cries. More likely he would detect a distortion in the handling of his fighter, or the control tower would radio to announce a pesky external passenger. Now the pilot tried his best to bring "the kite" back down in a manner that maximised the likelihood of the wind-blasted colleague being able to hop off.

There was seldom the time, personnel or equipment to forensically examine the results of a prang in order to figure out if a fundamental design or engineering fault had caused the demise of a particular plane. To this day a debate continues as to how, in July 1943, General Sikorsky, the Polish resistance leader (no relation to the Ukrainian-American helicopter designer, Sikorski), came to expire in the Mediterranean minutes after taking off in a Liberator from Gibraltar, whilst his pilot inexplicably survived. Lots of theories from technical to treachery float about on the internet.

Operational manuals for Second World War military aircraft were generally light on what to do if everything went wrong and you could not continue onward at a viable flying height. A bomber aircraft's prime function was to carry very heavy objects and jettison them above target points. All the design effort was focused on satisfactory procedures in the air. A retractable undercarriage aided aerial performance. But if the undercarriage would not lock down into landing mode and instead stayed stuck inside the underside of the wings or fuselage, or the whole mechanism dropped loose and could not be locked, then fate would take its course.

In the cockpit were tiny lights to indicate the state of the undercarriage: green meant good to land, red said something's not right below – anticipating that a massive amount of forward momentum and a huge force of friction were about to unpredictably play with the huge machine. Sometimes luck allowed "the crate" to complete an upright, contained halt. Often it didn't. A wing could scrape the ground immediately and be ripped away from the fuselage which would then swerve violently. Now you've got a distorted device under extreme arbitrary forces, all capable of initiating a flip, cartwheel or worse.

If you need to touch down away from an airfield - wheels locked in landing mode - the tyres might function and keep the machine in a viable configuration, but projections in the terrain could stab the aircraft into the ground, cracking it into monstrous cascading segments and a bloody mess.

Big bang theory

The bomb is a fiendish device: explosive chemicals confined within a casing that will blast outwards in all directions doing damage from its fragments and contents to anything in range - which might be a hundred metres or more. What a cruel, vile, anti-social instrument. It makes no distinctions regarding its targets: anyone thereabouts will be the victims of its destructive power. It will make more and bigger holes in a human being than a single bullet from a gun. And therein lies its appeal. At a stroke, it brings violence to the enemy en masse. Whole groups of people, not necessarily just armed forces, will be hit and hurt, or killed by its impact. It abruptly devastates and mindlessly eliminates its recipients. They will be damaged, disabled, destabilised; possibly completely destroyed by the ugly, dreadful thing. What a useful tool.

And isn't the aeroplane the perfect means for conveying vast quantities of these terrible objects to places and people you wish to defeat. Hence bomber aircraft were the 20th century's ideal instrument for dismaying and exterminating foreigners fast and furiously.

By 1939, science and technology had not reached a point whereby the biggest aeroplane could carry many bombs. The Germans concentrated on dive bombing: flying a single device down towards a specific target, and releasing it at the last moment to maximise the likelihood of it reaching the desired destination; the plucky pilot then endeavouring to pull out of his dive and rapidly climb to avoid hitting the ground; and, of course, being too close to the bomb when it explodes. This was the snag: on that rising arc, after the weapon has been released, the plane moves relatively slowly, so if opposition fighter aircraft are in the vicinity, they can quite easily pick off a Stuka as it hauls through its climb.

It proved more practical to release bombs from a height well above your intended target while travelling at great speed over that location. Chances of any particular bomb landing precisely where you wished were low. You could only expect to position explosives in a neighbourhood – what you might call Post Code bombing - so the proportion of the weaponry going astray was enormous.

Britain had learnt a lot from being bombed by the Germans. Disgorging containers of high explosive (H.E.) was not the best way to devastate urban areas: instead a combination of big bangs and many fire-inducing canisters worked far better. The bomb breaks open the building, then incendiary sticks can ignite exposed timber. An hour later, when the emergency services are in the midst of trying to remove the injured and dampen the flames, it pays to send over a second wave of bombers to blast the survivors and their rescuers, and so disrupt and demoralise the recovery effort.

Britain learned this, but failed to grasp Lesson Two: the survivors will struggle on as best they can. Dropping bombs on urban streets would kill some people, injure more and dismay the rest; leaving many homeless. But would the survivors stop going to work and instead flee the city to live in a bivouac out in the country? Might they rise up in resentment at the regime that got them into such a mess, and so plot attempts to bring down that leadership – overthrow it? Change the country's governors for others who will stop the bombs?

That wasn't what happened in Britain. The evidence – as carefully studied in Birmingham and Hull - was that, in the aftermath of bombing, most people, if they could, stayed in what was left of their houses, and went back to work as soon as possible, and didn't built up resentment against their political masters. Yet the UK now tooled up to bomb the towns of the Third Reich in the belief that it would only be a matter of time before those munitions plants would grind to a halt from damage and absenteeism; for those urban areas to be abandoned and for the distraught refugees to take action to excise their politicians.

But the Germans, like the Brits, didn't do that. Even with ten times the amount of ordnance being rained upon them as, for example, was decanted upon Coventry in one fateful night, those German citizens did their best to stay where they were, live in what remained of their homes and return to work as soon as was practical – not under duress, but out of choice. Like the Brits, if nothing else, they needed the money. Of course, fundamentally, there was also an animal-like instinct to re-enter and remain within their familiar domestic burrow. Yet Bomber

Command continued to pursue their strategy, believing it would bring the war to an end more quickly.

The Tallboy was a weapon to be reckoned with - a deep penetration device, dropped from 18,000 feet to achieve a velocity of 750 mph and so ram into the surface of the earth by eight metres before exploding. More than 800 were unloaded over the Third Reich.

In the summer of 1943, a Washington press release announced that "air experts" had plans to deploy bombs "twice the size and with many more times the destructive power" from bigger and more powerful aircraft: "air power on a scale which will make Germany's worst nights seem trivial."

However, many men in UK squadrons preferred a smaller weapon: the aircraft did not jump about in the sky upon the release of modest weights, and a quartet of 250 pound devices were potentially a more fruitful payload than one 1,000 pounder, because you were four times more likely to hit something useful.

Only a very small proportion of the population of the UK considered mass bombing of the Third Reich to be morally wrong or simply fruitless. In 1941 a group of pacifists set up the Committee for the Abolition of Night Bombing. They had support from George Bernard Shaw who advised Times's readers that by killing at least thousand Germans each night it would still take more than one hundred years to exterminate the nation. A few Bishops argued against the RAF campaigns. The Bishop of Bristol considered Bomber Command's work immoral, but the city's Mayor disagreed.

A handful of MPs and Members of the House of Lords argued cases to delimit the bombing; some simply pointing out it could result in post-war bitterness by the defeated side. Perhaps the most eloquent critic of RAF endeavours was author Vera Brittain who, following the widely celebrated Hamburg raids, wrote a booklet, first published in the USA, which spelt out the ugly scenarios that successful raids must have caused on the target populations. 'Seeds of Chaos' was briefly reviewed in the respectable UK papers but more or less ignored across the popular titles. A petition opposing random bombing of German urban areas mustered 15,000 signatures - nothing for Whitehall to worry about.

Achtung!

Hitler had never anticipated that his military adventurism might result in British planes attacking the Fatherland, but as BC performance improved the Third Reich realised it was necessary to erect an effective defence barrier; some elements matching what the UK had done to resist the Blitz, plus plenty that was much more powerful and sophisticated.

Thousands of anti-aircraft (flak) guns were emplaced across all possible paths of incoming bombers, the first wave aboard ships patrolling the North Sea shores. On land, big fixed batteries were established at vantage points on prospective routes, supplemented by railway truck-mounted guns, to be shunted to likely hot spots of intrusion.

German flak guns were finely-engineered weapons with long barrels able to rapidly blast big shells great distances. Loading procedures were automated - no crew blundering around with heavy cartridges - and the guns could be radar controlled, not needing sight of an enemy aircraft to be assigned a trajectory that could result in a hit. The 88mm anti-aircraft gun, built under licence from Bofors of neutral Sweden, fired shells four miles skyward. With a velocity of 700 mph these took six seconds to reach the aircraft then explode into a thousand shards of steel, all capable of piercing the wings, fuel tanks and fuselage, plus the machinery inside and the people working it.

Alongside the fearsome guns were extraordinary searchlights, projecting a shaft of brightness ten miles into the sky. Like the guns, the lights could be radar-controlled, to keep their chosen plane harshly illuminated, often temporarily blinding the pilot, bomb aimer and turret crews.

The RAF had believed that a cluster of bomber aircraft flying in close formation should present the enemy with an insurmountable force. The intruders would resemble a giant aerial battleship, bristling with guns which no small fighter would dare approach. But this notion failed to allow for the contrast in capacity between the opposing planes. Consider the manoeuvrability of a motorbike compared with a furniture lorry: the light craft, controlled by one man with a bunch of guns at his command, can fly much faster than a bomber and weave far better to overwhelm the slow machine, not designed for furious manipulation.

The Luftwaffe's quantity of aircraft sometimes did not match the UK fleets but they managed to do a lot more damage with their available complement due to the determination and ingenuity of their pilots. The RAF shot down some enemy fighters, but only a small number compared to the many British craft brought to a sudden end by German guns.

Luftwaffe commanders established a perimeter grid of air space stretching from the Baltic to Spain, each segment with dedicated systems and personnel. The approach of every British bomber was telegraphed ahead by warning squads – radar, sound and sight - enabling the patrolling fighters of each aerial rectangle to swiftly swoop down on the visitors. Jutting from the nose and wings of the night-fighters were hefty cannons serviced with long belts of large, fast-delivery shells. Most effective was the later assembly of cannons mounted behind the cockpit and angled upwards to give the pilot a perfect shot at the underside of an Allied plane above and ahead. Before the crew of the bomber had registered that Jerry was close, this cunning weapon would blast at the wings of the big aircraft, setting fire to the fuel tanks. The Luftwaffe man just had to nip sideways to avoid the disabled plane dropping on him.

German aircraft often had lots of heavy gear (including radar) aboard which meant their fuel tanks only allowed them to operate for an hour or so. They also needed to land to re-arm, but would be swiftly up in the air again to carry on where they had left off, plugging a few more Tommies. One German ace could destroy half-a-dozen BC craft in a single night.

To minimise the damage from falling foreign bombs, the Third Reich strictly policed its urban black-out rules while creating elaborate concrete bunkers across cities and factory sites able to accommodate thousands of workers and other civilians. German boffins distorted or jammed British radio and radar waves, and developed detection devices capable of alerting Berlin to the movement of RAF planes when they were still taxying on English runways.

Local bureaucrats, backed by security forces, were good at getting order back to a street that had suffered bombing by using political prisoners and slave labour to repair domestic buildings. Fast way to alleviate those who had lost their homes and possessions was to assign them dwellings from which Jewish families had been forcibly removed, and to provide displaced citizens with the furniture, wares and clothes of their missing neighbours.

As we know, a lot of British bombs never blew up. Three out of ten just lay where they had landed looking menacing. What was the Nazi answer to this? They forced Jewish people to try to defuse them.

A further dis-incentive to bombing civic buildings: the regime populated the top floor of important structures with captured foreigners. So a regional Gestapo headquarters would have a prison on its roof full of innocent women and children – a cruel human shield to keep the bombers at bay.

Loving the Lancaster

BC crews valued the skipper who had the capacity to weave and drop when the situation demanded it, even though the manoeuvre had the potential to cause the craft to collide with another plane somewhere below. The Lancaster was considered the best machine for dramatic dodges in enemy airspace. Generally the pilot tried to warn his crew, but sometimes the yank on the yoke came abruptly and was only followed by an explanation. A severe swerve could hurl crewmen toward the nearest hard object. A navigator might fall right through the fuselage, banging and crashing all the way. People would be wrenched off oxygen feeds and heating power; knocked out and/or badly wounded. Air sickness might be triggered, and you vomited wherever you found yourself - but no complaints; just gratitude that the aircraft is still flying and there's a chance it might land intact - thanks to a brilliant skipper, typically aged just 22.

The iconic bomber, costing £59,000, was produced by three factories in England, each at a rate of around ten a week - sufficient to replace the craft lost on the nightly raids over Germany. RAF engineer Ted Miles told me that every Lancaster delivered to his Lincolnshire airfield was in first class condition upon arrival.* The plane was considerably better than its predecessors, though weaknesses included the range and power of its guns, and a tendency to skew on take-off, but pilots were trained to offset this by over-powering the port engines. The inner port engine provided the power for the intercom system, so if this unit failed the crew could not talk to each other.

Perhaps the most serious inadequacy in the Lancs design was the hatch from which crew were meant to bale out when necessary. The hole wasn't big enough: an average man could not easily get through while wearing his flying gear and parachute. Had the designers failed to take this into account when first constructing the machine? When was this fatal flaw discovered? The deadly characteristic came formally to the attention of the Air Ministry when a number-cruncher identified discrepancies between the crew survival rates from different aircraft: the Lancaster had by far the worst record for fellows reaching the ground by parachute. Regrettably the figures were not acted upon for a long time; only towards the end of the war was the hatch improved.

However, Commander Harris considered:

> "The advantage which the Lancaster enjoys in height and range enables it to attack with success those targets which other types cannot tackle except on suicide terms."

Its most celebrated outing was the ambitious dam breaking mission. Could the RAF drop a weapon on to reservoirs holding millions of gallons of water that would cause the contents to be released and thus muck up munitions production in the valleys below? Alas, the operation did not go as well as planned, or as the film indicated.

The very best air crews were picked and one of the most respected skippers was chosen to lead them. Guy Gibson did not personally choose the air crews, as the film suggests. And the airmen were not all Brits: two pilots were Canadian and several crew members came from other nations. It was not Gibson's idea to use intersecting beams of light to determine the necessary flying heights; this technique was already being applied elsewhere in the RAF.

Yes, Barnes Wallis came up with a new-fangled bouncing bomb that took an awful lot of engineering and practice to make it function. Eventually, on the 16th May 1943 nineteen specially adapted Lancasters crewed by 133 first class airmen took off with the aim of breaking three dams above the Ruhr valleys. One plane turned back because, on crossing the Dutch coast, a single flak gun managed to sever the crew's intercom system which meant they could not follow Gibson's instructions. Flying very low to remain undetected by German radar, one aircraft crashed into power lines. Another was hit by flak over the dams. Two of the crew were able to bale out and so became prisoners of war.

Some bombs bounced towards the Eder dam, one functioning as Wallis wished to breach the wall. One plane was hit by flak above a nearby town. The fuel tanks and bomb exploded in the air, causing the rear turret to cascade away from the fragmenting craft. The gunner managed to parachute down, albeit with severe burns. He became a prisoner and survived the war, but later committed suicide. Another crew, struggling with navigation, spotted a reservoir below and so released their weapon towards its wall, but this was not the right dam; however the bomb missed anyway. One plane got completely lost and so turned back for England. The skipper was abruptly sacked and re-assigned, along with his crew, to standard BC missions - all of them dying on ops over the next few months.

Eleven Lancasters were lost that night; 53 airmen died and three became POWs. 1,300 people drowned in the valleys along with 6,000 farm animals, but the impact on industry was minimal. However, the mission did demonstrate to the Nazis that their enemies were wily and resourceful, game to tackle daring endeavours. Such ingenuity and courage must have given Hitler more to fret about.

7,370 Lancs were constructed during the war. Afterwards, many were broken up for scrap. Only 35 of the vital aircraft completed more than a 100 missions. 3,341 were lost in action. For thousands and thousands of fine young men, the final moments of their cruelly short lives were in a Lancaster.

*The author's trigger for commencing this project was his interview with Ted Miles who explained that at his Lincolnshire airfield he and his colleagues were responsible for seeing off 30 Lancasters each evening: "… and typically 29 would return, so we had lost one valuable plane and seven trained men". The author was shocked, and ashamed to have gone through life unaware of this extraordinary statistic.

Eliminating Adolf

Why on earth was it that, in a country stuffed full of weaponry, no-one grabbed a gun and got up close to Hitler and fired a shot at him that killed him? How come no individual in that whole nation had the hate and determination to personally assassinate that dreadful man?

Yes, he had his fans – an extraordinarily high number of them - but he had no shortage enemies too; people who loathed him, for what he had done to them, to their lives, livelihoods, family, home, to their friends and neighbours; to Germany's standing in the world. There were hundreds of reasons to despise Hitler and want him dead – not just for revenge, but for the benefit of mankind; for the future of Germany – if Germany was to have a future.

Millions of people had been forced into work they detested, thousands of houses had been destroyed by enemy bombs. Tens of thousands of citizens of a minor ethnicity had been rounded up and sent off to strange camps in Poland where - rumour had it - they would never come out alive. But no individual with a festering grudge against the Nazi regime sneaked into a rally or street crowd to successfully reach the lunatic who had caused all the problems and let him have it – whatever the consequences.

In 1944 a bomb was furtively left under a table where Hitler was due to speak. He wasn't standing next to it when it exploded, so he survived. But he was very upset, and an investigation was undertaken into how this had happened and who had been responsible. The Gestapo narrowed it down to 5,000 people - all of whom were executed, just to be on the safe side. Five thousand? That's not a terrorist cell, that's a mass movement.

Anyway, they got rid of those trouble-makers, which was a lesson to everyone else: Don't try to kill Hitler, or you will die too – not to mention your grannie. Nevertheless, that must have been an unsettling moment for Adolf – to think that someone (apart from the Jews, the Poles, the Dutch, the French, the Brits; Russians, Americans and Greeks, to mention a few) might have had it in for him.

Could Bomber Command or the USAAF have dropped a bunch of bombs on Hitler? They would certainly try, but two problems. First, where the hell was he? His movements and whereabouts were generally kept secret. Hard to know where he might be for long enough to get a plane or two overhead. Secondly, accuracy: as we know, getting one bomb to drop on one designated building was nigh impossible.

Some historians argue that it was better the Fuhrer was not murdered around this time, as his frequently bad decisions were steering the Third Reich towards defeat. If its dictator had been exterminated in these years, perhaps his underlings might have grasped the nettle and made a better fist of fighting back, whereas, by April 1945, they were devoid of appetite to battle on, and doubtless saw the suicide of Hitler as a welcome relief for them and the remains of their country.

In November 1944, the Americans were alerted by a sympathetic Italian that a Mr A. Hitler was due to spend the night at a particular hotel in Milan. They sent off a fleet of planes to give the place a blasting, but it turned out the infamous traveller stayed somewhere else that evening, so only others in the vicinity were killed or injured. Yes, vicinity – no explosives impacted on the targeted accommodation.

In April 1945, the RAF sent 400 planes to blast Hitler's beloved Berchtesgaden. Sadly, the evil proprietor was not at home that day, but I would argue that this insult without injury nevertheless had the capacity to unsettle the Fuhrer's sense of his own invincibility, genius and prospects. If those horrible British flyers could do so much damage to his lovely terraced pavilions with Alpine views, how was he going to succeed in bringing them to their knees and subjugating them to the Third Reich way of things? Perhaps they were indestructible and he wasn't? Rather than being crowned Emperor of Europe, was it possible he might soon be made to look extremely stupid in some international court of justice? Perish the thought!

Excuses, excuses
Sometimes an aircraft displayed alarming indicators of trouble minutes before take-off, so the skipper might decide to steer the machine off the strip to examine the issue that was rattling him or someone else aboard. This behaviour cast a shadow on the ground crew. Had they left something undone? Failed to finish a job or check the integrity of a system?

However, questioning the serviceability of a plane before take-off also meant other people might question the commitment of the men aboard. On one occasion a station commander drove over to a halted aircraft and demanded that the pilot get on with his job. When the skipper argued for delay, the commander dragged the fellow from his cockpit, had him arrested, then took the controls and, still in his shirtsleeves, got the aircraft back on the runway. Without wearing flying gear, the officer flew the craft to Germany, unloaded its cargo and returned to base, to supervise the court martial of the reluctant flyer.

Of course, things might start to go wrong aboard a craft soon after it left the ground. When a heavy load of ordnance is roared forwards and upwards, extreme force on mechanisms can overwhelm the drive systems or fracture fuel pipes near hot metal and initiate sparks and fire. That plane would try to come down again, its terrible cargo still inside.

Mechanical difficulties could emerge halfway across the North Sea. Was it practical to carry on or should we abort this mission and return for a hazardous landing? There could be heated language over the intercom. Skipper's say was final, though not necessarily popular. If the boys got back in one piece, they usually agreed to keep shtumm about any angry debate in the air.

Minor incapacities were frequently tolerated: wonky instruments, freezing oxygen feeds. However a pilot's sudden illness might necessitate an early return. Unless someone else could realistically take the craft over Germany, there was no point in continuing. If a problem occurred beyond the English coastline, the crew might elect to disgorge their ordnance into the water and fly back relieved of its weight and danger.

But coming back early was seen as a poor show, and the men would be grilled about possible dereliction of duty, collective cowardice or cynical indifference to pursing the commands of the squadron – even though aborted missions did not count on a man's tally of sorties; the total of which was taking him towards a point when he would be relieved of combat duty for a while at least.

Most crew understood most aircraft systems and would try to mend any troublesome elements en route: jammed leverage rods, fouled guns, trapped turrets. The worst prospect lay out on the wings: a failed engine could be shut down, but if one was in flames someone might be game - once the craft had reached its slowest viable speed and height - to get out there with a fire blanket. Wearing his parachute and roped to the fuselage, the volunteer could hack handholds and footholds in the wings with an axe. Sometimes the wind and effort beat them back. Sometimes they got to the engine but the blanket blew away. And, of course, some heroes never made it back inside.

A proportion of returning craft and men were lost close to their own airfields. Another plane might appear from low cloud almost in front of a landing bomber and cause the destruction of both machines and everyone aboard. A badly damaged plane might prove unable to execute a landing and crash into the ground, trees, or buildings. An ambulance was always parked near the runway – "the meat wagon".

A powerful perspective on American endeavours to constructively cross the North Sea can be found in Dick Grace's autobiography, 'Crash Pilot'. He flew in France during the Great War, then thrilled crowds across the States as a barn-storming stunt pilot, before staging air stunts for Hollywood films. Despite his years and injuries, he joined USAAF's 8th in East Anglia:

> 'God was never more important than at this time. Kids who weren't too religious became very religious. I didn't come in contact with one heretic or atheist. Scoffers were few. When the line that holds you to life is thin and the knife is poised to part it, people change. I changed. You got to know that you were living by the grace of God and for no other reason.'

Saluting the Soviets

For the first couple of months of 1943 the front page headlines of the Daily Mail concentrated on reporting Red Army successes with pushing back the Germans towards their border. The paper also noted that the Russians had managed to shoot down more than 4,000 Luftwaffe craft through the winter months. But in May the Mail alarmed its readers:

HITLER HAS NEW PLAN TO INVADE BRITAIN

Apparently he was toying with cutting his losses in the East and erecting a mighty military wall to inhibit any further Soviet advance into German-occupied territory, which would enable him to transfer 75% of the Luftwaffe to the West to challenge British and American air forces, and so have another go at getting his troops on to English beaches.

The newspaper also allocated front page space to a message of appreciation to Churchill from Stalin:

> 'I welcome the bombing of Essen, Berlin and other industrial centres of Germany. Every blow delivered by your Air Force to the vital German

centres evokes a most lively echo in the hearts of many millions throughout the length and breadth of our country.'

Winston promised Joe to convey these encouraging thoughts to the Air Ministry. Below this report, the Mail noted that the RAF had lost eleven bombers somewhere over Holland the previous night. The newspaper revealed that German women had been counselled by Reich authorities to avoid making reference to the Allied bombing of the Fatherland in their letters to their men on the Russian front. It would dismay the Wehrmacht soldiers to know that the domestic harmony they were fighting for was being hammered from the air.

Perhaps the most distinctive example of how the criteria of the era impacted on the presentation of the Russians by the British press came in the form of the Mail's front page lead of Tuesday 28th September 1943:

DNEPROPETROVSK SUBURB STORMED

Another Red Army westward advance - in those days this was good news.

Rays of hope

One of the most enduring myths of the Second World War in Britain (particularly prominent in Worcestershire) is how our brilliant boffins invented radar and thus befuddled the German war machine.

The notion of some ray that could be directed towards a plane was initially contemplated as a means of damaging that craft and/or its pilot. This ambition emerged in the 1920s as a neat solution to the fear of enemy fleets entering domestic air space loaded with massive bombs to devastate civilian populations and their property.

Scientists got to work on turning the Death Ray fantasy into reality, but they didn't get very far. What they did discover was that a radio beam directed at an object in the sky would bounce back, and evidence of that returning signal could be identified on a cathode ray screen. However this was not a unique British breakthrough; the Americans and Germans were way ahead in devising equipment that showed the whereabouts of aircraft many miles away.

UK boffins called the concept "radio direction finding", and established laboratories near Bournemouth to develop a viable system; but Churchill feared their experiments could be bombed by the Luftwaffe and so insisted they re-locate inland – to the handsome premises of a private boys school in Malvern, Worcestershire.

There is now a modest museum within the nearby National Trust's Croome Park where you can see films made in the 1940s designed to show airmen the cathode ray images that could indicate an enemy plane was somewhere over the county. The capacity of those embryonic contraptions was severely limited - wobbly oscillations peppered with interference – only able to suggest that some aircraft or other might be 20 miles away. Hardly game changers.

Hundreds of experts across Europe worked on hampering the technology of their opponents, not least by examining the kit aboard crashed enemy planes. Could we manipulate their frequencies to use them against our foes? One fleet of Luftwaffe bombers decanted their ordnance over factories in Nottingham when they had been intended for the Rolls Royce works at Derby. Beam bending by the British had caused the mis-alignment. Recognition of this tweaking only emerged when captured German pilots were secretly monitored discussing the difficulties of reaching particular targets.

To listen to broadcasts each half hour from stations in the UK, BC wireless operators had to reel out 20 metres of trailing aerial from the back of their planes - another awkward element to the night's stooge. Meanwhile the Germans had worked out how to listen to the radio conversations between RAF airmen and their control tower.

One group of UK scientists working on a new direction finder undertook a domestic flight to evaluate the prototype. The plane crashed killing all aboard, and put the programme back by months. Ambitious devices were developed - early versions the size and weight of an Aga oven - and each sooner or later became known to the other side. British air-to-air radar, once functioning, was, for a long time, unable to distinguish between a RAF bomber and a Luftwaffe night-fighter.

Malvern is full of folk who are the offspring or neighbours of brilliant scientists who helped develop radar. The town's current generation sometimes refer to those electronic experts as the war's "unsung heroes". Undoubtedly they did a great and vital job, but next to climbing into a Lancaster as a rear gunner to cross the North Sea in the dark hoping to reach Berlin in one piece, fiddling with valves and circuits was ... unsung, perhaps, but heroic? Not quite.

The curse of Kursk

"We are determined to continue the war until a clear and definite solution is reached so that we and our descendants can be sheltered in the future from a conflagration of this kind. The enemy will shortly learn to his cost what Germany and Europe are capable of in the field of arms production. After the winter we shall resume our march forward to assure the freedom and existence of our people. It will be then that a Power will collapse, and that Power will certainly not be Germany."

... Hitler's message to his fan base at the start of 1943, but within weeks a bunch of his best generals had been forced to surrender to the Russians following the battle for Stalingrad. Further reverses jabbed at their boss through the spring, obliging Adolf to pick the Soviet city of Kursk as the place for finally halting the Red Army's retrieval of its territory.

The Battle of Kursk began in early July - the biggest confrontation of armies the world had ever seen, involving 3 million soldiers, 13,000 tanks and, ultimately, 12,000 aircraft. German skills and equipment were superior, but the Soviet Union could deploy greater numbers, and had substantial and heroic support from bitter partisans behind the German lines, destroying supplies by road and rail every night.

Casualties were enormous and the likely outcome was not at all clear when, five days into the Kursk confrontation, American and British paratroopers landed on the island of Sicily south of the Italian mainland, to be met by local soldiers eager to surrender. Here was the soft underbelly that Churchill had believed exploitable. Hitler realised Mussolini needed shoring up and so extracted forces from the Kursk battlefield to head south and stop the Allies crossing to the Italian peninsula. The Wehrmacht generals considered it madness to weaken their Kursk armies at that critical time, but that was Hitler for you.

The arrival of German forces on Sicily seriously slowed the Allies' advance, which was not going smoothly. Nearly half the gliders transporting Allied paratroopers from north Africa fell into the Mediterranean; few of the men aboard reached shore. Meanwhile British warships patrolling the island shot down several Allied transport planes. But the biggest blunder was allowing a mass Axis escape over to the Italian mainland which, in theory, Allied aircraft could have intercepted.

The distraction of Sicily disturbed the balance of power around Kursk, and allowed the Soviets to slowly prevail, but at enormous cost. The Germans suffered half a million casualties at Kursk that summer, which was just 5% of all Russian losses during this year.

Max Hastings emphasises that the Red Army was the 'main engine of Nazism's destruction'. He also points out that the "soft underbelly" on the Italian peninsula, proved alarmingly muscular. The Allies 'were inexplicably and culpably ill-informed about the geographical, tactical, political and economic problems they would meet there'.

Only soft spot was Mussolini's own belly. Rome was bombed by the Allies on the 19th July. This inspired local political leaders to arrest the Fascist dictator a few days later. By the autumn, Allied forces, including huge contingents of Indian troops, had established themselves on the southern end of the Italian mainland, and began to occupy airfields which would allow them to commence sorties northward into Austria and Germany.

Eisenhower soon declared that there would be no more aerial bombing of Italy by the Allies, and in October the Italians announced they would assist their previous enemies in the fight against the Nazi regime, which had by now decisively lost the horrendous battle of Kursk.

Following orders
If you have watched a few episodes of ITV's 'Foyle's War' dramas by Anthony Horowitz, you may conclude that the south coast of England was peppered with German secret agents bent on undermining British efforts to execute the conflict. In reality, there were not many subversive characters doing dodgy things at night to aid the Nazis. Nevertheless the UK Air Ministry was always concerned about security on air fields, and insisted every squadron exercised immense discretion regarding who knew what: casual talk might cost lives. Operations were

revealed on a need-to-know basis. When instructions emerged from HQ, air crews would assemble for briefings, the meteorology officer explaining weather prospects without knowing exactly where the lads were aiming. He was then dismissed, the door was locked and now the men were assigned targets.

Ground crew were never told where their planes were heading, but could estimate distances from the quantity of fuel allocated. Neurotic station commanders often feared sabotage: enemy sympathisers or angry neighbours sneaking through the fence; disgruntled staff - even an insane airman - deliberately causing harm to a machine.

BC fellows appreciated good reasons why their squadrons were doing particular things; if an identifiable factory at a specific chart reference was making something to aid the enemy, they valued the clarity of purpose as they headed out at dusk. No-one liked being ordered to tackle something without an adequate explanation; however the top brass considered 'Window' so secret, it was imperative that no inkling of its existence could become known to the opposition in advance of its first deployment.

Someone in a laboratory (while chewing chocolate?) had waggled a bit of silver foil in front of apparatus and discovered it interfered with radio waves on certain frequencies, including the wavelength used by German radar to detect the approach of enemy aircraft. Imagine the possibilities if a fleet of bombers could cross the North Sea and not have their imminent arrival exposed by electronic devices!

Further fiddling in the labs determined the best shape and size for the foil strips to maximise their capacity to befuddle the defenders. Furtive test flights and launches were conducted to determine the best height from which to release the strips, and how far ahead of the bomber planes the material should be decanted.

The preparation and supply of the packs of foil to squadrons was treated as top secret. The relevant crews were discretely informed that their aircraft was carrying an unusual but vital cargo to be cascaded out at a precise time and place.

They did what they were told, and it worked marvellously well. Thousands of buildings in Hamburg were destroyed on the night of 27th July 1943, and 14,000 citizens died, whilst hardly any air crews were shot down by the Luftwaffe because the Germans had not seen them coming, thanks to the effectiveness of the foil.

The subsequent incendiaries started enormous fires causing hot rising air to rapidly and violently suck in more oxygen from the sides. Wind speeds of 150 mph developed, capable of pulling people off the street and into the flames. The temperature in the middle of the giant firestorm covering several miles reached 1,000 degrees centigrade.

The city's President of Police reported the results:

'The streets were covered with hundreds of corpses. Mothers with their children, youths, old men - burnt, charred, naked with a waxen pallor like dummies in a shop window. They lay in every posture, quiet and peaceful or cramped, the death-struggle shown in the expression on their faces.

'The shelters showed the same picture, even more horrible in its effect - the final distracted struggle against a merciless fate. Although in some cases bodies sat quietly, peacefully and untouched as if sleeping in their chairs, killed without realisation or pain by carbon monoxide poisoning. In other shelters, positions of remains of bones and skulls showed how the occupants had fought to escape from their buried prison.'

300,000 homes were destroyed, 2,000 shops were damaged; 500 factories, 300 schools, 100 municipal buildings, 60 churches, 25 hospitals. A million people fled the stricken city. These were the lucky ones. Hamburg became a vista of 6,000 acres of smoking rubble.

The whole German political hierarchy found the intensity and scale of the bombardment deeply worrying. Of course, they also figured out how their prediction system had been immobilised and so swiftly amended defence techniques. Next deployment of the strips brutally demonstrated to the RAF that the enemy had cracked Window. And towards the end of the year, fragments of foil scattered across German countryside was harvested by surviving children to decorate their Christmas trees.

Rocket men

The Treaty of Versailles had specified that Germany was not to undertake any engineering designed to produce big guns. However there was no reference in the delimiting document to self-propelled ordnance or rockets. So here was menacing activity that could be explored by Third Reich scientists, and one in which they made extraordinary progress. All top secret, of course, however once they had some prototypes to test in the air they were forced to expose their gear to the outside world. Good place to practice was a deserted peninsula, Peenemunde, in the Baltic Sea - not many people about, and a long way from nosey foreigners.

Over in Britain, rumours circulated about Nazi development of giant ordnance devices, but there was no evidence. Then an RAF reconnaissance flight passed over the peculiar peninsula and snapped some strange shapes under construction: big, long canisters, sometimes on trailers, sometimes sticking upwards. Could these be rockets, or just an elaborate fabrication designed to direct British bombing to a lump of land where effort and equipment would be hugely wasted?

Some of the site's forced labourers now smuggled out messages about extraordinary propulsion ambition in progress. The British War Cabinet decided these alarming developments must be neutralised, ideally by eliminating the experts. No further reconnaissance flights were undertaken so the Germans were not alerted to RAF interest. It was assumed the facility could generate a smoke screen in the event of approaching enemy planes, so BC practiced blind flying on mock targets, relying entirely on pathfinder flares. The true goal was the quarters of the scientists and engineers: if they could be killed, that would seriously decelerate the programme.

On 17th August, squadrons were despatched to the peninsula to destroy the complex below, regardless of any difficulties or challenges. The airmen did not know what lay below; just that it was a big site full of stuff that could do the Allies harm. If the crews failed to succeed in their task that evening, they were told they would have to return the next night and, if necessary, the night after that, and so on until the necessary job was done.

To draw Luftwaffe fighters away from the vicinity, a few RAF planes were sent to other destinations in advance of the main force, which took a route that did not directly point them towards Peenemunde. At the last possible moment the boys swung over the peninsula, but weather conditions were bad and the pathfinders struggled to place flares accurately, causing the first wave of bombs to fall on a camp full of Polish slave labour, including the men who had alerted the Allies to the plant. 500 were killed. Later waves of ordnance were better positioned, though creep took more and more weaponry away from required destinations. The Luftwaffe swiftly re-routed to Peenemunde and gave the latter attackers hefty resistance: of 600 Allied aircraft sent out, 40 failed to return and 200 crew died.

Nevertheless, the sorties made some big holes in the facility, and killed some key workers, including the chief engine designer. Biggest scalp was a Luftwaffe commander who, shamed by his failure to adequately protect Peenemunde, committed suicide two days after the raid. This was portrayed in the German press as a sudden fatal illness. Meanwhile Peenemunde managers detonated explosives round their premises to make the site look completely destroyed and thus not worth a return visit.

But it turned out that the whole mission had taken place six months too late, because most of the rocket testing work had been completed and the finished designs for manufacture were already at production factories across Germany and Poland.

However, the rough endeavours helped delay the deployment of the dreaded V1 and V2 rockets until after D-Day, when the Allies could enact plans to capture the launch sites. Valiant airmen in effect saved many British lives that August night. The raid again demonstrated RAF audacity and courage, and extinguished some vital enemy scientists, though not Wernher von Braun, who would later help launch USA astronauts to the moon.

Additionally, of course, the surprise peninsula intrusion would have further cheesed off the Fuhrer - in essence, a trajectory on the desired arc.

All American heroes

'The objectives of both the American and British Bomber Commands are strictly military. We have rejected the policy of reprisals... Instead we strike at the enemy's industries and communications, at the nerve centres of his resistance, with such force as eventually to destroy his capacity and will for bloodthirsty war and criminal oppression.'

... the UK Air Minister's foreword to 'Target Germany', a 1944 HMSO booklet summarising the first year of American bombing endeavours in Europe. Readers anticipating the marketing of triumph might have been surprised by the candid documentation of difficulties for USAAF 8th Bomber Command, commencing with the long build-up due to provisioning demands: each new bomber station cost $5 million to construct and contained 400 buildings, 2,500 men and 50 aircraft, plus huge quantities of spare parts and gasoline. The whole complement of 750,000 personnel across the UK required 225 tons of food each day, as well as eight tons of soap, and eighteen tons of cigarettes or candy.

By the spring of 1943 the Americans were ready to tackle missions deep into foreign airspace from Britain. They sent 100 bombers to assault an aircraft factory in France. Sixteen failed to return, but the booklet's authors did not yet know if any crews had become prisoners of war. The text explains that many bombs were fused so as to not explode immediately, to give the forced labour time to run away. Accuracy in this daylight raid was considered to be excellent. A navigator noted: "As the English say, we really pranged the target."

By May, the Americans could muster 200 bombers on day raids, spread across different locations to disperse Luftwaffe defenders. On 14th May, four 'military or economic hubs' were attacked and eleven bombers failed to return, though the surviving crews reckoned 60 Luftwaffe fighters had been shot down. The publication acknowledged RAF help while facing the formidable resolve of the defenders:

'Almost without exception, enemy fliers displayed suicidal recklessness in attack. They will probably continue to do so as long as they have sufficient aircraft to make a fight of it – not necessarily through affection for the Nazi regime but rather because of a certain occupational loyalty to the job which all fliers feel, an unwillingness to let the unit down.'

The narrative conveyed work in progress. On 17th May, ten planes were sent to raid a factory in Holland and none came back. We learn of wounded pilots being lifted from the controls so other men could continue the flight. The gunners standing at an open gate halfway along the fuselage had a broad vista of impending danger but were most exposed to enemy fire. One suffered a cruel end when his parachute accidentally opened and billowed out of the aircraft wrenching him away with a deadly jerk.

The Americans learned not to mix their two bomber aircraft types as the differences in performance made it difficult to sustain formation. Yet there was a price to be paid for close formation flying: Luftwaffe bombers would appear above a cluster of US planes and drop ordnance on them. The book quotes the notion that German airmen occasionally flew captured Liberators up into the American bomber stream to shoot at identical aircraft, but post-war interrogation of Luftwaffe officers revealed this to have been a myth; the imagination of disconcerted men in alarming circumstances.

One image that exercised US airmen - confirmed when the de-briefings took place - was the sight of a young woman swimming naked across a river in Romania - spotted from low-flying aircraft on their way to bomb oil installations.

July 1943 saw the biggest loss of US machines on a single day: 88 Fortresses failed to return, though 300 Luftwaffe planes also went down. One photograph conveys the shocking final moments of an American bomber dropping through the sky devoid of its tail-plane.

Aerial photos show explosion craters across landscape - pictures intended to demonstrate the density of application by the raiders, but also revealing a high proportion of ordnance landing in parks, sports fields and farms.

On 17th August - twelve months on from their first tentative outings - the USAAF undertook 'Anniversary Raids': major assaults on ball-bearing and Messerschmitt factories. Again 300 Luftwaffe defenders were hit, but this time just 60 American planes failed to return.

That first year of US missions saw the release of 17,000 tons of explosive on the enemy, and the elimination of 2,000 Luftwaffe planes, but at the cost of almost 500 US bombers; hence 4,481 of their crewmen unaccounted for.

Only one Hollywood-like moment portrayed in the text – an American gunner still confined to his plastic bubble above the fuselage as his craft hit the sea and started to sink. The man continued to fire his guns at Luftwaffe planes overhead until the water took him below. Patently one of thousands of heroes, for whom we must forever give thanks.

Swinging the pendulum

Early in 1943 the four-page Daily Mail revealed that RAF crews were "browned off" with their short range transport and munitions target flights to France – a few planes dropping a few bombs to cause a bit of a nuisance somewhere or other. The boys wanted to "kill Germans in Germany" preferably via the medium of the new Mosquito, the De Havilland "wooden wonder" built by cabinet makers, and capable of zipping through enemy airspace far faster than opposing fighters. But by April the Mail's front page could announce:

THE NIGHT-AND-DAY AIR BLITZ CONTINUES
'The greatest air offensive in history was continued unabated yesterday by the Anglo-American Air Forces. For 72 hours bombs have been crashing down on Hitler's Europe in the West almost non-stop at a stupendous rate.'

Two weeks later, front page news of an 'Intruders Raid' on London. Then in May:

'Day and night last month a total of no more than 100 German aircraft succeeded in carrying bombs across any part of the British coastline.'

The Mail reckoned this could be due to a shortage of replacement parts for Luftwaffe aircraft, caused by the relentless Allied raids on German factories. Despite news of 'Casualties in London bombing', Daily Mail Air Correspondent Colin Bednall reported:

BATTLE OF THE REICH IS ON
'The unprecedented activity of the RAF and the USAAF in the last week is no longer regarded just as strategic bombing but as the Battle of Germany itself. The whole internal structure of the enemy is being methodically wrecked in preparation for the final assault.'

In July, the Mail exposed discussions within the Third Reich military about the possible deployment of gas bombs as retaliation for the suffering caused by the Allied phosphorus incendiaries "which exceed the horrors of gas warfare." Additionally the Germans were apparently building a "Vengeance" bomber fleet to bring home to Britain the "policy of frightfulness where it originated". And the newspaper returned to a taxing question:

CAN BOMBING WIN THE WAR?

Authoritative views concluded that the defeat of the Nazi regime would require a land invasion.

On Friday 9th July, the Mail reported a strike of night-shift workers in the Ruhr protesting against their vulnerability to RAF raids. 180 of the selfish troublemakers were summarily shot. Next day, trouble at home:

BOMB HITS CINEMA

'Many die' in a 'south east English town'.

But a couple of days later:

100 MILES OF SICILY COAST OURS

Misery for Mussolini. The following week, promise of more:

YIELD LEAFLETS RAINED ON ITALY

A few weeks later, data on Mediterranean successes:

800 AXIS PLANES ABANDONED IN SICILY

Soon, further encouraging numbers: the USAAF claimed that, amidst the destruction of 100 of their Fortresses, they had managed to take down 500 Luftwaffe fighters; while in North Africa the Germans were assessed to have lost 12,000 planes against 2,000 RAF craft.

By August one can detect in the Mail's presentation of events that victory lies somewhere ahead: the Germans were backing off from the Russian thrusts while, in Berlin, Reich officials were evacuating one million women and children, anticipating that worse was to come.

Mid-August brought revelations about the 'Anniversary' raids:

GREATEST DAY BLITZ ON EUROPE

However:

THIRTY-SIX HEAVY BOMBERS LOST

Soon, tales of the Luftwaffe combing its administrative ranks for ex-pilots who could be drafted back into front line duties. Next, a report on 15 Luftwaffe planes harassing London, alongside rumours of a secret new German rocket gun in development. Yet, behind-the-scenes, evidence of mutual co-operation between the protagonists: a prisoner-of-war swop had been arranged; 5,000 gravely wounded Allied men would be exchanged for 800 sickly German prisoners rounded up in north Africa.

Then news of a senior German officer calling a strategy meeting which Hitler would attend but not chair. Was the Fuhrer losing his grip? November saw more exposure of the 'Gloom and Terrorism reign':

> 'A Berlin woman clerk, dining with friends in a café, made a pessimistic remark about the German leadership. The Gestapo heard. Her office was visited the next day and she had to sign a declaration: "I am guilty of treason. I know that I deserve death. I expect execution." She was left unharmed but is liable to be arrested at any time. Anyone in an official position is shot immediately and given no opportunity for such a confession.'

Meanwhile, evidence of mounting assaults:
GREATEST DAY RAID ON REICH - MORE THAN 1,000 PLANES

Next day, 5th November:
4,000 TONS BOMBS DROPPED BY ALLIES IN 12 HOURS

This news was supported by a sketch of 300 railway trucks – the equivalent transport necessary to move that ordnance at ground level. The Air Ministry supplied a quote:

> 'Bomber Command's striking power is now 12 times greater than in 1939.'

But it was still not all one-way trade. Within twenty-four hours:
BOMB HITS LONDON DANCE CLUB

The following day, quotes from Hitler's recent Munich rally oration:

> 'Some people in Germany may believe in an enemy victory but, with thousands falling at the front, we shall show no mercy in liquidating a few hundred criminals. If the German people should break under the present test, I would shed no single tear for them.'

A Moscow newspaper described this as 'the speech of a cornered rat'.

For you the war is over

There were three ways a bomber airman could inadvertently arrive on enemy territory. Firstly, his plane might start to malfunction, and the skipper would decide there was no alternative but to try to land on what looked like reasonably flat ground somewhere ahead. If you descended safely, you were required to attempt to destroy your plane rather than allow it to fall into enemy hands. After shifting any injured crewmen away, you broke a fuel line and put a match to the petrol. Special kit aboard might contain a delayed detonation device which you could trigger before you jumped out.

Local people would have heard and seen you come down. They might approach the crash site or alert the authorities. Should you run and hide or give yourself up? The instruction was to attempt the former: to seek a way back to your home country somehow; because the moment you were arrested, you were no more use to the Air Force, and instead just an irritating burden for the opposition.

Most likely means of landing on foreign soil was by parachute descent. Escape from a damaged flying craft was part of your training but, like many other aspects of military aeronautics, the gap between classroom theory and front line frantic life-saving was immense. Parachutes were awkward to wear, dreadful to shove through hatches, and often unpredictable once deployed. You would hope to cruise downward and not to be shot at by people on the ground or from enemy aircraft. You wanted to land somewhere flat and soft, but could you see a suitable surface and direct the chute in that direction? Always a high likelihood of hitting the ground very hard: broken feet, legs, arms, shoulders, noses and backs were common.

Should your parachute fail to deploy – due to bad packing or inept handling – you would probably hurtle down, slam into the ground and be dead in seconds. But miraculously sometimes a fellow survived the failure of a chute to function properly.

Then there were the flukes, who left the plane with no parachute, or with their back pack torn away, or the chute caught on the tail-plane - causing the wearer to be careered through the sky behind his falling aircraft, but able to cut himself free rather than be towed to his death.

Occasionally even free-fallers reached earth without fatal injuries, perhaps cascading into the tops of tall conifers.

What could the fellow suddenly on enemy soil expect from those who discovered him and challenged him? In the early years of the war there was generally civilised treatment of aerial arrivals. The airman had been at work and something had gone wrong. He would be arrested, interrogated, and placed in detention. No need for this to be unnecessarily unpleasant.

In the Home Counties, a Luftwaffe officer was being escorted by soldiers when their train stopped at a suburban station. An English woman on the platform, seeking Spitfire donations, rattled her collection box at the carriage window. The captive lent out and sarcastically dropped Third Reich coins into her container.

The relentless assaults on German cities by 1943 recalibrated capacity for sympathy. British and American airmen who had baled out from a bomber might be assaulted by an angry crowd wanting revenge on the raiders. One English pilot chose to wear a lounge suit and casual shirt for work, in order to pass himself off as a civilian if he was forced to land on foreign soil. Others laughed at this, until April 1943, when it happened and it worked.

RAF men were given lessons in how to survive in enemy territory. You could try passing yourself off as a local and steal a bike to move fast; though the Germans had every cycle marked with a code to determine if the rider owned the machine or not. If you were aboard a railway carriage and you wanted a nifty exit, then your pre-mission practices at jumping from a vehicle at 30 mph might help. Should you be caught, in the unlikely event that you were not stripped of all your belongings, you would discreetly pass on to the most senior officer in the POW camp the miniature camera and compact hacksaw hidden in the heels of your boots.

Compare this with the Far East where the more fortunate captured Allied airman might be swiftly beheaded.

Hornets' nests

The landscape around the Pacific was often far more rugged than in Europe - mountains rising directly from the sea, thick with vegetation full of treacherous wildlife; while weather extremes made the worst Atlantic storm seem inconsequential.

The Japanese had imposed themselves in tiny pockets of civilisation on slivers of land all the way down to the fringe of Australia. They had not met much resistance and established small fortresses served by crude airstrips to complement their fleets of aircraft carriers able to transport hundreds of fighter planes to any point in the ocean. The Allies faced a vast scatter of ferocious enemy outposts everywhere between China and Indonesia. Driving the Japanese back towards their home islands would be a monumental undertaking that would see brutal prosecution and dreadful attrition on both sides.

However, the daunting kernels of Japanese resistance would prove vulnerable to weak support: shortages of the equipment needed to maintain a frontline force far from home. A plane made in Japan might be an admirable piece of hardware, but it often turned up on location without associated crates of spares, so could soon become inoperative. And there was little standardisation of aircraft parts, each model of plane requiring its own unique complement of replacement fittings.

The Japanese had a long way to go in developing effective cockpit radio communication. Most pilots relied on hand signals to indicate intentions to their aerial colleagues, supplemented by a chalkboard for specifics. But an advantageous aspect of many Japanese army aircraft was their ability to utilise short, lumpy, sloping patches of ground for take-off and landing. In parallel, Japanese navy pilots had perfected the knack of darting from the decks of aircraft carriers, then getting back down on to rocking, rolling platforms in heavy seas.

American instincts were to operate bigger planes on bigger ships in safer conditions. On the pockets of land that needed to be occupied to advance towards enemy strongholds, it was essential to carve out long, flat, firmly-surfaced runways capable of allowing large aircraft easy access. Only the celebrated Dakota had the ability to land in tight spots and get up again without mishap. This distinctive Yank machine would deliver critical supplies including cranes, diggers and concrete, so huge teams of construction workers could create viable Allied air strips. The Japanese forces often had no gear that mechanised the turning of jungle into airfields. Instead the Imperialists forced locals to hack down trees and shift soil so first wave pilots could attempt a landing. Then the luckless natives were obliged to pull the planes into leafy corners so they would not be visible to enemy reconnaissance flights. Flying over strange islands dense with foliage, trying to spot hornets' nests, was a key element to advancing the wars in the Pacific. Those below knew that aerial exposure could destroy their surreptitious battle plans, and so much of the groundwork was conducted at night, then tidied at dawn, to leave no trace of activity visible from above. But malarial mosquitoes emerge in the dark and exposure to fever saw off thousands of Japanese and their captives.

No American serviceman went anywhere in foreign parts without a logistics operation in place, assuring him of food and drink, ammunition, medical supplies and operational spares whatever might befall him and his colleagues. In contrast, the Japanese military hierarchy never adequately addressed how to keep front line forces sustained on inhospitable territory; hence around 90% of Japanese army deaths were from non-combat causes.

In February 1943, the Americans, with considerable support from Australia and New Zealand, got their first foothold on the southern edge of the abruptly established Japanese Empire. Commitment and courage captured an airfield, which meant big planes could start to operate northward. Sinking Tokyo's aircraft carriers was an essential goal: well-placed US torpedoes or bombs could remove a hundred planes, their crews and vessels at a stroke. 'Skipping' bombs over water so they bounced into the sides of ships was practiced and perfected. Occasionally the weapons failed to explode, but their impact into the hull could incapacitate any sailor inside that battered bulkhead.

Over the year, the Americans managed to remove dozens of giant Imperial ships from contention, but this was often a painful process. Max Hastings indicates the nature of the opposition in 'All Hell Let Loose':

> 'The Japanese, who had been merciless in victory, now showed themselves determined to cull every possible human life from their inexorable descent towards defeat.'

The Americans supported the modestly-equipped Chinese Air Force to counter the Japanese along the Asian continent, resulting in hundreds of the Emperor's planes being destroyed on the ground by surprise assaults from unexpected directions. The Americans and Australians also eliminated many parked planes on tiny islands. It is estimated that 7,000 Japanese planes were destroyed in 1943, while a similar number of the Empire's pilots died on over-ambitious missions or aerial accidents.

Reflecting the pressure of problems closer to home, only on two occasions during the year did events in the Far East command the front page of the Daily Mail. On 5th July:

'Japs See Skies Black with U.S. Planes – The Americans have established complete air superiority in the Solomon Islands.'

And on 18th August:

'Greatest Raid of Pacific War – 225 Jap planes parked on New Guinea. 120 destroyed. 50 damaged.

10,000 bombs dropped. 1,500 Japs killed. 3 Allied planes lost. The opening battle for air supremacy.'

Swatting in progress.

That extra kilometre

Luftwaffe night fighter pilots could not hope to disrupt a whole fleet of enemy aircraft streaming through their airspace. All they could achieve was damaging a few planes so they would not bomb or get back home, rattling the rest in the process. The German airmen manoeuvred, fired, swerved away, then tried again until they were out of ammo or short of fuel and needed to land. After which they would head back up and aim to pick off some more. The best Third Reich pilots notched up more than a hundred "kills" against RAF bombers; one celebrated Ace shot down seven Lancs in half an hour.

By 1943, Hitler's regime had around 500 planes dedicated to nocturnal defence. A year later – despite the mass bombing of German aircraft factories – the number of available planes was 800. At the end of 1944, when the Allies were devastating vast areas of enemy industry, Luftwaffe defender numbers peaked at 1,250.

A crashed Lancaster or Liberator, with the bodies of its crew scattered about, made a good photo story for German newspapers. Patently it was better to impede intruding RAF and USAAF squadrons before they reached their targets, but the Germans would also intercept aircraft attempting to return to Britain, because every Allied plane damaged, every opposing airman injured or killed, was one less problem to worry about tomorrow. So Luftwaffe flyers, if they had the fuel, would pursue Allied craft and jab at them all the way to their home airfields. At night the Germans even launched flares ahead of returning BC planes to lighten the sky and make their targets more visible.

The only resistance to the pluck of the Luftwaffe fighters came from the very top: when Hitler heard about his brave pilots chasing bombers back across the North Sea he screeched that they should not bother, because it was much better to have enemy planes crash on Germanic soil, where citizens could appreciate the capacity of the Third Reich to inhibit and hurt their ruthless, heartless opponents.

Always a catch

> 'Let us suppose that the industrial section of some great German city could be accurately bombed at dusk by several hundred American aircraft, set well alight, and then bombed a few hours later in the hours of darkness by 1,000 R.A.F. bombers. If the American bombers could start serious fires, the percentage of bombs dropped on the following night which hit the target would be most significantly increased. The displacement of factory workers and the destruction of the factories will continue on an ever increasing scale until the enemy can no longer supply the fighting men with their material requirements of all kinds or maintain the home front. The attrition will have become exhaustion and the end will be near.'

… the views of an ex-RAF Air Marshall after the Americans made their first substantial sorties into German territory with visits to Wilhelmshaven and the Ruhr in January 1943. Exploratory missions continued through the spring, but an attack on a Luftwaffe repair plant near Antwerp in April saw most of the explosives drop on a nearby residential area, killing nearly 1,000 people, including 200 school children. Then a Liberator ferrying the Commander General of US Forces in Europe crashed fatally in Iceland.

Regular, substantial USAAF missions into Germany - often aided by extra fuel tanks and fighter aircraft escorts - began in May. Heinz Knoke recalled one intrusion:

'I spot the enemy formation ahead. Some three hundred heavy bombers grouped together. They carry a total armament of 4,800 heavy machine-guns. I pick out one of them as my target. I come in for a frontal attack. I keep on firing until I have to swerve to avoid a collision. My salvoes register. I drop away below. Flames are spreading along the bottom of the fuselage of my Liberator. It sheers away from the formation in a wide sweep to the right. Twice more I come in to attack, this time diving from above the tail. I watch my cannon shell-bursts rake along the top of the fuselage and right wing. The fire spreads. The inside engine stops. Suddenly the wing breaks off altogether. The body of the stricken monster plunges vertically. One of the crew attempts to bale out. But his parachute is in flames. Poor devil! At an altitude of 3,000 feet there is a tremendous explosion, which causes the spinning fuselage to disintegrate.'

Some of the flaming wreckage peppered a farm close to an airfield, so Knoke landed and ran over:

'Their shattered bodies lie beside the smoking remains. One hundred yards away I find the captain's seat and the nose wheel. A little doll, evidently the mascot, sits undamaged between the shattered windows of the cabin.'

In June and July, USAAF losses were in excess of 5%; yet they continued to undertake missions into Germany or over to Norway seeking out identifiable military, munitions and logistics targets. However there was a fuel limit to the range of American fighter escorts, so the Luftwaffe lurked in the air space beyond this perimeter. On 1st August, American attempts to disable Romanian oil fields saw 54 out of 177 planes brought down; but the mission was well reviewed by the Mail:

200 RAIDERS SMASH PLOESTI OIL

'2,000 airmen aboard Liberators flying at 200 mph for 2,400 miles' released their ordnance from 200 feet in 'one of the war's most daring raids' which may have 'deprived the enemy of the major portion of his refining facilities.' No mention of any losses of US planes or people. In fact, the courageous endeavour slowed oil production for merely a month.

Aircraft designers experimented with amendments to their machines. The well-intentioned configurations sometimes helped, sometimes hindered: extra guns on the noses of aircraft reduced visibility for the bomb aimers; retractable radar detectors below the fuselage often skewed the performance of the plane. Despite the attrition, the Americans ploughed on; in early October losing 30 aircraft and their crews on each of three consecutive days. On the 14th another major attempt to flatten German ball-bearing output saw 400 Luftwaffe fighters blast away at the 300 intruders, of which 60 never returned.

In November, USAAF squadrons were established on southern Italian airfields - which promised shorter runs north to German territory - as experienced by young Joseph Heller, who would subsequently write 'Catch 22', drawn from those uncomfortable times. But one real life incident went beyond the New York novelist's portrayal of ironic horrors of war. An east Italian port, Bari, was being used by the Americans to unload supplies for the Foggia airfields and for their armies edging up the peninsula. Cargo handling was so intense the dock operators kept lights on for night work, which helped Luftwaffe bombers that flew south to hammer the port. One vessel was loaded with mustard gas bombs – only to be used in battle if the opposition resorted to this measure first. A single German plane dropped some bombs on this ship which blew up and unleashed the toxic chemicals on the sailors, dock workers and nearby civilians, many of whom were burnt and blinded. The Americans admitted to 25 ships having being sunk, but the offending consignment and its repercussions were kept secret.

Sent to Coventry

Bomber Command air crew were all volunteers. No-one was made to sign up, but once you had, there was no escape: you were obliged to follow orders and proceed with missions, however poorly you might judge the likely outcome of a stooge. If you demonstrated behaviour that indicated you were not fully committed to the cause, then your commanding officer would grill you to determine if this resistance was a misunderstanding, or reflected a fear of again entering those nasty skies beyond British shores.

Anyone arguing that goals were unrealistic, the dangers too excessive for the perceived desirable outcome, might be accused of a Lack of Moral Fibre; i.e. cowardice. This meant being 'Sent to Coventry': to an establishment for the evaluation and re-orientation of men who refused to proceed with their required functions because of the perceived hazards or futility.

To be labelled LMF might see you being demoted to a lower rank, with ground duties of a demeaning nature (e.g. cleaning latrines); or shunted across to the army, or assigned to coal-mining - perhaps the least worse prospect for someone unable to hide their fear any more.

So you would need to think very carefully before admitting to anyone in the service that you were terrified of getting in a plane again. The shame would stick to you for the rest of your life. Some secretly hesitant flyers surely reckoned it was preferable to die in battle or in an air accident than be branded LMF. Certainly landing in German territory and being bundled off to a POW camp would be a better option.

Airmen stuck at their tasks through determination, patriotism, comradeship, loyalty and commitment. But there must have been plenty who found flying far worse than they had expected, yet suppressed their misery until fate brought the nightmare to an end. The realistic feature film, 'Appointment in London' made in 1951, has Dirk Bogarde with many flights already chalked up, confiding to a lady friend that he is "afraid someone might see how scared you are".

Despite the daunting prospects and terrible odds that most air crew faced several nights a week, there were only around 200 cases of alleged lack of moral fibre each year – some fellows perhaps merely having expressed concern about a single mission and thus having their personal file marked as possibly flaky. The subtle notation might initially be no more than a carefully placed paper clip.

Let us salute the courage and achievements of all the Bomber Command volunteers. Hard for us to imagine the necessary grit required to proceed.

Reports from the front

Newspapers hungered for cheering stories of military daring with desirable results. Covering war required sophisticated co-operation between the armed forces and the press. How much access to what facts was it wise to allow? Could you rely on editors to leave out information that might be helpful to the enemy, or reduce morale on the home front?

In January 1943, the Daily Mail discreetly advised readers that Rosalinde Tedder, wife of the Commander of RAF Middle East, after kindly visiting a hospital full of injured servicemen in north Africa, was returning to re-join her husband in Cairo when her plane crashed.

On Thursday 8th April, the paper revealed undesirable repercussions of a USAAF raid:

> 'Reports received from Belgium indicate that the Erla aero engine works at Antwerp bombed by a large force of Flying Fortresses and Liberators on Monday were completely demolished. About 200 Germans, mostly engineers and technicians, are said to have been killed, as well as some 700 Czech and Polish workers.'

A week later:

> PLANE IN STREET: 8 KILLED
> 'Five airmen were killed and three women also lost their lives when their homes were destroyed by explosion after an aircraft crashed in the village of Huntington near York yesterday. Eye-witnesses state that when the aircraft struck the ground its petrol tanks burst and houses were sprayed with fire. Rescue work became almost impossible because of the heat.'

The same month saw the Royal Australian Air Force invite Movietone News to capture a demonstration of aerial audacity, but two formation planes collided, producing pictures which the Allies did not want on cinema newsreels. The incident and footage were suppressed for a long time. Next month General Andrews, the most senior American officer in Europe, was killed when his plane crashed in terrible weather: bad news, which had to be released despite its impact on morale. But a fortnight on, something to celebrate:

FLOODS POURING THROUGH RUHR
'Mine-Wrecked Dams Paralyse Germany's Key Industrial Area. Villages, Factories, Bridges Swept Away'

Way down in the copy, the Daily Mail noted: 'Eight of the Lancasters failed to return.' The leader article underlined the triumph:

'No more sensational feat has been accomplished in this war, or any other. The bombing of these targets holds that high dramatic quality which always belongs to supreme achievement. Not that the R.A.F. is out for cinematic effect. It is out for results, and in smashing these two dams, it has got them in a big way. The "huge waves" which swept down the valleys must have caused great damage.'

18th August warranted a big headline:

GREATEST DAY BLITZ ON EUROPE
Far below was more small print: 'Thirty-six heavy bombers lost'.

On 9th November, more grim civilian repercussions:

PLANE CRASH: 38 DEAD
'Thirty-eight people including the pilot were killed when a British Army plane crashed on a village near Poona, North-West India. The plane skidded for some distance, tearing down workers' flimsy huts and killing Indian women and children.'

A fortnight later, reports on promising British raids:

20th   BIGGEST BLITZ – RAF OUT AGAIN.
           Berlin hit by 350 'cookies'
23rd   BERLIN BLITZED AGAIN LAST NIGHT
24th   HITLER 'BOMBED OUT' BY RAF

The Fuhrer's house, adjacent to the Chancellery, had been set alight. After a night in his bunker, Hitler left the city at dawn. The raid also destroyed the Kaiser Willelm church, and the British Embassy.

25th   TROOPS TAKE OVER IN BERLIN

German soldiers were corralling refugees swarming through the streets. The Mail explained that 'Berlin has now become the most bombed city in the world', receiving 5,000 tons in a week from Lancasters. The paper allocated space to that diabolical propaganda guru, Goebbels:

> "It is true that part of our city has suffered heavy damage. Many of our people have been killed or injured. But one day the bitter time will come to an end. The flag of unshakability will be hoisted over the capital, and out of the debris of destroyed houses and streets a new Berlin will rise after victory, a Berlin more beautiful than ever."

Next day, Commander Harris proclaimed:

> "The Battle of Berlin will progress until the heart of Nazi Germany ceases to beat."

The Air Ministry now allowed some journalists to travel in the bomber stream to evaluate for themselves the tasks and their impact. The BBC's Richard Dimbleby went on Lancasters to Berlin and brought back vivid audio recordings. Meanwhile, a newspaper man, Lowell Bennett, filed this copy prior to boarding an outbound plane:

> 'Berlin is going to be attacked again tonight by hundreds of four-engined bombers which will avalanche down tons of explosives and incendiaries into the Nazi heart and capital. It may be one of the most concentrated raids of the war. I am flying in one of the last Lancasters, which alone will drop hundreds of incendiaries as well as 4,000 lb 'cookies'. We are about to take off to join the vast stream thundering towards the European coast in the darkening sky. This report is being made in the event of 'B' for 'Betty' and myself not returning.'

…which was what happened. The next evening, from the same Lincolnshire air station, the Daily Mail's Colin Bednall boarded a Lancaster destined for Leipzig, which enabled him to write:

> WE FLEW 'BY THE BOOK' IN A WORLD OF FIRE.
> 'I do not expect to have another experience so terribly fascinating and completely mesmeric as this.'

It was:

> 'a near-miraculous advance in the cold, remorseless application of
> science to this type of obliteration warfare.'

The Mail now alerted readers to Hitler's demands for a super-weapon from his scientists; then came news of the RAF 'pummelling' the 'secret weapon' coast; and on Christmas Day the Americans also blasted V1 rocket sites, providing the sort of headline everyone wanted.

A matter of numbers

The data on 1943 endeavours can read like a catalogue of horror – in the air and on the ground. Typical BC operations saw 750 bombers set out for targets across Germany; statistically 37 craft would fail to return, meaning about 250 airmen had been killed, 50 more captured.

On 30th January the Command flew stooges to Oldenburg "to create despondency and despair" among refugees from Cologne. Most conurbations in western Germany were assaulted again and again, not always accurately. Air Ministry whizz kids hit on the notion of a '400 yard, 50% error': evidence that half the ordnance landed within 400 yards (366 metres) of its intended target. The maths turned terror into neat graph nodules: thousands of citizens dead or injured, millions of buildings damaged, hundreds of airmen killed. Of every 20 new airmen volunteering for Bomber Command operations, nine would be dead before the end of the war, two would be in German prisons and a couple more would have sustained long-term serious injury.

90% of Lancaster sorties flown at night over Germany did not encounter a single Luftwaffe fighter; those that did had a 50% chance of surviving. Across the year, BC airmen had had a 17% chance of surviving their first 'tour' of 30 missions; merely 3% the second tour. Yet those extraordinary young men kept showing up to get on with it.

For the record, 29th April would prove to be the half-way point of the war in the Pacific (taking the start as the Japanese attack on Burma before Christmas 1940).

In the month of June, 100 British bombers were lost over the Ruhr, half in one operation against the Folke-Wolf aircraft factory. Through the summer, more air crew died than German bomb victims. July saw the Allied invasion of Sicily and the prospect of troops working their way up Italy to hit the Axis from below. Meanwhile, 630 BC bombers headed to Dusseldorf, and 29 did not come back.

Air Chief Marshall Harris was convinced that dense, relentless bombardment of Berlin would bring the war to an end: the enemy would sue for peace - it was just a matter of numbers. But the Nazi HQ was deep within Germany - plenty of space and time for Luftwaffe night-fighters to pick off Allied planes. Harris commenced his campaign in August with 1,500 sorties on the capital, which lost 114 planes - 14%: the deaths of 500 airmen and similar numbers of Berliners.

25th August: 160 BC flights to Nuremberg, 23 failed to return. 10th September: 500 to Dusseldorf, 38 lost; 13th: 400 to Bremen, 26 lost; 16th: 400 to Essen, 40 lost. If a bomber was heading over an already burning target, the pilot needed to be alert to the prospect of external pressure changing dramatically due to the up-draught of very hot air. A plane could suddenly fall by thousands of feet and even the best skipper might struggle to stabilise the craft again somewhere above the ground.

In September, Italy changed sides. And on one painful night over Germany, Bomber Command lost 300 airmen - the worst single operation for the RAF so far. However, this was surpassed in October by the Americans losing a quarter of their planes on one day mission.

November saw the downing of 170 BC crews; in December the Command's loss rate neared 10%. A big Berlin mission was conducted on Christmas Eve, which resulted in at least one Lancaster crew being buried in the German capital on Christmas Day.

The Americans argued that concentrated attacks on oil installations should swiftly reduce the enemy's ability to function, yet Harris continued to direct the majority of his forces to randomly destroy built-up areas (albeit with nominal military, government or logistics elements at the designated address.)

By the end of the year, the Command had flown 150,000 sorties, losing more than 3,000 aircraft while decanting 26 million incendiary devices over German housing. Champions of Bomber Command describe the raids as "considerable achievements", albeit "marred" with the "occasional air crew losses" or "regrettable" misplaced bombs. However Max Hastings considers Harris should have been removed from his post when he patently side-lined Air Ministry orders.

From a distance, with cold objectivity and no prism of patriotism or loyalty to family members or ex-colleagues within revered institutions, the activities can seem ugly, unproductive and in some ways self-defeating. Post-war analysts have questioned the wisdom of Churchill's unceasing demand for unconditional surrender. Miserable German citizens were never offered a viable alternative to the Nazi regime that might have encouraged them to attempt an overthrow of Hitler and his entourage. Thousands were killed, injured, and 'de-housed' and many factories were damaged, but there was no sign of the Third Reich war machine being disabled by the onslaughts. However the raids provided some relief for Soviet Union soldiers, because German planes, guns and troops had to be pulled away from the east.

The devastation inflicted on Russia was far more severe than anything in the west. Stalingrad and Leningrad under siege reduced starving people to eat the flesh of the dead. The resilience and determination of Soviet Union forces would be the critical fulcrum of the Second World War: not the Battle of Britain, nor the arrival of the Americans, or the bombing of German infrastructure, or D-Day, but the millions of Soviet soldiers relentlessly battering the Germans back to their borders and beyond.

However, the records also show that many of the massive endeavours to hammer the German nation made an impact on Hitler personally. After the war, the diabolical PGG had his diary confiscated. It revealed a note penned after the brutal Berlin raid of late November that damaged the Luftwaffe HQ and its treasured aircraft museum, plus Adolf's personal railway train - "a heavy blow. The Fuhrer is much depressed."

Ladies and gentlemen, here is hard evidence for my thesis. Not a single sortie was in vain. The cumulative impact of all those flights across the North Sea to deliver ordnance and misery on the enemy population got to the man at the top. He was on the road to despair. It was hopefully just a matter of time.

1944

SHIFTING FRONTIERS

For the Daily Telegraph, biggest news for the first day of the year was:
RUSSIANS RECAPTURE ZHITOMIR BY STORM
A secondary headline revealed:
U.S. BOMBERS HIT PARIS WAR PLANTS
'Large formations of Flying Fortresses and Liberators again escorted by American, R.A.F. and Allied fighters, attacked two ball-bearing plants in Paris and an airfield on the west coast of France yesterday. Their operation was part of the great design in the intensified round-the-clock air offensive against enemy targets.'

No mention of panic in the Home Guard when dozens of parachutists appeared in the Kent sky. The defenders feared these were invading Germans, before realising they were Americans abandoning damaged bombers returning from the continent. The first Telegraph leader column for the '226th week of the war' focused on:
'THE ROAD AHEAD
German capacity for fighting has been reduced by the Allied air offensive which, as 1943 went out, developed greater weight and deeper penetration than ever. The Luftwaffe still fights hard and no doubt will fight harder to avert collapse as long as possible, but Germany has been compelled to exchange the pride of aggressive power for hopeless endurance.'

Readers were alerted to Hitler's seasonal message: The bomber onslaught on towns "has bitten deeply into all our hearts". He blamed his recent military difficulties on Italy's defection and the "shameful treason against Mussolini". The Fuhrer warned that Britain's politicians wanted the greater part of the German people to be exterminated, their children taken from them, and for millions of Germans to be deported to Siberia:

"However great the horror of today, it cannot be compared with the ghastly calamity which would hit our people if this coalition of criminals were ever victorious."

Anticipating an invasion, Adolf added:

"I can tell you, with the fullest confidence, that wherever the Allies land they will receive an appropriate welcome... Retaliation will come."

On the evening of 1st January, 400 Bomber Command aircraft headed to Berlin, but 28 were shot down, including many pathfinders, one of which blew up along the marking route, scattering flares and confusing the bomb-aimers. Next day, 300 headed for the German capital, but 60 turned back with "problems". On 20th January, 700 sorties saw 35 picked off by night-fighters on the way. Next night, 60 intruders were shot down around Magdeburg. January was the worst individual month of the war for the Force with the loss of 350 planes. 15th February saw the biggest RAF mission to Berlin: 900 planes dropping 2,600 tons. Four nights later, of the 800 bombers approaching the Messerschmitt factory at Leipzig, almost 10% were lost. Through the winter months Harris dispatched 30-odd missions to Berlin which killed 6,000 people there and made one million homeless, the battle costing the RAF 1,000 aircraft with the loss of more than 6,000 men.

Hitler ordered Goering to send fleets of bombers to London. Hermann mustered 500 planes, many manned by novices. A late January raid only managed to decant 10% of its ordnance on London, which killed 100 citizens for the loss of 40 craft. Intermittent efforts followed, but each mission further depleted Luftwaffe capacity. February saw 1,300 sorties which killed more than 500 Brits or visitors. One bomb blew out windows at 10 Downing Street. It all fuelled appetite for further endeavour in the opposite direction.

What the hell was that?

As we know, to impede big American planes bristling with gun turrets Luftwaffe airmen had learnt that approaching them head on was best: blasting at the cockpit, pulling away the moment the intruder swerved, already out of control because you had wounded or killed the pilot. In April 1944 the Americans lost more than 2,000 bomber aircraft flying from East Anglia, though defeated 500 German fighters in the process. An American bomber crewman now had a one-in-four chance of surviving his tour of duty unscathed.

Air commanders on all sides were aware that it paid to give airmen rest periods, otherwise their judgement and performance would decline. By 1944, the Allies were maintaining these principles much better than the Luftwaffe. Bomber Command required air crew to undertake a tour of 30 missions before any down time. They would later be recalled for a further 30 missions, after which they could serve the rest of the war in a non-combat capacity. Statistically, chances of completing two full tours were alarmingly low. In 1942 less than half the BC crews would survive their first tour; only one in five would get through their second. By 1943, just 17% of new airmen would see out a 30 operation tour. A mere 1 in 40 would sustain their second exposure. All constantly faced this high possibility of death, with little or no means of minimising their vulnerability to such terminal prospects.

German airmen experimented with a bomb suspended on a cable below their aircraft. The theory was to swing this towards an intruding plane then release it on an arc which the enemy would be unable to avoid. One American recipient of the pendulum weapon managed to return to base because the bomb failed to explode and merely knifed a length of cable into the US fuselage. The Germans concluded the manoeuvre was too difficult, but right to the end of the war American crews dreaded the prospect of giant cheese cutters.

More fears were stimulated by crews believing some Luftwaffe planes were radio-controlled: no pilot aboard, no human beings inside. Instead it was somehow operated remotely, either from another aircraft or from the ground. The Germans never attempted such science fiction, yet American airmen kept bringing up this nightmarish notion at briefings.

Occasionally an Allied crew might spot the explosion of something ahead or alongside which looked like an aircraft. A theory developed that the Germans were sending up fake plane-like structures to blow up in their faces and spook them. The alarming occurrence became known as a "scarecrow". To calm the men, senior officers would sometimes acknowledge this nasty tactic and advise the crews to ignore it: stay calm and carry on. After the war, interrogation of Luftwaffe officers explored this unpleasant diversion but no German interviewed had any knowledge of giant fireworks. Allied airmen were witnessing their own side's craft blowing up, which they perceived at the time as a cruel enemy trick. There were no scarecrows.

Bloody Berlin

The period perceived as the Battle of Berlin lasted from November 1943 to March 1944. Heaviest individual night for Bomber Command losses on these missions was 24th March '44, when 77 craft were shot down. Not all of the eliminations occurred over Germany; one was caused by a London anti-aircraft battery.

A week later, attempts to attack Nuremberg proved to be the worst night for losses for the Command in the whole of the war. Of 795 aircraft setting off, 95 were shot down, another 71 were seriously damaged and 12 crash-landed. Much was blamed on misleading weather predictions. Cloud cover had been anticipated, but moonlight allowed the Luftwaffe to spot the bombers approaching, while vapour trails made their route clear.

Thousands of Berliners died, or were injured and/or made homeless by BC's endeavours. Yet a degree of civility remained in some quarters. After one British bomber crashed, killing some of its crew, the captured survivors were subsequently allowed to attend their late colleagues' funerals at the Berlin War Cemetery.

Some unhappy airmen described bombing Berlin as "sheer bloody murder". Harris eventually recognised that his strategy was not succeeding; there was no evidence that the Germans were caving in. Max Hastings considers:

'It is almost impossible to overvalue the ingenuity and determination with which the defenders responded to the bomber offensive. In late 43 and early 44 the German night-fighter force came close to the decisive defeat of Bomber Command, just as the Luftwaffe day-fighters almost achieved the defeat of the 8th Air Force.'

Harris would have pursued other city assaults, but Allied High Command now needed the bombers to concentrate on preparation for the invasion of the western shores of the continent and deliver convincing attacks on deception locations.

After the war, the British government study of the 'Strategic Air Offensive against Germany' was damning in its assessment of the 'Battle of Berlin':

> '...from the operational point of view, it was more than a failure. It was a defeat.'

But I would argue that in essence what Bomber Command had been doing did bring about a vital achievement: Hitler lost heart, lost hope; soon lost the will to live. And those around the Fuhrer - shoring him up, swearing loyalty - immediately sought a way of getting out alive; begging for mercy.

Harris helped bring this about – along with the 125,000 men who served under him. He was a determined strategist, providing the world with the evidence that Britain could hit back and hurt. Arthur Harris's forthright application to the horrendous task he accepted undoubtedly helped bring peace and harmony to what was left of Europe.

Grounded

> 'The Enemy is known to attach the utmost importance to the interrogation and search of prisoners, but he can learn nothing from a silent and resolute prisoner with empty pockets.'

... from the War Office's 'Responsibilities of a Prisoner of War'.

In all, 33,000 American and 13,000 British and Commonwealth airmen were detained on German-occupied territory. Each captured man was taken to a Luftwaffe interrogation centre near Frankfurt where the Red Cross would gather names of newcomers to alert home nations and families, but this could take more than a month.

Each prisoner was kept in solitary confinement until interrogations, which often took the sweet-and-sour formula of one questioner seemingly friendly, the other cold and hard. As combat continued, the Third Reich had to set up more camps for the unwelcome visitors, most of who considered they were treated tolerably by the guards. Some inmates reckoned escape schemes were top priority; others avoided such effort because life became very unpleasant when staff uncovered evidence of a departure plan.

Prisoners could send postcards home, and the Red Cross supplied inmates with food parcels. Guards were known to pilfer or confiscate such goodies, while Allied officers who took on camp management responsibilities were also often suspected of snaffling the contents of those precious packages.

Back in Britain, some military clerks spent their entire war investigating the whereabouts of colleagues who had not returned from a mission. Any chaps who managed to escape from a German prison camp and reach home would be interviewed by War Office planners trying to understand the confinement regimes in order to enable more men to break out.

The stipulation of not taking personal belongings on a mission was frequently ignored, perhaps most foolishly by an American who flew wearing a jacket emblazoned with the slogan: 'Murder Inc.', to match the nickname on his plane. When this guy was captured, the Nazi propaganda machinery could unleash vivid confirmation of American intentions.

To convey the nature of incarceration, the Daily Telegraph mounted a POW exhibition in May 1944, including 'an exact reproduction' of a German camp, complete with sentry boxes and towers - all in the grounds of London's royal Clarence House: 'Adults 1s, children 6d.' The display was opened by the Duke of Gloucester, then visited by the Queen, 'wearing a slate blue coat and dress with a smoke fox fur and a thistle spray brooch in her matching hat'. This coincided with news of 50 POWs shot by the Gestapo after trying to escape from Stalag Luft 3. The Telegraph noted:

> 'The deaths were concealed until a representative of Switzerland paid a routine visit to the camp a month later.'

Rather than having been killed in the course of escape or while resisting arrest, it was suspected they had been executed. Subsequently this was confirmed, and a week later the paper ran a front page follow-up:

SHOT PRISONERS DUG FOR 15 MONTHS

...commenting:

> 'Those in charge of the camp should be put on trial after victory.'

Off the rails

> 'There are still trains carrying munitions, tanks, oil, food for the Hun. We
> need many planes to stop them in their tracks. More planes, more work,
> more savings by us on the civilian front. The more we save – in all things
> – the better we shall support our train busters in their dare-devil work'

... a newspaper advertisement by the National Savings Committee,
advocating self-denial for a purpose.

The Air Ministry frequently identified a rail line somewhere in
Europe that was an essential artery for conveying enemy troops or
armaments. War Office aviation charts for Germany used black lines for
rail routes - the most prominent element of the representation of the
landscape. Next came roads in red, then hills in green, rivers in blue and
buildings in grey. Reach the right valley and you could spot the train
line through it. Follow this and you might identify bends and joins, and
so work out what bit of track you were above. Discharge your cargo and
it might reach the railway corridor, but your average bomb will not do
much damage to a gravel-embedded wooden sleeper holding a heavy
steel rail in a series of iron brackets, and a few forced workers will soon
replace the compromised metal and timber. Crews achieving a direct
hit on a munitions train discovered alarming repercussions: the
composite explosion could punch up into the plane. One kite flipped
over as a result of blast, but the skipper managed to right it again and
continue on his way.

In March and April 1944, squadrons were assigned to Operation
Chattanooga, applying their skills to rail yards that could aid the
Germans defend their frontiers after D-Day. This meant taking bombs
to built-up areas, which was always asking for trouble. Fifteen
locomotives and 800 wagons were destroyed at Le Mans yards, but 100
civilians were also victims. Across other junctions, 200 Allied planes
obliterated 2,000 freight units but killed 1,000 French people; while 100
Royal Canadian Air Force bombers blasted Belgian rail complexes
extinguishing nearly 500 locals.

In Italy, Operation Strangle was designed to muck up munitions
support for German armies resisting the Allied advance up the
peninsula. Between March and May, 20,000 sorties dropped ordnance

on Italian rail lines, sometimes breaking 70 lengths of track a day. The beleaguered soldiers quickly made good those routes, though often left them looking useless. Then Allied spotter planes would identify more munitions trains heading south, which meant the lines were viable again. On the odd occasion when Allied bombers damaged a bridge, the Germans would make a part-repair at night but leave one section missing, only to be re-inserted when the next train was ready to pass.

No return journeys were tackled; Third Reich factories were churning out enough locomotives for Italy-bound trains to make a one-way trip.

We kicked their asses

1944 was the year when the greatest quantity of American planes, airmen and ordnance took to the air, and when the U.S. Eighth Army Air Force based in East Anglia grew to be the single biggest aerial fighting command, with more machines and personnel than the R.A.F.

Not every American plane was perfect. Some engines had flaws that became exposed on long flights and in novice hands. Some US pilots were given extra training in preserving their engines by not pressing them unnecessarily hard. The goal of the bombers was defined as getting at least 50% of their ordnance to land within 300 metres of targets. When faced with Luftwaffe fighter planes and dense anti-aircraft fire, this prospect was painfully challenging. One January mission saw 650 US bombers trying to raid enemy aircraft factories; 60 lost in the process. Some German planes now deployed rocket launchers, able to disable a big bomber from a good way off.

The Americans needed more practice, better engineering, and kinder weather. They got a window of high pressure over Europe in the middle of February and made the most of it. 1,000 US bombers took to the skies on a succession of days, aiming - with clear sight of the terrain below - to damage aircraft factories and facilities throughout the west side of occupied Europe. 200 US bombers were lost during 'Big Week'. And through the nights, the RAF lost 200 planes while carpet bombing near those factories.

Roger Freeman's histories log heroic episodes when pilots were killed or injured and other crew members, peering through blood-splattered windshields, tried to bring back their craft in one piece. Returning American planes were vulnerable to Luftwaffe fighters lurking over the

French coast. Two returners collided over Great Yarmouth, eliminating all 21 aboard.

Freeman records some remarkable survivals. One American airman lost consciousness in the bomb bay while trying to dislodge jammed ordnance. He came round when free-falling, and yanked his parachute open just in time to land in one piece. Another airman's plane blew up, throwing him alone clear. He was holding his parachute but managed to strap it on to his back and so slow his descent into a tree.

The USAAF's first trip to Berlin in March consisted of 31 planes of which five failed to return. Next outing to the capital was made up of 700 bombers escorted by even more fighters. 80 planes were lost. When so many aircraft travel together in close formation, some buffeting is inevitable. Turbulence, often caused by the aircraft ahead, combined with novice piloting could see planes collide. Sometimes both could head home with broken wings or tails; other times neither journeyed further.

Hairy exchanges saw many Luftwaffe defenders eliminated by the valiant gunners aboard the US bombers, or by their escorting fleets of audacious fighters. Germany lost 40% of its western perimeter aircraft in the first six months of 1944. In one month, a quarter of all assigned Luftwaffe fighter pilots died while trying to resist the intruders. •

Clusters of planes in bad weather might drift and lose a clear sense of their position. Some disorientated American aircraft released their cargo above urban areas in Switzerland. On discovering the errors, the USA government offered apologies and compensation to the neutral nation, but not before the tiny Swiss air force shot down several of the alarming visitors.

All American endeavours from East Anglia were scheduled to happen in daylight, but occasional long runs with late starts and route diversions meant some planes did not get back across the North Sea until after dark – which enabled some daring Luftwaffe fighters to follow them. One April evening saw fifteen German planes bring down nine 'heavies' then damage nine more on the airfields, killing 38 American servicemen in the process.

The month of May saw a horrible own goal caused by bad weather: at take-off, one bomber failed to rise and instead rammed through fencing and crashed into the woods beyond, its full payload of ordnance aboard.

In heavy mist, ground control signalled to halt further take-offs. The next plane, already half-way down the runway, braked and came to a stop. The following pilot did not see the order to wait and proceeded with his take-off, so hitting the stationary craft mid-runway. Twenty-one crew died and it took three days to fill the cavity in the tarmac.

For D-Day, the Allies deployed more than 3,000 aircraft. Fearsome resistance was expected from the Luftwaffe, but it proved insignificant. Most German planes had been assigned to defend the Fatherland, and it took several days before they were ready to operate back in France.

Bombing front-line German defenders required the greatest of accuracy by Allied air forces. Of course, a proportion went astray. Perhaps most cruelly, one bomb exploding amongst Allied troops might indicate to the pilots behind that this was the required destination and so further ordnance was delivered there.

The month of June saw the highest number of American sorties from Britain in the whole war: around 30,000. Whilst German aircraft factories, despite their pummelling from above, were still turning out formidable quantities of machines, the training programmes for German pilots were becoming briefer, often due to fuel shortages caused by the American assaults on oil plants. Goering was desperate for a positive public relations story and aspired to see at least one hundred US planes being brought down by his flyers in a single day. The master-mind threatened his crews that failure would have them flung into the army for service on the Russian front. Hermann's gruesome ambition did not come about, though on one occasion 25 USAAF bombers were shot down by 90 Luftwaffe fighters in just three minutes, and on another day a total of 73 US fighters were lost.

By July, the 'Mighty Eighth' was mustering more than 1,000 bombers protected by fighter escort fleets of 700. The raiders would head for a variety of destinations to dilute the defence effort, much of it now staged by novice German fighter pilots with only a few weeks of combat experience.

A test flight over Lancashire brought about the worst UK air crash in the war: a Liberator was overwhelmed by bad weather and came down on a village school, killing 23 adults and 38 children, mostly from the fires generated by 3,000 gallons of gasoline.

During the autumn, US planes began to encounter the devilish new German jet fighter - which could zoom through the sky but was menacingly difficult to manage. Rattled Luftwaffe users complained that they struggled to get the roaring beasts to slow down enough to tackle a viable landing.

Meanwhile, American and British fighter pilots started to wear special high pressure suits which stabilised the blood flow in their bodies when in the midst of high speed turns, hence overcoming the repercussions of the G-forces that could cause an airman to pass out.

Reach into German territory was eventually enhanced by additional fuel tanks fitted below US fighter wings. Rather than carrying just enough juice for the planned trip, the tanks were filled and, when an opportunity arose, were dropped still half-full on an enemy airfield or railway station, so the pilot could then fly over again to strafe the large, reinforced-paper capsule and set it on fire. Many fearless and fast-thinking American fighter pilots deployed sophisticated teamwork. One guy saw a colleague's craft descend to earth behind enemy lines. The mobile airman swiftly landed in an adjacent field to pick up his pal for a lift back to base.

The most daunting challenge for the Americans were punchy flak batteries deployed around prospective targets. A quarter of all bombers were at some time hit by flak, causing on average one in twelve to crash mid-mission. But in case you might imagine that every German anti-aircraft crew were a superbly-functioning killing machine, consider the following: one disgruntled flak operative was accused by his officers of failing to follow orders. He was brought before a tribunal which determined that the shoddy fellow should be executed. However, the German judicial system allowed a guilty party to choose their method of death. So the prisoner - continuing to be awkward - requested a firing squad of anti-aircraft guns. Hence he was chained into the top of a tall wooden turret some distance from a flak battery and the crew were told to fire at him. His ex-colleagues took pot shots intermittently but none of the shells struck as required. Perhaps the defiant offender had a bit of wriggle room on his platform. He died of starvation three weeks later. This German's ass had not been kicked, unlike many, many thousands of his fellow servicemen.

Clear skies?

In the spring of 1944, all western Allied air forces were brought under the single command of General Eisenhower, the invasion supremo. There would be no more independent air operations for the foreseeable future. To assemble thousands of vessels ready to leave English ports during one night and cross the water to France, without crippling aerial harassment on the way, meant the Luftwaffe had to be kept at bay.

During the build-up to the invasion it was imperative to repel all attempts at German aerial reconnaissance over any part of southern England. The accumulation of all assets close to Portsmouth and Southampton were carefully obscured, while fake military contingents along eastern Scotland were fabricated to suggest to passing Luftwaffe crew that nautical ambition towards Norway was on the cards.

Bomber Command units were required to wreck transport infrastructure across western France. 9,000 sorties were undertaken, some of which caused high numbers of civilian casualties: 250 on 26th March, 450 on 9th April, nearly 500 the next day; but the total number of French deaths in the "softening up" did not quite reach 10,000, and thus was considered tolerable by both Churchill and Eisenhower.

Months of pummelling German airfields, fuel plants and aircraft factories hugely reduced the Luftwaffe's capacity to monitor or menace the Operation Overlord build-up. Fighters ensured that barely any German planes managed to pass over southern England in April or May 1944; none in the first week of June. Meanwhile bomber crews assaulted the whole length of the western continental seaboard so the Third Reich could not anticipate any specific invasion landing points.

On D-Day itself, only about 60 Luftwaffe aircraft attempted to approach the massive armada and these were soon seen off by Allied aerial escort patrols. It was as near as anyone could have hoped to the novelty of clear skies.

Once Allied troops were on French soil, the priority became maintaining a 24-hour mobile shield of steel above and in front of the spearhead. By now the Luftwaffe was out-numbered ten to one; nevertheless they occasionally undertook sorties to hamper the Allied advance, but soon faced wild-west cowboy-like sweeping challenges from American pilots in Mustangs.

As Allied armies edged through occupied territory, expecting their air forces to aid their advance, bombers occasionally unloaded their cargo in the wrong place on the wrong people - hitting fellow servicemen on the ground unknowingly. On 14th August, the RAF was required to weaken German defences facing front-line Canadian troops. The Canadians lit yellow identification flares but the approaching bombers mistook these signals for pathfinder target indicators, which resulted in nearly one hundred Allied soldiers being killed by British airmen.

A serious shortcoming was the failure by some senior airmen to work sufficiently closely with the relevant generals in directing craft to target pockets of German resistance. Shoddy parameters saw the occasional bombing of American soldiers by American airmen. A system of smoke markers was established so that flyers knew that the coloured cloud was rising from their own front line - they needed to aim beyond such indicators. However the Germans soon propelled similar smoke bombs behind American lines, causing US planes to again pound their own side. When air controllers used radio from forward positions alongside ground troops they could much better direct aircraft to desired locations, but some officers chose to stay at the back.

Also staying at the back, Adolf Hitler feigned delight at the appearance of Allied forces on French soil, assuring his generals that he relished a decisive scrap that would swiftly result in any surviving landing craft passengers being shoved back in the sea.

The course of the war

On 7th June, The Daily Telegraph encapsulated the critical news for its 700,000 purchasers:

ALLIED INVASION TROOPS SEVERAL MILES INTO FRANCE

Prior to this, in 1944, the newspaper had featured progress on the Russian battle line for 56 mornings, and the state of play in Italy on 38 occasions. Following D-Day, advances inward from the French coastline dominated the front page on 150 days.

Across the year, the Telegraph proudly championed the Royal Air Force. On a dozen separate days, RAF successes over German territory warranted front page prominence. A week after D-Day, an article explained that 400,000 tons of bombs had been dropped by the R.A.F.

since the start of the war; and at the end of the year, the paper reported that the same tonnage had been delivered during 1944 alone.

Its broadsheet format allowed the newspaper to cover other issues elsewhere on the front page, so further Russian advances unfailingly commanded space. The tone of the text almost always indicated positive prospects for the Allies. Focus on set-backs was rare and mostly given lower profiles. A January headline about the USAAF:

NAZIS' MAIN FIGHTER FACTORY BLASTED

… was one of the few occasions when a secondary headline exposed bad news:

'59 bombers missing'.

Hitler's Germany was presented as being in difficulty due to Russian troops and Allied bombers. A week after D-Day, Stalin's appreciation of his Allies' initiative was documented:

"One cannot but recognise that in the whole history of war there has not been any such undertaking so broad in conception, so grandiose in scale and so masterly in execution."

A few days later, the Telegraph acknowledged a potential new difficulty:

'The R.A.F. has been quick to accept the challenge of the aerial robot – a jet-engined monoplane generally described as a midget machine which is shaped like a Spitfire.'

However, the impact of the Nazi rocket menace was given very little coverage. Instead, readers learned that the Force had found solutions: 'R.A.F. fighters shoot down robot planes', 'secret counter-blows against robot plane', and 'robot runway destroyed by bombs'. Then news of army achievement:

'Robot bases captured in Normandy'

Early in July, following a report that 2,700 flying bombs had killed roughly the same number of British citizens, the Telegraph reported Churchill's speech on joint tactics:

'I consider that the Government were right in not giving a great deal of information about the flying bomb until we knew more about it and were able to measure its effect. The newspapers have in an admirable fashion helped the Government in this, and I express my thanks to them.'

Ranting and rocketing

Did Adolf read a lot of science fiction as a boy? Because he kept pressing his R&D teams to tackle stuff that seemed far removed from viable military reality. One of the nuttiest notions was a giant gun that could be emplaced in France to fire shells across the English Channel and over Kent to land in the middle of London. Perhaps he'd seen something like this in a comic. His whizz kids eventually came up with a weapon so big it could in theory do that job. But it was unwieldy (as they could have told him initially, but thought better of it) - extremely difficult to move, then point in the right direction; its enormous shells distinctly dodgy and inclined to stick in the barrel. One of Bomber Command's most successful and swiftly executed operations was to destroy those monster gun emplacements in July '44.

Hitler had also barked at the lab rats to supply rockets for launching towards London. The talented technicians eventually produced such scary machines, but struggled to have them take off properly and head in the required arc. The desperate dictator kept assuring his gloomy political entourage that he had great tricks up his sleeves. He knew the Allies would soon try to invade. Wouldn't it be great if he could propel this explosive spanner into the midst of their works!

Then it was the 6th June 1944, and the Americans and the Brits and all their Empire friends were on French beaches and still those rockets were stuck on their stupid ski slope ramps. Adolf ranted a lot, and before the week was out, the bullied boffins set off their first V1. Okay, it went a bit astray but it was a marker: proof of remarkable rabbits in the Fuhrer's magic hat.

The V1 carried 1,800 pounds of explosive at 400 mph. It rose to 3,000 feet and could therefore travel 160 miles - enough to reach Buckingham Palace. Engineers tweaked the engines, fins, pay loads and firing mechanisms then started to blast rockets off regularly. On 13th June, one of the spooky new menaces came down in Bethnal Green killing six locals. On 17th June, 200 'pilotless planes' rained on to London. Bomber Command was charged with destroying the launch sites, which were hard to spot and harder to hit. More than 130 aircraft were lost in attempts to eliminate the ugly ramps erected amongst trees.

Ten thousand V1s were launched between June 1944 and March 1945 (when all the sites were finally overrun by Allied troops). 6,700 "doodlebugs" crossed the Channel, but only 2,500 reached London. However, collectively the weird machines killed around 6,000 civilians and injured 17,000 while damaging 23,000 houses.

Elsewhere in the Nazi workshops, to tackle the problem of declining fuel supplies, some scientists came up with a plane that they reckoned could be powered by coal dust. We can imagine Adolf kindly explaining to them that they must be mad.

Who knows when Hitler first displayed his ranting tendencies - perhaps it was in the trenches during the First World War when he became frustrated by his officers' failure to prosecute the land battle better. Maybe he ranted against the formidability of his foes. Certainly ranting about Jewish people, communists and foreigners worked well for him in the 1920s. This led to a relatively calm period for his flaky psyche when his terrible agenda of social engineering and territorial seizure began to be implemented. But when set-backs were reported to him, the ranting returned. He became convinced he was being let down by the shoddy performance of inadequate officers – all of whom faced a scorching when they turned up at HQ.

Next out of his box of tricks came the V2, missiles designed and built by the German army; absolutely massive, making the V1s look like rejects from a discount fireworks shop. Bomber Command undertook 16,000 sorties against the rocket sites, sending down 60,000 tons of ordnance on them.

The first V2 to head in the right direction left the surface of the earth in September 1944 and soon arrived in Chiswick. Over the next six months (again, until their sites were completely overrun) the Wehrmacht launched 2,000 of these monsters, half of which reached Britain, causing 2,750 deaths and 6,500 injuries. It was not enough to turn the tide, but it was certainly vengeance of a sort that should only appear in comics.

An Intelligence arm of the American Air Force specialised in surprise activity that might in unconventional ways disrupt the enemy. One of their more bizarre propositions was to fill an aircraft full of pornographic magazines and decant these over Hitler's headquarters. This plan never got the green light, so we can only wonder if a fluttering mass of dirty pictures might have had a benign effect on the Fuhrer's temperament, or would have resulted in yet another big rant.

Self-defeating

When you're zipping through the sky at several hundred miles an hour, aware of fellow pilots around you while looking out for enemy craft somewhere ahead, it can be difficult to comprehend the wider picture, the general state of play within the action to which you are contributing. So information from base is essential to give context and direction to your endeavours. Good to have someone on the ground with a grasp of the wider circumstances to alert you to what should be done next. Headphones feeding you warnings and commands increase your effectiveness in the air. Likewise, whatever you can communicate back – short and to the point – may aid controllers trying to manage what is happening in their skies. The right message at the right moment might save your life or others. However, the enemy could possibly tune in to these conversations: hence there was need for discretion or codes.

In the later part of the war, the Brits deployed fluent German speakers to issue spurious radio commands to Luftwaffe pilots to direct them to wrong rendezvous points. The instigators then enjoyed listening to the heated exchanges between the German air crew and their confused ground controllers.

Of course wireless communication was always vulnerable to interference. Perhaps the worst repercussion of radio failure was prior to D-Day when nearly 400 Allied bombers heading for a German military base required routing advice along the way. An American army exercise in Sussex was using that fleet's wavelength for local training, so no messages could to be radioed between the UK controllers and their aircraft over Germany, which enabled a swarm of Luftwaffe fighters to shoot down forty of the intruders in just twenty minutes.

When so many admirable attempts were undertaken to confront enemy forces it was inevitable that some endeavours would go horribly wrong. Most frequent was misjudgement by anti-aircraft crews shooting up shells at friendly aircraft. AA spotting skills were flawed; their listening training unsatisfactory. With clouds in the sky, rain in their eyes, despair in their hearts, did they allow an aircraft safe passageway because they weren't sure whose side it was on, or blast away at it to discourage it from proceeding? They did both, and each option could be wrong. The RAF and USAAF publicised identification painting schemes for the undersides of their fighters – black and white panel designs to help ground crew recognise friendly craft overhead, but land or ship-based guns still shot down some colleagues.

Night bombers heading for Germany in the dark had twitchy gunners in their turrets. One man might believe a nearby plane was about to attack, so he blasts off rounds at that craft - where its crew could assume the source must be an enemy fighter and so fire back.

Undoubtedly the most ironic conclusion to a bomber's career was being bombed from above by another aircraft on the same side. Throughout 1943 and 1944 this happened again and again. In the dark it was common for one fleet of planes to approach a designated target at a particular height and thus unwittingly decant their payload while other aircraft on the same mission were passing below. Incendiaries falling from above could land and burn on the lower plane's wings. A high explosive canister could puncture the fuselage, be triggered by the impact and/or cause the ordnance of the lower aircraft to explode. One ghastly scenario was the incendiary device that crashed through the window of a plane - frenzied crew then trying to cast it out before they and the plane were burnt to destruction.

Curtains

Unlike civilian flights of today, most aircraft journeys we are exploring were expected to form a loop. The craft takes off from Airfield A with the goal of returning to Airfield A sooner or later, in one piece. Intriguingly, Roger Moorhouse's book about assassination attempts on Hitler embraces two dramatic occasions when the future for the world, and for the instigators, hinged on a one-way flight.

In March 1943, Henning von Tresckow, a senior army officer, contrived to have a parcel put aboard an aircraft that would be taking the Fuhrer from a meeting back to his command centre. Henning had constructed a bomb inside the package, but told a pal it contained two bottles of brandy which he wished to transport - for convenience's sake - aboard Hitler's plane.

Henning had been plotting this for some time. Whilst he could do most of the mechanical preparatory work himself, he realised that the elimination of the Fuhrer's regime required more than just his death. It needed a system standing by to usurp the power structure - so that another leading Nazi could not simply step into the breach. Hence the plotter had mustered a secret cell of supporters all motivated by the horrors of Nazi action and convinced that a different government was in Germany's best interests. These people were on stand-by to seize power in the minutes following the revelation that Hitler was no more. They had squads of soldiers briefed and willing to arrest the remaining Third Reich leadership. The nation would be assured of common sense prevailing, and peace would immediately be negotiated with the enemies of the empire.

The device was primed to explode once the plane had been in the air for half-an-hour. Henning watched his pal take the parcel on board; then Adolf stepped inside and the aircraft took off.

Now a tense time for Henning and his mates - thinking about their responsibilities in the days ahead. They've severed the head of the Nazi monster. One day, they might admit to their action – the deadly parcel – but that can wait. Immediately they must ensure a civilised regime replaces the despicable hierarchy. For two hours Henning paced up and down. He was changing history. He blew Hitler up in a plane. The world was about to turn. And he, Henning, was at its axis.

The phone rings. Hitler's plane has reached its destination, no problems. Business as usual. Never in the history of flight has the smooth landing of a plane been such bad news. Lots of swearing and thumping of walls, I'm guessing. Then Henning has to break the news to his hyped-up co-conspirators. *"Don't proceed. The target remains intact."*

Doubtless more swearing and thumping, but a degree of relief in some quarters – which is what Moorhouse detects around various failed endeavours. The instigators were glad they had tried, but relieved they did not have to tackle the enormous consequences. Meanwhile Henning got another pal to extract the dangerous parcel from the Fuhrer's offices. Turned out that a fuse hadn't worked - a tiny hiccup of gigantic significance.

A later revolutionary attempt sees a would-be assassin on a plane contemplating how his forthright action has changed history. Claus von Stauffenberg was a well-respected officer who occasionally attended meetings chaired by the top man. Claus hated Hitler, and all the chaos and pain he had caused. The angry officer always carried a briefcase to meetings and, because he was so well thought of by the hierarchy, he was not required to have his case searched. Perfect.

Like Henning, Claus had contemplated the consequences. He had a gang of supporters standing by to take command of the empire the moment Hitler was kaput. Now there was a lot of fiddling around with the briefcase and its contents – testing, experimenting. Claus even went to one of Hitler's meetings with the bomb in his case, then walked out with it again – just to check that it was possible to do that. Yes, why didn't he just set the thing off when he was in the same room as Hitler and be done with it? If only.

Instead, he practiced a lot. Then the day came when the real thing would happen: 20th July 1944 – six weeks after the Allied invasion of Normandy. He'd set the timer to go off just minutes after he left the room. What could go wrong?

As he exited the building, Claus heard the bomb explode. Wow! He hurried on to the airport and jumped on a plane for Berlin. He was going to rendezvous with his co-conspirators and set about taking over the levers of power.

So Claus now experiences a psychological maelstrom similar to that of Henning's fifteen months earlier, evaluating his vital place in the narrative of the Second World War: Who won't always remember where they were when they heard Hitler copped it? *"From the ashes of the Third Reich, let us henceforth erect a new Germany, a new Europe, within which all peoples can play a valued role - even Britain, which might like to join us in forming a common market."* - Claus surely worked on such speeches as the flight approached Berlin. And, of course, we know how this story ends. The bomb did not do its job. Yes, it went off, but not near enough to Hitler to kill him.

Claus hopped off his plane and joined his pals at HQ to announce they could commence the seizure of the troubled empire. But the gang wanted independent confirmation that the Fuhrer was a goner. Claus now lied to them, saying he had been nearby when the bomb went off and had seen Hitler's inanimate body being removed by rescue workers. The maniac was definitely dead. But Claus couldn't rally them. They'd got cold feet. And now someone's on the phone. *"Oh my God, it's Adolf"*, who was – surprise, surprise – ranting about traitors in his midst. He had survived the briefcase bomb.

Some plotters ran off, others were rounded up, including Claus. That evening, he and three more traitors were court-martialled and taken to face a firing squad. Claus didn't last the day.

So much for those fancy speeches he'd sketched out on the plane. What a flight - the tension, terror, triumph thundering through your head when you think you've killed Hitler and will go down in history as the hero of the western world. Instead, it's curtains for you, whilst the bastard marches on.

Spaghetti hoops

1944 saw the Allies edge their way up Italy, watched, helped or hampered by locals who often weren't sure whose side they ought to be on. Some Italians bore bitter grudges against their previous compatriots and undertook furtive action to make German lives difficult or short. Sabotage raids were applied to Luftwaffe-held airfields; assaults were made on Nazi air crews relaxing in local trattoria.

A proportion of Italian airmen chose to join the Luftwaffe in attacking the new intruders, while others threw their lot in with the Allies; though generally allocated tasks that avoided them having to bomb domestic locations.

The Germans' job was to not move an inch backwards. Instead they hunkered down, with a resolve that it is difficult for a civilian in peacetime to fathom. For days on end they might be hammered by bombs from above, interspersed with head-on artillery fire, yet they did not collapse in bloody chaos or back off. A dozen German soldiers might spend long hours jammed into reinforced concrete pill-boxes while ordnance shook the ground around the structure. The moment a bombardment eased off, those men would be back in business deploying their weaponry against Allied lines.

The Axis powers had lost 1,000 planes in Sicily, and replacements were slow in coming because, as well as that long peninsula poking down into the Mediterranean, the Third Reich had its eastern and western fronts to service. At the start of 1944, the Germans could only muster 500 planes to hold Italy against 7,000 Allied craft, which were supported by a third of a million air personnel. The Luftwaffe did a formidable job with the resources available. However, new radioguided missiles clamped below some aircraft fuselages proved horribly erratic, some exploding the moment they left the ground.

Goering decided his pilots weren't trying hard enough, and pulled a cross-section of them back to Berlin for court-martialling, to set an example to the others. Roman soldiers would have recognised this random application of punishment. It was also applied by the Nazis to Italians living in towns where any evidence of counter-insurgency emerged: decimate the natives - kill one in ten villagers so that no-one will make trouble again.

The Mediterranean Allied Air Force pummelled German-held airfields and eliminated hundreds of planes, only occasionally decanting ordnance in wrong places. The Luftwaffe managed a few spectacular assaults, not least on Corsica when 35 planes blitzed Allied airfields damaging 60 craft and killing two dozen personnel.

The Allies massively bombed Cassino to punch a way forward, but this created mountains of rubble which made streets impassable. And still the Germans fought back relentlessly, resourcefully. In response, 15,000 bombs might be dropped in an hour to try to dislodge defenders.

Across two summer months the Allies lost more than 400 planes to flak while flying 100,000 sorties. But air superiority eventually removed almost all the Luftwaffe from the skies above the vineyards, allowing American generals to re-assign anti-aircraft units to artillery work.

While trying to kick out kernels of fearsome resistance around Rome, it was inevitable that a few bombs would accidently arrive on Vatican property. In case anyone got the wrong impression, Allied press officers pointed out that lots of air crew were practicing Roman Catholics.

Made in Japan

'Many have chronic dysentery, and almost all show chronic fatigue states. They appear listless, unkempt, careless, and apathetic with almost mask-like facial expression. Speech is slow, thought content is poor, they complain of chronic headaches, insomnia, memory defect; they feel forgotten, worry about themselves, are afraid of new assignments, have no sense of responsibility, and are hopeless about the future.'

- a doctor's description of American airmen who had spent too much time stuck on grim little islands in the South Pacific – clearly at odds with the spirits of the film of the same name. How come?

The real-life airmen had been facing enemy pilots who showed no fear of collision or any other consequence. This was the fundamental problem in fighting the Japanese, who persevered whatever the outcome, seeing honour in dying for their Emperor. What could you do in the face of such madness? Out-number them with bigger, better machines and well-trained, generously-supported personnel.

Mitsubishi had produced a great fighter aircraft: the Zero - capable of 370 mph and five hours in the air. However, when the Americans first examined a crashed Zero they discovered the airframe was constructed 'like a fine watch', which meant, unlike Spitfires or Mustangs, the machines took a long time to put together. Japanese factories could only turn out 200 a month; not enough for the rate they were disappearing across the Pacific. And all that quality finish did not offset the fact that the Zero easily caught fire and so quickly exploded if hit by a few bullets; whereas western craft were built quicker and cruder but far more resilient. Allied airmen learnt not to tackle a Zero head on, but to swoop down on the Jap gem and blast off a few rounds before scarpering.

Zeros were especially handy aboard aircraft carriers. This was a great idea: a mobile airstrip for 50 planes that could be positioned anywhere in the ocean to batter something a few hundred miles away. Best to send up half your planes and keep the rest back to protect their floating home - a theory which seldom went to plan. Biggest snag with an aircraft carrier is the giant tank full of high octane aviation fuel. A proper airstrip locates its fuel depot well away from the action, but that's not possible on a boat. You're stuck with massive quantities of petrol sloshing about below the flight deck. Any sensible sailor skippering a carrier works on a core principle: whatever you do, keep flames away from the fuel. Okay in peace, but once you've taken your precious vessel into a war zone, heaven help you if someone heaves a bomb on your deck or stabs a torpedo into your side.

Another nasty factor when flying planes from carriers: many of the aircraft have wings that fold. There's a big hinge halfway along each wing so the whole thing can fit on to the lift to bring them up from the decks below. Occasionally, during a severe manoeuvre in the sky, the bolts locking the hinges in flight position gave way.

Shocked by Pearl Harbor, the Americans hated the vulnerability of US ships to aerial assault, and so determined to capture islands across the Pacific from which they could operate airstrips not subject to being sunk. Most manoeuvres above this ocean were modest affairs compared with the enormous air fleets battling across Europe day and night. And unlike that continent, here most of the action took place over water where, of course, everything was fluid - never clear where ships might steer; where best to locate your flak guns.

First substantial air combat had seen Chinese pilots working in tandem with Americans, using US-built aircraft to harry Japanese planes helping Imperial troops get deeper into China. The Japanese made life miserable for the natives in the territories they had invaded. Soldiers were trained to be ruthless against what they perceived as lesser creatures in China, Malaysia and Indonesia. Bayonet practice was sometimes conducted on captured locals to toughen up front line troops. Rising Sun brutality was not confined to prospective partisans; old people, women and children might be randomly assaulted and executed. At home this was passed off as removing alien species from the Empire; to other nations it was portrayed as preparation for returning Asia to the Asians.

In the first months of 1944, outings from US carriers saw off hundreds of enemy craft. Japanese occupiers of islands held very basic airfields, often without camouflage cover yet short of warning systems or anti-aircraft batteries. So a swift, surprise attack by Yank heavies could splatter 50 Imperial planes sitting round the strip. When the Americans got a foothold on an island, they sent teams to fake the construction of air strips at the far end - kicking up dust to attract in the

Zeros - so that the real new US airfield could be worked on 30 miles away without interruption.

Washington planners decided that the Mariana Islands - far north of Australia and well east of Hong Kong - could provide their big bombers with a launch platform for directly assaulting Tokyo. So American and Australian crews began strafing the Japanese airfields on the Islands in June 1944 - which initiated a major battle around the Philippines.

Tokyo's top aircraft carriers were sent to intervene. Amongst the fearsome ships was a stonker that had originally been shaped up as a luxury passenger liner for the Japan Mail Steamship Company. Most of its planes were immediately put in the air to challenge the US navy's carriers heading in from the east. On the first day of engagement, the Americans managed to see off 350 carrier-based enemy craft and most of the 50 Japanese planes operating from the Islands. Next day another 270 Imperial airmen splashed into the Pacific, not necessarily in one piece. US forces succeeded in sinking three enemy carriers. 100 American planes ditched in the sea, generally because they were out of gas. However, most of the Allied airmen were rescued during this largest aircraft carrier battle in history. And the Japanese converted mail liner sank, killing 250 aboard. It blew up when aviation fuel leaked from the storage tanks.

Bigger American planes now appeared from improved airfields in China to drop ordnance on Japan's domestic steel works, but their strike rate was poor with 15 out of 75 craft crashing. Two months later, the Americans made a second attempt to pummel a Tokyo steel plant from China and nearly 100 American airmen were lost. Those who managed to parachute from their burning plane might be shot at. If they landed alive, they faced torture and starvation before execution.

Meanwhile, on the new American airstrips on the Marianas, Zeros strafed dozens of big bombers on the ground. Mitsubishi churned out 11,000 Zeros during the war, but the latter half were flown by novices after all the well-trained men had bitten the dust.

Japanese industrial output had been just 10% of that of the USA in the 1930s. Tokyo commissioned ten aircraft carriers to pursue their Pacific ambitions; the USA produced 27 carriers in reply. No way was Japan going to succeed following the Marianas mauling. Had the Emperor sued for peace after three of his biggest boats sank, he might have saved the lives of six million people across Asia, including a million of his own citizens.

Japan's largest-ever aircraft carrier was launched in November 1944. 265 metres in length and weighing 66,000 tons, it was going to carry 50 rocket-propelled flying bombs to resist the American advance, but a US sub fired torpedoes into the Godzilla-league ship after it had been at sea for just ten days. 1,400 of those aboard drowned, including hundreds of civilian ship-yard workers still fitting out the internal structure. Those rescued were abruptly interned on a deserted island so news of the disaster would not leak out. The nautical monster did not prove to be a great machine made in Japan.

Another day, another challenge

After Hitler's insane invasion of Russia, Britain's Fighter Command undertook small scale, short raids into north-west France. The Hurricanes and Spitfires could be an occasional irritant at railway yards, army camps or munitions factories, but there was plenty of opposition resisting these intrusions. In the first five months of 1941 more than fifty Fighter Command pilots were lost over France. Between June and September, the fatalities jumped to 300.

Some Spitfires were fitted with an auxiliary fuel tank to increase their range. This was sculpted on to the underside of the port wing, but it seriously affected the handling of the aircraft. The imbalance of weight combined with the mismatched wing surfaces meant pilots struggled to fly their craft in a straight line, and the experiment was abandoned.

On 27th September 1941, ten Fighter Command aircraft had been lost on a single harassment raid of enemy ground facilities. Then the Command was supplied with a new American plane, the Bell Airacobra, which failed to behave as promised in the brochure. After just four outings, the RAF withdrew it from service.

The well-intentioned sorties into continental air space remained problematic and painful. On 8th November, during attacks on Lille, nine Command craft were downed and seven pilots died. Across 1941, the RAF lost 560 fighters on daytime operations, and 200 more planes in other arenas; whereas the Luftwaffe only suffered 200 losses altogether on its western front.

In April 1942, the Luftwaffe undertook their Baedeker raids on British centres of cultural heritage. RAF Fighters attempted to thwart these assaults but with limited success.

From January to May '42 the Command lost nearly 300 aircraft on daylight raids into France. On 19th August, Operation Jubilee was mounted on Dieppe - a brave attempt by the Allies to gain a foothold on continental Europe - but the Germans vigorously repelled these endeavours, Fighter Command losing 100 aircraft and 50 pilots. The same month saw the start of American bombing missions against the German empire setting off from East Anglia. This required British Fighter squadrons escorting as far as possible - which was not very far - into enemy air space.

The Command tackled all responsibilities with courageous determination, though was frequently dismayed at the level of losses - which mounted to 500 planes across the various theatres during 1943 - until November, at which point Fighter Command was formally disbanded. The squadrons were then split into two segments: one designated as the Air Defence of Great Britain, the other allocated to 2nd Tactical Air Force to support British and Canadian invasion troops.

A week after D-Day the first doodlebugs appeared over Kent, and ADGB was tasked with intercepting them: flying towards the V1s to shoot them down, or tip them off course with a flick of the wing. Several pilots became very proficient with this real-life arcade game. Their flight logs noted dozens of 'destroyed bugs'. Just as well, for the Germans were launching around a hundred a week.

Then in September along came the V2, conveying a ton of explosive. A thousand were propelled toward Britain over the next six months and RAF planes could not stop them. AA batteries might pick off a few, but most came down randomly, causing hell and pain to those who could not run away fast enough.

Eleven months after its demise, Fighter Command was re-instated as an institution, replacing the ADGB and assigned to escorting Bomber Command raids over Germany. Of course, few of the airmen now in the cockpits had any personal experience of the Battle of Britain. Such was the nature of the attrition of those times.

Red skies

'In the terrible years of the Great Patriotic War, I swear to you my country, and to you my party, to fight to the last drop of blood and my last breath – and to conquer. Forward to victory. Glory to the Party of Lenin.'

... the declaration of intent from newly-created elite forces being mustered to defend Russia, among which were a new generation of formidable airmen and women. The time had come to move from quantity to quality; yet quantity was always critical across a country 4,000 miles wide.

Stalin always treasured the May Day parades which included a fly-past of his latest bombers, fighters and support craft; even prototype helicopters. Behind-the-scenes, Moscow was working on eight-engine whoppers capable of crossing the continent to assault Japan. In the 1930s, the Russians had managed to embrace French and Italian designers, while American and German engines were purchased - not least BMW power units. As well as putting in an appearance in the Spanish Civil War, the Soviets had sold 400 of their aircraft to the Republicans, and when Japan assaulted Mongolia in 1938, Stalin assigned 1,000 craft to resist the invaders.

But many early Russian planes were alarmingly unreliable; some so treacherous that pilots occasionally refused to climb aboard. Radios were rudimentary and often had to be supplemented with hand-signals or flares to alert fleets as to what they should do next.

After the aircraft factories were re-located eastward, quality control problems plagued production. However air and ground crews alerted the makers to inadequacy – including, occasionally, screws hammered into engine block joints when threads failed to match.

By the end of 1943 Stalin claimed his forces had eliminated 60,000 German aircraft for the loss of 40,000 of their own. By 1944 the Russians could deploy 13,000 planes; and in that year their factories delivered 18,000 new fighters. Through the war, the USA provided their ally with 15,000 craft; Britain contributed 5,000, including 1,000 Spitfires. But the most critical aircraft for Russia was all their own work: a slow, heavy, armour-plated machine designed to destroy enemy tanks. Awkward to manoeuvre, unable to fly high, the beast was armed with big rockets for launching in front of German Panzers. 1,000 were manufactured each month and despite a high attrition rate they proved decisive around Kursk.

The Soviets mustered 6,000 planes for their 1944 Belorussia assault to bash the Germans back into Poland. Alongside help from French, Czech, Ukrainian and Polish air squadrons, the Russians worked their bombers in shifts, one crew manning them by day, another at night.

Stalin could not persuade the Americans to supply him with a fleet of Super-Fortresses, but as luck would have it a couple of the great US planes were forced to land on Soviet territory following a raid on Japan. Russian engineers took the machines apart and used the formula to build their own version within a few years.

Collaboration with the Americans generally worked well, but when US bombers attacked a Berlin oil plant in June 1944, then continued on to Russia for re-fuelling, pursuing Luftwaffe planes were not intercepted by Soviet defenders. This enabled the Germans to strafe the bombers when they reached their designated airfield, so destroying 40 planes and igniting half a million gallons of petrol - which killed 25 Russian fire-fighters and lit the sky red.

Hush hush

There's nothing worse at work than making a big mistake and not being sure whether to reveal this to your colleagues and/or your boss, or hope no-one has noticed. We all know that feeling.

However bad your blunder, it will not have been as wince-making as that of a fellow called Bernard, one of many BC Lancaster gunners taking another unpleasant night journey to somewhere in Germany on 19th September 1944. By now, the bombers were often escorted by Mosquitos - smart planes which could swiftly see off enemy aircraft – making a vulnerable Lancaster gunner feel marginally more at ease in those hostile foreign skies.

Bernard's Lanc had reached the target area okay and released its deadly cargo. Now the boys were on their way back over Holland - where maverick Luftwaffe fighters might be lurking. Thank goodness those Mosquitos were out there somewhere. You could seldom see the

Mossies in the dark, but in theory they were nearby, scouting the skies for enemy activity.

But Bernard took nothing for granted and did not relax even after many hours of cramped, cold peering into blackness. He kept his eyes peeled. And suddenly his worst fears were confirmed. Looming up from nowhere was an aircraft. What was it? So hard to see in the dark. A Junkers maybe? Those German machines had far better weapons and could see off a British plane before its gunners could point their lousy pea-shooters in the right direction.

Bernard had a fraction of a second to be decisive. The fate of his plane was at stake. It was all in his hands. At any second the other craft could blast him and his mates out of the sky. So Bernard squeezed his triggers and mercifully the guns worked. He got off a spray of rounds into the front of the enemy machine, which immediately swung away. Looked like a Junkers, and it was going down. But as it fell away, Bernard noticed something about it that reminded him of ... a Mosquito.

Now Bernard's skipper is on the intercom wanting to know what's happened. *"Seen him off, boss. One of those damn Junkers. Reckon he's done for."* Stuff like that. All the crew congratulate him for his audacity; swift effective action. But was it a Junkers?

The BC lads get back to base and report for de-briefing. Bernard explains how he saw the German plane and managed to squirt off rounds that seemed to make it fall out of control. Lots of free beer for this gunner, no question.

Through the night, other planes from the mission returned and intelligence officers gathered the data on what happened to each crew.

Of course, it can take weeks to account for every man and aircraft that did not get back each night. Only some time later, the audit on that evening's mission confirmed that one of the escort planes had been shot down over Holland - a Mosquito, piloted by someone very special: Wing Commander Guy Gibson – Gibson, the Dambuster; Gibson, the national hero.

On the same night when Bernard had blasted that menacing Junkers out of the dark sky, Gibson's Mosquito had been shot down. Was it definitely Gibson? Yes, because the celebrated pilot had done something forbidden - hidden his identity tag in his sock. When the

Dutch found his body they discovered the tag, and so buried him in a marked grave.

The RAF eventually received confirmation of his death overseas. This was such a terrible blow to the Force, and the nation, that two months passed before Air Marshall Harris informed Gibson's Squadron, requesting that the news did not go beyond the officers' mess. The loss stayed secret until early in 1945 when prospects of Allied victory ahead had reached a point whereby Whitehall considered the country would not be too demoralised to hear of the demise of the great Guy Gibson.

Meanwhile, Bernard became increasingly convinced he had made a dreadful mistake. Yes, he swigged down those beers, but tried to cast off the congratulations.

After the war, Bernard lived with the anguish of his horrible secret. In his old age, he tape-recorded his recollections of that terrible night. His widow later played the tape and learned of the burden her husband had kept to himself for fifty agonising years.

War-tested'

'The invasion of France and Italy was made possible by the enterprise and engineering skill of designers and craftsmen in our factories and workshops.'

No small claim by Gilmans - 'pioneers in industrial flexible drive equipment'- from Smethwick, near Birmingham, in their advertisement in the 9th November 1944 edition of 'Flight', the 'Official Organ of the Royal Aero Club'. The weekly publication contained commercial messages and editorial coverage of the state-of-play and prospects across the British aeronautical industries. Vickers-Armstrongs devoted a page to proclaiming 'Dive-Bombing Spitfires Help to Drive Germans from Coast', but much display advertising showed businesses supplying the military now emphasising their capacity to contribute to a future peacetime economy. Blackburn Aircraft's "war-tested" Cirrus engines were:

'... proving their worth in spite of exceptional difficulties. They have operated throughout France, Africa, Sicily, Italy and now in France again, often in desert conditions, rarely with hangar protection and with the minimum of maintenance. Tomorrow, when the clubs get going again and the air is free, the sturdy Cirrus units will be available for private and business aircraft in a handy range of sizes.'

Rumbolds of Kilburn explained:

'The skill and manufacturing capacity in light alloy manipulation... are at present tied to the war effort but the project department is ready to investigate... schemes for the passenger arrangements in aircraft of any category.'

The Bristol Aeroplane Company took space to announce they had dedicated their Piccadilly showroom to a display of parachutes. Meanwhile, at London's Devonshire House visitors could view a dented and charred (and presumably disarmed) example of a flying bomb, in a display designed to encourage donations to the London Federation of Boys' Clubs: 'The cine film showing bombs being hit by ack-ack is a real thriller.'

The editorial pages commenced with praise where due:

'All branches of the Royal Air Force are doing such fine work every day and all day that there is a danger that the nation may become blasé. That in so many of its operations the Royal Air Force has to strain aircraft and crew to the utmost is too often overlooked entirely, or at any rate insufficiently appreciated.'

'Flight' evaluated newspaper coverage of Bomber Command's attack on the Tirpitz in a Norwegian fiord on 29th October:

'Generally speaking, the Press did not make a great deal of this amazing operation... one of the most astounding ever executed by the Command. The Lancaster bombers must have been carrying a considerable overload in order to be able to cover 2,400 miles each with a bomb load of 12,000 lbs. Not only must the take-off have been difficult, but the Rolls-Royce Merlin engines must have kept running at somewhere near full power for the whole of the awkward flight. We on-lookers can only marvel and say: "well done, Bomber Command; well done, Avro; well done, Rolls-Royce."'

A few pages on, admiration for the accuracy of Mosquito crews in pummelling a Gestapo HQ in Denmark:

'In those buildings were housed the Gestapo records, which would enable the organisation to seize such Danes as they considered dangerous. Most of those papers were, it is hoped, destroyed; and it may also be hoped that a goodly contingent of Gestapo villains were in their offices when the bombs fell.'

There was appreciation for recent Allied bombing of Cologne, now just a few miles behind the American battle line: 'for all practical purposes, Cologne has ceased to exist'. Readers were advised that the Super-Fortress flights from India to bomb Japanese installations in Singapore docks was the longest daylight raid yet undertaken by military aircraft.

Air Commodore Frank Whittle was pleased the first use of the jet-propelled fighter had been to destroy flying bombs, but hoped the products of his work could do more to serve the causes of peace. Air Training Cadet Leonard Wells of Cumberland had been awarded a British Empire Medal for his rescue of a pilot from a burning aircraft which crashed near where he was at work on a farm. The young man climbed on the wing of the blazing machine and dragged the pilot from the cockpit, thus saving his life.

Reports from the Aeronautical Society's conference on civil aviation recognised that the training of future station managers was a difficulty:

'They had to be able, in addition to their ordinary work, to entertain kings, ambassadors and people of every condition.'

Another participant could visualise:

'... a sort of Continental mail order house which could deliver daily and in a few hours anything which a customer anywhere in Europe ordered'.

'News from Inside Axis and Enemy-Occupied countries' revealed that the Luftwaffe were closing down training schools and sending cadets to help on the ground on the Russian front, while Berlin boffins had developed a fluid that might enable airmen see better in the dark.

A photograph of Lancasters on a runway, 'each about to carry bombs to Ruhr cities', is captioned: 'Five ton lorries'. Alongside, Service Aviation Announcements listed Promotions, Appointments and Awards, including Acting Squadron Leader G. Campbell who had a Bar added to his Distinguished Flying Cross for his contribution to an August operation against enemy facilities in France:

'Despite heavy anti-aircraft fire the attack was pressed home with good results. Shortly after the bombs had fallen the aircraft was struck. It immediately became almost uncontrollable and height was lost rapidly. Petrol poured from the pierced tanks, and the starboard engine caught fire. The situation seemed hopeless. Coolly and skilfully however Campbell effected a crash landing. As the aircraft touched down, it burst into flames. All the crew with the exception of the top gunner had got clear. Without hesitation Campbell entered the wreckage in order to release his comrade. Unfortunately he had succumbed. The brave pilot displayed conduct in keeping with the best traditions of the R.A.F.'

This edition of 'Flight' lists 210 recipients of a DFC; plus 66 people awarded a Distinguished Service Medal. Below this is printed the week's Roll of Honour: the Air Ministry regrets to announce Casualties "in action" due to flying operations against the enemy; as well as: "on active service", including ground casualties due to action; and, in addition, non-operational flying casualties, fatal accidents and natural deaths.

The alphabetical listing (name, rank and medals) of RAF victims shows 132 killed in action, 229 missing; 76 killed on active service. Next, losses for the Air Forces of (on this occasion) Canada, Australia, South Africa, New Zealand, the Women's Auxiliary Air Force and the Air Transport Auxiliary: more than 200 further casualties. All merely part of the price, in just one autumn 1944 week, for edging the country towards a conclusion to hostilities. So much for a sense of operations coming to an end; the whole thing almost over.

Of war-tested survivors, what prospects ahead? In the classified advertising, we find:

'R.A.F. pilot, 4,000 hours, singles/twins; 2,500 hours instructing; interested in post-war employment; age 35. Box 7060.'

Good luck to him.

Sieg Heil

A giant swastika symbol created by Luftwaffe aircraft flying in formation over a Nazi rally had delivered a chilling wartime newsreel image across the cinemas of the world. Below, Hitler smirks at this indicator of prowess; Goering gloats at his Force's daring demo. Capable of stunts like this, why shouldn't the Third Reich conquer the world?

After one Messerschmitt was shot down by an RAF fighter in Belgium, the Brit flew overhead in order to assess the results of his 'kill' and saw the German pilot clamber from his cockpit then fire his pistol up at the passing British craft like a crazy comic book character. Despite maniacal determination, the German Air Force eventually declined in effectiveness. The assault on western Europe in May 1940 had caused the loss of 20% of the force. The Russian invasion halved capacity. By the autumn of 1944, 15% of Luftwaffe's front line flyers were being lost each month, and the ability to replace crew and machines was limited.

A quarter of a million German homes had now been destroyed, 2 million badly damaged. Half a million Italians were forced to work on repairs; rubble used to build barriers round abandoned neighbourhoods to keep out looters, who would be shot on sight. Lime was sprayed on bodies in the streets to inhibit the spread of disease. There were now five million evacuees across Germany – some moved by the state, the rest on the run from danger. They all needed water, food and shelter, and were too exhausted to challenge the regime.

Along the way, the Jewish population had been stripped of their belongings, their dignity, their identity. Transported like cattle – but worse – to faraway compounds; no longer people with civic and commercial roles. To be hounded by functionaries immune to decency; indifferent to suffering, shock, screams.

Families were broken up, herded by gender into queues assigned for mass murder chambers; their bodies then removed by work parties picked from the stronger arrivals – those able to carry, dig and bury, for a few days or weeks at least – all facing gun barrels poised to eliminate them should they resist.

Heinz Knoke's recollections underline his obsessive commitment to the advance of the Reich, not least due to his love of its leader:

'I do not suppose the world has ever known a more brilliant orator. His magnetic personality is irresistible. We listen to the spell-binding words and accept them with all our heart. We have never before experienced such a deep sense of patriotic devotion towards our German fatherland. Every one of us pledges his life in solemn dedication to the battles which lie ahead.'

By the spring of 1944 Knoke had accumulated twenty-five 'kills' of enemy aircraft, but on 29th April an American Thunderbolt brought him down. Wounded, he clambered from the wreckage and was taken to hospital. A fortnight later, as he began to recover, he was told the Allies had arrived on the beaches of Normandy:

'Every European fighting the Asiatic hordes in the East has been stabbed in the back by the invasion of the West.
'

Then he learnt of the assassination attempt on his Fuhrer:

'A wave of intense indignation sweeps through the German people. What could be the motive of the conspirators? The very existence of the Reich is at stake. On its survival depends the delivery of Europe from the threat of Bolshevism.'

However, the injured pilot recognised 'follies and excesses':

'Despotism without conscience has been revealed among the Nazis in the background around Hitler. Disgusted and indignant, the German fighting soldiers and officers turn away from those whose brutal war crimes and atrocities are now exposed. These criminals, whose activities were as a rule restricted to the concentration camps and labour camps in rear defence areas, have dishonoured the name of Germany.'

By August the ace was back on duty, but noted:

'The German Fighter Command is slowly bleeding to death in defence of the Reich; our cities and factories are being razed to the ground practically without opposition with deadly precision by the British and Americans.'

He was transferred to Czechoslovakia where partisans blew up his car, further injuring him:

'Each time there are some who do not return, but there are never any questions or complaints. I am more than willing to go out and fight again.

With the task completed and our homeland free once more, we can pay fitting tribute to the memory of our heroes and comrades.'

Knoke survived to write his book, then entered politics - for a Nazi-type party which was declared illegal in 1952 because of its racist agenda.

The Reich Ministry of Public Enlightenment and Propaganda portrayed Allied bombing as instigated by Jews in the west, manipulating politicians and the armed forces. 400,000 German citizens died from that campaign, alongside 60,000 foreign workers. Half a million were maimed and 50% of buildings in major urban areas were destroyed.

So much for the swastika.

Where is this going?

In October 1944 the German town of Duisberg logged its 2,000[th] visit from RAF planes. Surely they had had enough? Photo-reconnaissance flights identified where the damage had been done and where there was more to do. Many of the hairy picture-gathering outings were from Membury, now a service area on the M4 motorway. One in eighty photo trips got shot down, some by the new German jet planes that could zoom up high and pick them off.

Army veterans have told me about moments of drama, perilous action and shocking violence from their front line action. But they also reveal long stretches of time when they and their colleagues weren't doing much. They were awaiting orders, maybe on exercises. Months, even years, might go by before they would be in hearing distance of enemy forces. For air crew, it was not like that. Because every time you took off you were in danger. Every mission tackled by every pilot presented a life-threatening challenge. Some historians allege there were some hopeless operations by airmen: missions which had little prospect of success, and instead subjected valuable personnel to unwarranted danger. But I am not inclined to consider any air service as unnecessary. Each time a plane took off with the aim of reaching opposition targets, the enemy were required to evaluate that intrusion. Could they deter the attempt, and if so how? What might happen next? Which forces might be deployed in the wake of this endeavour? Where could resources prevent further assaults?

I don't think there were any futile flying gestures by the RAF or USAAF during World War Two. Some operations were patently less successful than others, but every flight to challenge the enemy obliged the Axis commanders to take account of that threat; to fight back immediately or later deploy additional assets at that location. No man or machine in the Allied air forces was expendable, but it was sometimes imperative to commit a craft wherein its chances of survival might be grimly small.

In 1940, British aerial endeavour demonstrated that its empire was not defeated, and that message got through to the Americans and Russians, while it was also recognised across Europe by millions living under subjugation of the Nazi regime. Every Allied airman's death contributed to the depletion and defeat of their enemies.

Germany had been manufacturing eleven different types of military aircraft. By 1944 that number had jumped to 27, while fighter speeds had risen from 340 mph to 540; maximum altitudes had increased from 34,000 feet to 41,000. Yet if one imagines that the devilishly cunning Luftwaffe had the capacity to appear suddenly at any airfield and there cause havoc while our boys were still in their bunks, note that throughout the war the important air base of Duxford in Cambridgeshire did not receive any attacks.

By 1944, the German aircraft industry - despite all the bombing - consisted of three million square metres of air frame production inside reinforced underground factories; elsewhere was even more space for making aero engines. In this year, they turned out 38,000 new planes - their biggest annual quantity - most destined for a short life on the eastern front. Meanwhile, Bomber Command decanted 200,000 big bombs. By now the RAF was beginning to retire airmen who had clearly done more than their share. A bunch of Poles who had admirably flown British kites for several years immediately signed up to American units near Norwich to continue the Allies' cause.

Through the summer, the Allies deployed 14,000 planes in western Europe, while the Luftwaffe could only assign around 1,000 for its defences. But there were still many harrowing outings. Five raids were made by BC on the city of Stuttgart. On the final occasion the

Luftwaffe shot down 39 of the attackers, 8% of the total. On 20th July, nearly 14% of BC bombers sent to attack the Homberg oil plant failed to return. 28th July: 300 BC bombers hit Hamburg but 7% were lost. Similar losses a fortnight later at Brunswick, then at Russelheim. Then on 12th September, 240 BC crews managed to kill 10,000 people in Darmstadt and make 70,000 homeless.

A September edition of the Kent Messenger pointed out that the county had suffered more doodlebugs than London. The capital had received 2,200 while Kent was peppered by 2,400. A map showed the location of each weapon's impact; the greatest density between Folkestone and Hythe, where 125 bugs plunged down, though not all exploding.

A Daily Telegraph journalist, Edmund Townsend, was reported missing after baling out of a blazing bomber whilst dropping supplies to troops at Arnhem. For several weeks he lived:

> "...the life of a fugitive from enemy search parties - probably the first war correspondent to have been shot down on his first flight with the R.A.F."

He hid in ditches, chicken sheds and pigsties, before joining 20 other men on the run to be secreted back to Allied lines by Dutch patriots.

Fleets of between 400 and 1,000 BC planes were frequently sent to sites in the Ruhr to further devastate already ruined locations. Meanwhile, Berlin received visits from small numbers of big Russian bombers flying from re-acquired Soviet airfields. In October, BC headed to Bergen to try to destroy U-boat bases, but in the process killed dozens of Norwegian civilians. In December, the Command flew to the town of Heilbronn to attack railway facilities, and killed 7,000 people in the area, which must have disrupted train schedules to some degree. Statistically BC were now doing a much better job. Air Ministry number-crunchers estimated 90% of bombs landed within 500 yards of their target. However, Professor Overy would later fundamentally dispute those figures.

In the autumn, Allied planes raided the Osnabruk airbase from where the scary, new-fangled Me262 jet fighter was making tentative flights. A lot of potentially menacing speed came to a sudden halt.

Own goals continued to deliver misery. In November, a Dakota ferrying wounded American and Polish soldiers back from north-west Europe to England crash-landed, killing all aboard.

What happened to Glenn Miller? No-one knows. In mid-December the popular band leader climbed into a plane at a small grass airfield outside London in order to join his colleagues in Paris, and was never seen again.

On Christmas Eve, Allied bombers set out to break up the German advance into the Ardennes. 2,500 planes dropped 5,000 tons of ordnance, but 21 Allied aircraft were shot down by American AA guns. Meanwhile, Bomber Command tried to deliver seasonal crackers to Cologne. In bad weather, 39 planes set out but six failed to return, two colliding en route. On Christmas Day the crew of a US bomber baled out over France, believing their plane was a goner. In fact, the stricken machine proceeded all the way to Wales before crashing. Plenty more Allied air accidents up to New Year with cold weather freezing vital parts mid-mission.

The Americans published their 1944 achievements in Europe: 360,000 sorties, dropping 400,000 tons of bombs while shooting down 7,000 German planes. So no-one would be surprised at their capacity and targets, the USAAF alerted people of its intentions by decanting across the continent a billion leaflets which in total weighed 1,700 tons.

RAF historian Mike Rossiter points out that by December 1944, due to improved performances and declining defences, German towns 'could now be almost effortlessly obliterated'.

Yet still those stooges needed to continue.

1945

WHEN WILL THIS END?

"The world must know we will never capitulate, and despite setbacks will never leave the road on which we have embarked. What millions of our people have to suffer in grief and pain is enormous, but so are their achievements. I also know that German cities will rise again to new splendour. The Nazi State will re-build everything wrecked within a few years."

... Hitler's New Year message.

Soon a series of extraordinary things would happen: the instigators of the conflicts would be vanquished; Britain's war-time leader would be voted out of office. Both the reviled European dictators would be dead; and a fine American President would pass away.

The world would soon discover disgusting, inhuman behaviour by fanatics, and would have demonstrations of new bombs which made all previous ordnance seem trifling. By the end of August, planet earth would be at peace, albeit shattered and fragile.

In January, the Daily Mail revealed that Germans were told that anyone failing to support the Nazi war would be "destroyed". It was:

'a chill warning to a half-defeated people that surrender could mean only worse miseries than to fight on blindly: therefore it was better to fight on. To what a sorry pass has Germany of 1945 been reduced. With all our difficulties, how Allied prospects shine and glitter by contrast.'

The Times reported that the American people begin their New Year confident as ever of ultimate victory:

'... enheartened by the turn in the tide of battle on the western front, but with much of the exuberance wherewith they began 1944 gone out of their optimism.'

Many in the USA had assumed the war would have ended by now. There was growing absenteeism in some of their munitions plants.

The Daily Mirror had front page news of a return visit by U.S. airmen to the French town of Nantes:

'This time they were laden with tons of candy and cake instead of tons of high explosive. They were hosts to 3,000 school children at a party. They held another party at an orphanage for 741 children – some of whom lost their parents in air raids.'

Bomber Command's New Year began with troubles: two Mosquitos destroyed on missions on 1st January, one on take-off; then five Lancasters crashed, two on take-off. On 6th January, 600 RAF bombers headed to Hanover and 30 were lost. But across the month, BC conducted 25 operations against German targets, consisting of 6,000 flights, and only 85 craft were lost - just 1.4%; the least painful ratio since mass missions began.

'War Illustrated' explained the force's new effectiveness:

'A Master-Bomber's responsibility is like that of a commander in the field. In an attack on a German industrial city, he ensures that the incendiaries are evenly distributed over the whole area and thus cause maximum destruction. When bombs demolish a factory, he makes sure that bombs to be delivered a few seconds later do not waste themselves on the same building.

'He stays over the target the longest, endures to the full the worst of which the enemy is capable, and must remain unflurried and coldly calculating to the very end... perhaps the toughest task of all. Thanks to this fighting "master of ceremonies" two or three hundred planes are achieving as much as a thousand bombers were doing not long ago.

'It is possible for the Western-based Allied bombers to attack whatever German defended urban stronghold the Red Army Marshalls may indicate for reduction from the air.'

Every day, British newspaper front pages now focused on events across western Europe – the edging forward of Allied men and machines. Valentine's Day was no exception - when the Daily Express allocated a small front page headline to:

DRESDEN GETS NIGHT RAIDERS

This was nothing special. The following day, the 15th, the Mail made brief reference to the RAF 'softening up' locations for Russian advances, whereas the Telegraph led with:

NON-STOP AIR BLOWS AID BOTH FRONTS
650,000 R.A.F. FIRE BOMBS ON DRESDEN

This was adjacent to a photograph of the remains of the town of Cleve, recently bombarded 'as a preliminary' to its capture by Allied troops. The Mirror declared:

GERMANY'S WORST AIR BLITZ
- 9,000 flights to aid two fronts.

All good news. Whereas the Express highlighted trouble in the Pacific:

THE HORROR OF MANILA
'Mass murder of men, women and children by Japanese.'

Underneath was a smaller headline:

GREAT RHINE-DRESDEN BLITZ

The Times found space for this news in the third column of its fourth page:

SMASHING BLOWS AT DRESDEN
– ATTACKS BY R.A.F. AND U.S.
'British and American bombers have struck one of their most powerful blows at Dresden, now a vital centre for controlling the German defence against Marshall Konev's armies advancing from the east. "There were fires everywhere, with a terrific concentration in the centre of the city," a Pathfinder pilot said.'

Next day, the Express again prioritised the Far East:

U.S. NAVY PLANES HIT TOKYO

Below this, a single column explained:

DRESDEN 'bombed to atoms'

'As the menace to Berlin grew last night, reports from both Allied and German sources told how Dresden, planned by the Germans as a "substitute capital", is dying. The German Overseas News Agency said: "Dresden is a heap of ruins. It has been smashed to atoms." Since Tuesday this city, hitherto almost untouched, has been carpeted by heavy and super-heavy explosives and incendiaries. The Germans went on to complain of the loss of art treasures and beautiful buildings. But the truth is that Dresden is a major city in the war effort. As a rail and road junction it has been used to pump German troops into counter-attacks against the Soviet army.'

The Mail ran a story headlined:

THE DEATH OF DRESDEN

… but devoted more space to MPs debating Transport Command flight crashes.

Next day, the Express created a verb from the east German name:

WEST WALL 'DRESDENED' BY LANCASTER FLEET

'Ruhr cities in the path of Anglo-American armies were blasted yesterday by R.A.F. and U.S. Eighth Air Force heavies.'

Here was a handy term for a fruitful outing. The paper noted that 50,000 people had perished in the last three days. The climax of attempts to overwhelm the Nazi regime was clearly approaching. A week later, readers were advised that the war had so far lasted 2,000 days. Who wouldn't want it over soon, no matter how? A fortnight on, the Express's Stockholm correspondent reported:

DRESDEN IS DEAD, NAZIS HOWL

'The Germans came out with a new line in propaganda screams today when the newspaper Das Reich printed a long article on 'The Dresden Catastrophe'. It gives a picture of bomb havoc never before equalled in a German publication. But the horror is laid on so heavily that suspicion is at once aroused. Dresden is represented as a purely cultural centre with no mention of its great war factories or its importance as a transport centre behind the Eastern Front. In the inner town not a single block of buildings remains intact or even capable of reconstruction. The town area is devoid of human life. A great city has been wiped from the map of Europe. Tens of thousands who lived and worked in the city are now buried under its ruins. Even an attempt at identification of the victims is hopeless. There were 1,000,000 people in Dresden at the time, including 600,000 bombed-out evacuees and refugees from the east. Today we can only speak of what once was Dresden in the past tense.'

Someone had added a zero to those figures. The Telegraph quoted the same report and provided some editorial context:

> 'The stranglehold is closing upon Germany's potential. Given fair weather, it will not operate much longer.'

More than 25,000 people died in the city. The British Deputy Chief of Air Staff had encouraged the endeavour by arguing that a series of heavy attacks "...may well result in establishing a state of chaos."

If anyone thought it unnecessary to press on relentlessly, a week after the Dresden missions, the Express presented readers with a front page map locating prison and civilian internment camps across Germany, some of which 'have already been overrun by the Russians'. We were yet to learn of conditions inside.

Ten days later, the diabolical PGG announced: 'The enemy air terror has reached inhuman proportions, and can hardly be borne.' But he could promise bigger V-weapon launches in retaliation, and declared:

> 'We smile at threats that our leaders will be brought to trial and the death penalty. If the enemy won, the suffering and sorrow which would befall our people would be so great that it goes without saying our leaders would go before them into honourable death.
>
> We are not ashamed of our setbacks. They only happened because the European West and the plutocratic-Jewish-directed U.S.A. covered the flanks of the Soviet rabble and today tie our hands. Otherwise we would be able at any time to crush Bolshevism.'

So hints of suicidal thoughts within the hierarchy. These would prove profound.

On 3rd March, the Express reported that Cologne 'had two blitzes yesterday in the mightiest daylight air assault on the west and east fronts... including the Red Army-objective cities of Dresden and Madgeburg'. So Dresden remained a target. The Opinion column of the paper proclaimed: 'The American air forces command the admiration of the world'.

Those Dresden ops of 13th and 14th February were merely another punch at Germany's staunch resistance to its invaders. The sorties were exceptionally light in terms of RAF casualties – just 40 British aircrew failed to return. But questions were later raised about the virtue and legitimacy of blasting refugees. Max Hastings describes it as:

'...the most futile and most distasteful phase of the bomber offensive, in which airmen disastrously damaged their place in history.'

'February 1945 marked the moment when far-sighted airmen and politicians began to perceive that history might judge the achievements of strategic air power with less enthusiasm than their own Target Intelligence departments.'

However William Chorley considered:

'... critics of Bomber Command have used Dresden as the stick to berate the actions of Harris and sully the achievements of thousands of aircrew who did so much to ensure that victory over a despotic regime would be accomplished whatever the cost.'

I will hereby defend the bombing of Dresden, because the assault further dismayed Hitler. The brutality, devastation, deaths and injuries imposed on the people in that location propelled the evil Fuhrer along a crumbling path of despair, driving him closer to the point when he concluded all was lost. Dresden surely shoved Hitler closer to suicide, which was what brought the war to an end. The vigour of the assaults may also have sown seeds for the huge Wehrmacht surrenders a few months later.

The destruction certainly demonstrated to Stalin that the west was doing its bit as he continued to press millions in uniform to fight their way towards Berlin. Soon after the Dresden missions, the Prime Minister's wife was invited to visit Moscow to meet military and medical representatives, and evaluate the results of Mrs Churchill's Aid-to-Russia fund which was equipping hospitals in Rostov that: "will stand as a permanent memorial to the united sacrifices of our two countries".

The eventual overcoming of the city did not attract much attention in the western press when it took place, perhaps because it occurred on VE Day. In The Times of 9th May, a single paragraph noted that Stalin considered the recently captured Dresden 'an important communications centre and a strong bastion in the German defences in Saxony.' '

A Guardian newspaper editorial in February 2015 reflected on the 70th anniversary of Dresden's darkest hour:

> 'The dilemmas that faced commanders in February 1945 were agonising. The raids would have devastating human consequences but they might help bring a devastating war to an end.
>
> 'New generations have a responsibility to ask how the Dresden raids or events like them can be justified and to reflect on what they say about us today. None of this is easy. What is not right is to quietly write a difficult episode out of the heroic wartime narrative that we prefer to pass on to future generations.'

Dresden was, tragically but simply, another of the appallingly high prices to be paid to help bring peace to Europe.

Made in America

Could a man be plucked up into the air by a hook on the end of a flying rope? The USAAF experimented with such a prospect as a means of retrieving lone servicemen stranded in hostile environments. Adaptations of parachute harnesses were fixed to loops of nylon strung between posts - so a plane flying very slowly could pass overhead to grasp the loop. The technique was trialled with sheep, the first of which was strangled by the wrench of strapping when it left the grass. Once the sheep trials were complete, a paratrooper volunteered to climb into the contraption. Lieutenant Doster braced himself, hoping the approaching plane was going slow enough not to jolt his legs off, yet not so slow as to stall with the sudden resistance. He was picked up in one piece, and winched into the aircraft, but it was concluded that such transport methods were best left to stunt events in peacetime.

Instead, the Americans, with help from Brits and Aussies, developed a team of pilots, working with very small planes, able to land and take off on minimal strips of cleared land. These proved invaluable in Burma for supplying outlying troops and extracting wounded men or spare materials. The noisy but versatile little kites were affectionately termed "jungle angels" by the guys whose lives were saved with swift journeys back to medical expertise.

The USA made many of the smallest planes and the biggest. Most formidable was the Super-Fortress, designed to carry a heavier payload far greater distances than its predecessors. Originally intended for battering Berlin, it was allocated to airfields in south-east Asia from where it could fly to the heart of Japan. But the craft needed massive support facilities and early models were plagued with performance problems. It could travel 3,000 miles, carrying 10 tons of ordnance at 200 mph, but required huge quantities of fuel to be flown to the relevant airfield aboard other planes.

How best to use this new tool which had cost $3 billion to prepare for battle? Always valuing scientific data, the Americans built a mock Japanese urban area in a Utah desert to practice dropping different bombs from different heights in different ways. Because the typical Japanese home was a flimsy affair – wood and paper walls – it was decided that incendiaries would be the most efficient way of disrupting the status quo across cities where there were few underground shelters to match those of Nazi Germany.

The Americans now copied RAF Bomber Command techniques – blanket, blind bombing of built-up areas. Firestorms removed most of the oxygen from the immediate atmosphere. People dived into rivers and canals, trying to stay below the surface, but the intensity of heat boiled the water and its contents. Huge proportions of the ordnance went astray. Like the RAF, formulae were applied to evaluate the scatter. At the start of the year, only about 20% of bombs landed within 600 metres of an aiming point. Mercifully, for those left below, the USAAF ran out of incendiaries by the end of March, and factories back in the States had to be contracted to produce fresh stocks.

Other US boffins had developed napalm - a neat means of hurling fire across streets abruptly. Another laboratory was making progress with thermite magnesium bombs that could burn through steel and thus destroy aircraft factories.

Japan began to run out of planes and pilots to inhibit the huge enemy craft, so well armoured that most Nippon guns could not make serious holes in them. Some Japanese airmen applied the kamikaze principle to the intruders, ramming the monsters before they travelled over domestic airspace.

American airmen unfortunate enough to bale out over the Japanese mainland faced a vicious reception; one group were taken to a university medical department and experimented on without anaesthetics, in order that so-called physicians could learn more about the human body's capacity to deal with various battlefield traumas.

The size and scope of the American economy - as directed by committed politicians - would eventually ensure the defeat of their oriental enemies. Early in the war, Britain had provided a haven for German Jewish scientists, including those working on nuclear physics. They had perceived the possibility of an atomic weapon, but applying their theories was far too costly for the UK; however American leaders were willing to facilitate this prospect, budgeted to come in a bit cheaper than the Super-Fortress program. So the scientists crossed the Atlantic to put future-changing ideas into practice.

The United States of America had financial and industrial capacity way beyond any of its allies or opponents. Dozens of their Super-Fortresses crashed on the Himalayas while trying to reach mission-ready runways in China; dozens more disappeared beneath the waves in the Pacific without ever releasing a bomb. Off Europe's Adriatic coast was a narrow emergency airstrip for ailing US bombers returning from outings to Austria and unable to reach southern Italy. Often there was no time to tow a damaged plane from the island's strip. Instead men would hack the machines into sections to make the runway ready for the next arrival. You needed a lot of dollars to so readily break up your own assets, knowing your colleagues would soon be taking delivery of many more mighty machines made in America.

Last gasps

Once Allied ground troops had pushed forward from the Normandy beaches, they could re-capture the airfields from where the Luftwaffe had been raiding England for four years. In retreat, the Germans tried to destroy any assets they could not extract. Buildings were burnt down or, worse, booby-trapped, and lots of holes were made in runways; but those cavities could be quickly filled. The RAF and USAAF soon began to utilise these facilities, which promised far shorter hops to enemy lines and beyond. Then Goering issued an ambitious New Year proclamation:

"We look to the future full of hope and confidence. We have new squadrons in the air, and already the first fruits of dogged endeavours by the Luftwaffe are maturing."

Next day, he despatched 800 aircraft on a mad dash to blast the new occupants of the airstrips. The RAF lost 200 machines on the perimeters; the Americans saw the destruction of 50 fighter craft. But several hundred Allied boys managed to get airborne and gave some intruders a bloody nose. And more misery lay ahead for the Luftwaffe crews which escaped: skimming back over the Wehrmacht front line they were shot down by twitchy German soldiers who took them for low-level raiders. The Telegraph declared:

LUFTWAFFE HITS OUT: LOSES 188 PLANES

Next day The Mirror revised the figure up to 364, and described it as:

'... the greatest loss ever suffered by the Luftwaffe in one day.'

The Mail's Colin Bednall explained:

"It remains safe to say that the Luftwaffe can no longer sway the outcome of the war, but it can continue to be a powerful nuisance from time to time."

Retreating from the Russians, German troops failed to destroy some key bridges over big rivers that had aided their escape but now potentially eased their opponents' way forward. The Luftwaffe had no huge bombers like those of the Allies, so they stuffed some of their large transport aircraft with explosives, then fitted a fighter plane on top, from where the pilot of the combo would do the driving. He would release the lower aircraft once it was aimed at those bridges. But the technique didn't work.

The German Air Force became bogged down by Nazi secrecy: decision-making kept under wraps; Goering failing to studying detail and co-ordinate policy. Some officers even used bugging equipment in departmental offices to try to identify associates' intentions.

Despite shortages of men, machines and fuel, small Luftwaffe units continued to display determination and skill. On 21st February, 14 Lancasters were sent to bomb the Dortmund-Ems canal, but encountered night-fighters, including Germany's top ace Heinz-Wolfgang Schnaufer, who shot down seven of the bombers in 20 minutes. Through his service, Major Schnaufer was credited with more than 120 British aircraft destroyed in action.

On 4th March, 450 BC planes attacked targets in Germany. As the 443 survivors flew for home they were chased by 100 night-fighters which shot down 20 craft. The Luftwaffe crews then strafed and bombed dozens of RAF airfields and anything else they could reach. The Daily Express offered a filtered version of the outcome:

'Last night, there was a raid by piloted planes on England. Twice a plane approached an inland town but was driven off. One raider dropped flares over a coastal district but they were soon shot down by ground defences. Another raider dropped a number of small bombs which smashed roofs and blew out windows. For the attack, which ranged from Northern England to the South, the Germans appear to have scraped together all the planes that they could spare. Eight of the enemy planes were destroyed by the R.A.F.'

Other German airmen were trying to fruitfully ride their wild jets to inhibit American bombers. They attempted to zoom up and release a big rocket from a tube below the wing. Chances of the projectile impacting were very low, but a few worked, which made US fighter squads even more determined to strafe German airfields and eliminate the alarming gnats.

One of the last successful bomb raids on England took place on Saturday 17th March, when a single Luftwaffe aircraft released ordnance that killed a dozen people below. Tuesday 20th was the final recorded visit by a Third Reich machine, which dropped a few bombs on to a deserted road and a farmer's field.

One German pilot approached an American-held airfield, avoided the flak, and landed. He was immediately surrounded by ground crew and told them he would be delighted to help the US in any way he could.

By April, the Luftwaffe was reduced to ramming American bombers. The theory was for the pilot to jump out seconds before impact. A hundred German airmen volunteered for these last ditch attempts to save the Fatherland. Radio communication of the flights was monitored in France – women's voices coaxing the men to complete the task that might help their families.

On 4th April, the Daily Mail reported that Goering had committed suicide following a "stormy" discussion with his boss. Not true. Ten days later (as discovered in Third Reich documents two years later), Hitler told planners:

> "The Luftwaffe are a lazy bunch – nobody does any work – with red tape everywhere."

On 18th April, the Mail highlighted Allied aerial raids on enemy airfields which accounted for the Luftwaffe losing 4,000 planes across the previous 17 days. The records reveal that Hitler now ranted:

> "The entire Luftwaffe Command should be hanged immediately."

At the end of the month, the Mail announced:

> HITLER SACKS GOERING

While the Telegraph reported:

> GOERING RESIGNS

… noting:

> 'Twice during his adult lifetime he has been detained in asylums as a lunatic.'

A week later, the Germans would formally surrender - at 8.am on Sunday 6th May. For some reason, a Luftwaffe pilot flew over the front line above Allied troops at Bremen ten minutes before the deadline and so became the last German pilot to die from western ground fire.

One way trip

All sorts of horrible accidents occur during the shocking minutes of interaction between opposing forces in combat. People do the wrong thing at the worst possible moment and the results are far removed from the text-book behaviour that was intended. So it was, when American sailors first saw a Japanese plane come soaring down towards the side of their ship at an angle and speed that meant it would never be able to swerve away from the hull, and instead would crash hard into the vessel – all very unpleasant, but within the bounds of ugly activity that servicemen had to expect out in the Pacific when encountering the enemy.

Only slowly did the US Navy identify a succession of incidents which indicated a pattern: Japanese planes that showed no intention of discharging ordnance before scarpering. Apparently, those at the controls were deliberately propelling their machines towards the opposition's assets.

Confirmation emerged from a German news agency towards the end of 1944, after Tokyo briefed its Berlin allies about new techniques to repel the Americans: pilots of the 'Divine Wind' squadron had damaged nineteen US warships east of the Philippines in just one week, using the 'air torpedo' method. They each rammed their plane - loaded with explosives - into an enemy battleship as close as possible to the waterline, so the hole in the side would cause the vessel to sink.

Divine Wind was a translation of Kamikaze, severe storms that had in the past destroyed fleets of Mongolian ships attempting to invade Japan. The Germans reported that the planes were like a 'V1 with a pilot', and hundreds of airmen with the necessary 'noble purpose and special training' were preparing for the 'hour of their victorious death'.

Here was a lousy prospect. Up until now the business of flying military planes had been sold on the notion that it was a highly skilled, prestigious profession which, if pursued with care and judgement in a reliable machine, could achieve marvellous things again and again. Only bad luck might stop those aboard returning to base and describing to colleagues their experiences on that outing. Instead, this scenario treated a one-way trip as a triumphant conclusion to an aviator's career.

The US army knew the capacity of the Japanese soldier to fight to the last in defending an island, a port or airfield. Now the navy realised the principle of surrender was not something easily achieved in the Orient. It was imperative to inhibit any Jap planes getting anywhere near the fleets. The 'crazies' needed to be eliminated, or at least disabled, well away from their intended destinations.

Amazingly, the Land of the Rising Sun persuaded more than 4,000 young men that killing themselves at the controls of a plane they had directed into the side of a US ship would be a fruitful way to advance the Imperial game plan. But the Kamikaze craze did not proceed as well as it should have. There was always a dignified ceremony on the side of the runway prior to take-off: a speech about glorious achievement and going down in history; the declaration of intent from the airmen, shored up with salutes and bowing. Then up and at 'em - though no guns, armour or parachute on the plane, and not enough fuel for a return journey. But, once men have left the ground, how can you be sure they will follow through? Some might toy with jumping out of the plane and swimming to safety. Therein lies a tiny prospect of survival; perhaps even seeing the relatives again. Sod the war, bugger the Emperor - if they could paddle a plank towards the nearest atoll, they might live for years in the jungle; maybe meet up with natives and go native. Better than whamming into maritime superstructures.

Not every kamikaze achieved the stated aim. Most failed to fly their clapped-out planes to the necessary destination due to malfunctioning, bad handling, or enemy interception. But enough of the suicide squads got through to make a disconcerting dent in the American presence. The aerial lunacy saw the sinking of more than 30 US ships and the drowning of nearly 5,000 sailors.

In order to continue with his vital war work, the commander of the Divine Wind brigade patently had a fundamental responsibility to look after himself. Occasionally he had to be flown to distant planning centres to discuss the next batch of one-way journeys. He was travelling to such a meeting as a passenger aboard a military aircraft when it encountered a US fighter, which shot it down, killing those inside.

Western newspaper cartoonists reached a point whereby making fun of foreign self-immolators seemed fair game. Several sketches contemplated how convenient it would be if the Japanese leadership took the same sword-to-the-stomach route out as had some of their defeated jungle generals.

One would-be kamikaze contributor was plagued with misfortune. His first attempt to make a suicidal flight saw him aboard a crummy old plane that could not even get off the runway. A few days later, he was waved off in another aircraft, but this developed mechanical problems so he made an emergency landing at an army base. A fortnight on, there arose another opportunity to do his bit, this time in the company of two others – reflecting the gruesome outfit's realisation that peer pressure in the air might better keep the boys concentrating on the purpose of their missions. This plane left base, then started to malfunction and came down in the ocean. The crew swam miles to an island where they hung around for months before being rescued. And guess what? By now the war was over. So their services and sacrifice were no longer required.

Not many kamikaze specialists lived to say they'd done three trips, all with return journeys. But the bigger picture shows that, after the Japanese chose to assault Pearl Harbor, they were on a one-way trip to defeat by the world's most powerful nation. By March 1945, the USA had shot more than 20,000 Japanese aircraft out of the receding Empire's skies.

Under wraps

On Saturday 6th September 1944 the British Government had advised the nation it could "stand easy" from flying bombs. The newspapers reported that RAF intervention techniques had been highly effective. Most notably, a single Mosquito pilot had chalked up the destruction of more than 40 V1 rockets on their way over the Channel: the menace of the dismaying arrivals had been overcome. The following day, in Chiswick, there was a massive explosion out of the blue, but no-one connected this with rockets. There had been no characteristic droning noise terminating ominously before the device descended.

The Times reviewed the history:

AFTER THE BOMBS

'In the most recent phase of the battle of London – the eighty days' flying bomb attack – it is safe to say that Hitler's newest engine of destruction entirely failed to achieve the purpose intended. One quarter of the missiles launched behaved erratically or went wide of the mark; only

2,300 crashed in the area selected. Nearly 3,000 airmen were lost in trying to inhibit the V1 which intensified the housing shortage. On average each missile completely wrecked ten homes and damaged 500 others, thus depriving Greater London of 107,000 homes.'

But the Chiswick explosion had been caused by the first V2 to reach the capital. Then, on 18th September, the newspaper reported that five children and four adults had been killed by 'a flying bomb' two days earlier; however the Air Defence of Great Britain had managed to destroy three other 'missiles'. This was on the same weekend that the R.A.F. had conducted its first formal commemoration of the Battle of Britain.

The parameters and potential of the new intrusions were kept under wraps. These Wehrmacht rockets travelled too high and too fast for British planes to nudge them off course. It was imperative to destroy the launch platforms. However, as the RAF became more proficient at damaging such sites, German army engineers became smarter at hiding the facilities from enemy view; transporting rockets on trucks, kept in woodland until launch time.

British politicians wanted the Allied troops now edging across the continent to turn their attention to these menaces, but the Supreme Allied Commander considered the progress of his armies towards Germany outweighed arbitrary loss of life on English soil. In desperation, huge navy shells were detonated in fields north of London, in the hope that spies would hear the bangs and believe these were V2s arriving at the wrong place. The secretly alerted German launchers might then recalibrate southward, which could take the disturbances into Kent countryside.

Through the winter, the impact of the V2s was shrouded in secrecy; then, in March 1945, a small front page article in the Daily Express was permitted:

FLYBOMBS SHOT FROM HOLLAND?
'It is possible that flying bombs launched against England on Friday night were new-style missiles of much longer range fired from ramps in North Holland. Anti-aircraft guns went into action and several were shot into the sea. Others were blown up in the air.'

But it was more or less impossible to knock a V2 out or away. At the bottom of page 3, by a Selfridges advert for 'Attractive Junior Frocks', was a discreet summary of recent descents:

'A 17-year-old boy standing on the edge of a reservoir was suddenly engulfed and suffocated. Nearly all the windows of a girls' school were broken and people in a neighbouring house were cut by glass. A bomb fell on allotments causing damage to houses, a public house and a hall. Six people were killed and many were made homeless when a number of small houses were demolished. Dozens of other houses were made unusable. The bomb fell near where a previous one had destroyed property.'

Fifty RAF planes were dispatched to Holland to eliminate rocket sites near The Hague, but co-ordinate errors meant ordnance was released at the wrong location and landed on civilian housing, destroying thousands of homes and killing 500 Dutch allies. The Air Ministry swiftly proffered apologies for a "deplorable catastrophe":

"The British people and, in particular the R.A.F., express their deepest regret for this terrible accident. The R.A.F will do their utmost to ensure that no such mistake shall occur again and, in their attacks on this indiscriminate rocket weapon which the enemy are using from Dutch soil, will do all they can to avoid risk to Dutch people."

Eisenhower now assigned troops to tackle the tormentors, and, on 6th April, the Express noted:

WEEK'S LULL: Is this the end?
'Britain passed yesterday its seventh consecutive day of freedom from air attack.'

Inside, the paper documented British civilian bomb casualties for the previous month: 792 killed, 1,426 injured; but no breakdown to isolate the V2 victims.

On 11th April, the Daily Mail reported that Canadians had captured their first V2 site. Then on 27th April, with the defeat of Germany close, newspapers were allowed to expose the bigger holes that the rockets had made on civilian life over the previous months. The Express front page included a large photograph of a horrible mess in Highgate on 27th March when the London suburb had received a rocket. Page 2 presented: V2, THE FULL STORY, by Basil Cardew, who explained that the worst rocket impact had been at a Woolworths store in New Cross in November 1944 when 168 shoppers had died. Second most destructive landing was in Stepney where 134 had been killed in March 1945. The same month saw 115 deaths in Smithfield Market and 52 in Deptford. In all, the rockets had hit 35 hospitals and 45 churches - all much worse than contemporary reports had indicated. Cardew acknowledged:

"There is no denying that Britain's defence experts had no counter to the 1,000-mile-an-hour robot which reached heights of more than 60 miles in the stratosphere."

England was not the only destination for V2 weaponry. As the Germans struggled to perfect their launch and trajectory mechanisms, many rockets commenced short, wobbly flights before punching down not far away. More than 5,000 Belgian citizens were killed by the abrupt landings. But, of course, the diabolical PGG kept such impacts under wraps.

Into the ground

'A delegation of at least one civilian and one disarmed soldier must await the Allied spearheads outside the town with a white flag. All mines must be removed before the Allied tanks arrive. The military commander must disarm his troops and hand them over with their arms.'

Procedural instructions for individual towns in the west of Germany - broadcast at the same time as the Dresden assaults were taking place to the east. Around one million German soldiers had already surrendered to Allied forces. A few weeks later, Churchill sent a confidential note to his Chiefs of Staff pointing out there was a danger that Allied ground troops advancing across Europe towards Berlin could find themselves bringing freedom to not much more than piles of rubble. He was concerned that 'we shall come into control of an utterly ruined landscape.' In fact, the armies were already encountering acres of ruins in many western German conurbations.

The Prime Minister's observation was seen by some as an attempt to distance him from the mass slaughter of civilians and refugees that the

Dresden outings had caused. He was pressed to publicly describe his concerns in a less critical manner, and so fashioned a revised version of his views: 'We must see to it that air attacks do not do more harm to ourselves in the long run than they do to the enemy's immediate war effort.'

But patently the more an enemy-held location was bombed, the easier it would be for ground troops to eventually occupy that place. On 2nd March, 700 Allied bombers yet again blasted what was left of Cologne to make it reasonably safe for the Americans to enter - by way of bulldozer - the remains of the city on the 6th.

Churchill popped over to examine the landscape for himself. Whilst there he was persuaded to undertake a photo-opportunity worthy of today's tabloids: an artillery unit invited him to chalk a note on the side of a shell they were about to launch towards enemy lines. The PM thought for a moment, then wrote 'Hitler – personally' on the casing, before it was loaded into a howitzer and blasted in the general direction of Berlin.

On Thursday 15th March, the Mail announced:
RAF's NEW TEN TON BOMBS BLAST THE RUHR
Lancaster Crews Report: 'Fountain of Debris'

Next day, the Express's Alan Moorehouse explained:
GERMAN G.H.Q. BOMBED
– 6,000 H.E. drop on the brasshats
'The British and American Air Forces are turning the whole Ruhr into a mass of rubble, and are isolating it from the war. After a night and day of cataclysmic bombing, the attack goes on again this afternoon. Our soldiers on this side of the Rhine can hear the German sirens wailing on the opposite bank and see the vapour trails of the heavy bombers streaming across from England. Smoke, haze and rubble dust obscure the target. It is the beginning of the end of the blitz on the Ruhr that began two years ago, and it can only finish in one thing – dust.'

A couple of days later, the paper featured an aerial photograph captioned:
'The target-marker bombs snake down on the city spread below, and the target they mark is Berlin - shaking under its biggest daylight attack ever.

Smoke billows up from the Borsig locomotive works as 1,300 American heavies crash home 3,000 tons of bombs at a rate of a ton a second.'

On this same day, in the House of Lords, the Archbishop of York recommended that anyone seeing Hitler in Berlin should not hesitate to shoot him on sight. The following week, a special team of airmen transported the RAF's biggest ever bomb: the Grand Slam was seven metres long and weighted nearly ten tons. The Lancaster adapted to carry the device needed three miles of runway to acquire sufficient momentum for lift off. Its goal was a stocky railway viaduct supporting an essential German transport artery. The weapon worked.

In the House of Commons, the Conservative MP for Clitheroe suggested that the Allies should preserve a square mile of bombed Berlin as a permanent record of the war started by Germany. Churchill responded that such a notion was "rather silly."

On 10th April, the Mail noted:

'Tonight the Ruhr – once the pride of Hitler's war-machine – is glowing like a colossal torch. In ruin and in flames, the great industrial basin is coming down over the heads of the German troops trapped inside it.'

A fortnight later, the Daily Express declared:
HITLER BOMBED OUT

The Fuhrer's Berlin premises had been damaged. On 2nd May, a hundred BC craft blasted Kiel once more, so allowing British and Canadian troops to clamber across the remnants two days later.

Many Berlin citizens were now fleeing westward, to avoid the bombs and the approaching Soviet armies. But some stayed in the city. Perhaps they considered it would all end fairly quickly and calmly. Maybe they thought they'd be lucky, and that no weapon could impact on their reinforced shelter. Perhaps they could not bear to abandon their family homes. So they existed in cellars beneath their houses, creeping out briefly to seek water and food, hoping the next bomb wouldn't crash on top of them, or even land a hundred metres away to blast shrapnel and debris at them. Those killed had no prospect of a formal burial. Many bodies lay where they fell for weeks. Survivors recalled bloated vermin and big insects feasting on remains.

One person who chose to stay kept a diary. 'A woman in Berlin' describes the activity and philosophy of a German citizen seeking sustenance in the subterranean shadows just a few miles from where Hitler was still ranting at his generals. She would scavenge for food while avoiding drunken Soviet soldiers scavenging for sex. This anonymous account of courage, canniness, shame and shock provides a vivid perspective of the last days of the Reich empire.

After VE Day, Bomber Command put on aerial viewing trips for its ground crews. The boys and girls who had got the bombers ready could peruse the broader results of their labours. The passengers gazed down in silence at the devastated landscape, doubtless imagining what had happened to all the people who had once lived where that rubble now lay.

Almost over?

In March 1945, Sir Frederick Handley Page, anticipating the end was probably in sight, laid on a lunch for executives in charge of Halifax aircraft production. Speeches revealed that at the busiest period of manufacture the previous year, 40 factories had been involved. Every hour, three miles of sheet metal were rolled; 700,000 rivets were punched. 50,000 workers had in total turned out 2,000 planes, enabling Halifax fleets to unleash 200,000 tons of ordnance the other side of the North Sea.

Bomber Command was now at the height of its powers with 1,600 aircraft delivering 90 tons of bombs per hour. On 13th March, the Telegraph front page stated:

R.A.F. BLAST DORTMUND IN BIGGEST RAID OF WAR

On 20th March, the Express led with:

MIGHTY BLITZ HITS GERMANS FACING MONTY'S ARMY
'Anything that moves' target for R.A.F.

However, reduced commitment to the cause was now exposed in the form of a strike at the A.V. Roe aircraft factory in Manchester, where 28,000 workers demanded better pay. They were following in the footsteps of Spitfire builders in Birmingham who had walked out on a string of occasions. Chinks in presentational armoury also appeared in RAF ranks; several servicemen faced criminal charges for selling travel vouchers to spivs, who in turn sold them to people wanting to make illicit train journeys. Meanwhile, two doctors confided to a Daily Mirror journalist that WAAFs were more likely to be invalided out of the RAF than men because of emotional problems. The newspaper turned this into:

WORRIED WAAFS ARE BIG WORRY

The Air Ministry swiftly slapped down this unwelcome PR with accounts of fearless WAAFs who had undertaken parachute missions behind enemy lines to convey vital information and equipment to partisans. Perhaps it was one of these women who was enlisted by an advertiser:

'This W.A.A.F. girl writes: "I have been stationed at places where Eucryl Tooth Powder was unobtainable, but always, as soon as I used Eucryl again, my teeth regained their lovely whiteness".'

Through the spring of 1945, the RAF lost 600 planes on 70,000 missions - 7% of their total war losses. Early in April, a BC sortie to Norway saw German flak blast a big hole in one plane, causing an airman to fall out. But he snared his parachute against the metalwork and was conveyed back to base, where fellow crew members were amazed to find him, shivering in his chute beneath the fuselage. 18th April saw BC take its final revenge on the island of Heligoland – 1,000 craft blasted the hell out of what was left of the naval base. 20th April proved to be BC's final combat mission to Berlin, but the Command had no reason to believe there were not still many more deadly Ops to be pursued. And some poor bastards were now being lined up to re-locate to the Far East to help the Americans hammer the home of the Ninjas.

Meanwhile, Fighter Command was obliged to assign assets to awkward missions amidst the fast-changing front line, to aid Allied advance and delimit enemy manoeuvres. The Command experimented with releasing canisters of napalm on a German stronghold at Arnhem, but reported that flames rose alarming close to the deliverers. One fighter pilot, scouring the countryside for strafing targets, saw what seemed to be soldiers moving east, so sprayed them. But most of the men below were British prisoners, including an RAF crewman in captivity since 1940 and who now died. In the Baltic, Third Reich political prisoners were been herded on to a ship for mooring offshore. Fighter Command was advised the vessel was full of escaping Nazis, so dispatched squadrons to sink it, and succeeded.

In the final weeks, the Command maintained its commitment to prickly tasks, and continued to suffer a high loss rate - typically eight aircraft each day. The last date of action for Fighter Command proved to be 4th May, which was fatal: two aircraft shot down by flak, two collided. Reflecting the range of personnel, each dead pilot was from a different country: New Zealand, Norway, Poland and England.

On Tuesday 8th May, Victory in Europe (VE) Day, Field Marshall Montgomery (Monty) wrote to the Air Ministry:

"We have no Germans left to fight. The mighty weapon of air power has enabled us to win a great victory and to win victory with fewer casualties than otherwise would have been the case."

Eventually it was over – in Europe. Many bomber units were immediately assigned to emergency feeding missions and rescue operations across the continent. Airmen recall these endeavours as the most pleasing moments of their whole service – supplying sustenance and comfort to troubled people on the ground.

For Coastal Command it was business as usual. There were still dozens of German U-boats below the Atlantic which might not have received surrender messages and so could still launch torpedoes at Allied shipping. By a cruel stroke of fate, the first pilot to have been awarded a Victoria Cross for his actions in the Battle of Britain, James Nicholson, died in air operations over India on VE Day.

The King continued to award Order of the British Empire medals. One of the last went to Flight Lieutenant R.C. Dickson, a medical officer based on an English air station:

'One afternoon when an aircraft landed from an operational sortie, an explosion occurred and the aircraft burst into flames. Flt. Lt. Dickson immediately hastened to the scene and found one member of the crew lying clear of the wreckage. After giving this airman a cursory examination, Dickson gave instructions for him to be removed to hospital. By this time ammunition and pyrotechnics in the aircraft were exploding continuously. The petrol tanks were liable to explode at any moment. Undeterred Dickson went to the aircraft to help another member of the crew who was trapped with his boots on fire. Displaying complete disregard for his own safety, Dickson tore away at the fuselage with his bare hands, injuring himself in the process, and freed the airman whom he then dragged to safety. Flt. Lt. Dickson's courage and devotion to duty on this occasion undoubtedly saved two lives. He has at all times shown outstanding devotion to duty and has done much to maintain the morale of air crews and ground personnel during difficult periods.'

Horror

Thousands of German citizens, workers, soldiers, SS troops and Gestapo officers had devoted extraordinary effort to identifying all the Jews in the country and in the adjoining nations, then rounding them up and shoving them on to trains to obscure corners of the Third Reich, to be disgorged into what the travellers sooner or later realised were death camps - huge compounds where millions of innocent men, women and children were murdered. This was The Final Solution to the perceived problems of Jews in Germany - kill them all.

Did the average German citizen realise this was happening in their country? Most claimed not to have known. But where the hell did they think their old Jewish neighbours had gone to?

We have all probably glimpsed, at least once, the horrific images from Auschwitz and Belsen, as photographed by Allied officers who entered those hell holes as they advanced towards Berlin: piles of naked, dead bodies lying near skeletal people barely able to walk or speak.

In the early months of 1945, few people were fully aware of the ghastly nature of the concentration camps. The excesses of the Japanese against their military prisoners emerged in the press before any details of German sadism. The first Brits retrieved from Burma in February had revealed the brutality of their Oriental guards and those terrible tales soon trickled into British newspapers. Then, on 4th April, the Daily Express allocated space on page 4 to James Welland's report from Bielefed:

HORROR CAMP SLAVES

'The first Americans to arrive saw thousands of starving men weeping with joy and fighting amongst themselves for morsels of food lying on the ground. In the so-called hospital ward lay a score of emaciated men on wooden slabs. They were skeletons with feverishly bright eyes. Some crawled towards us to press our hands. Some prisoners were bayoneted to death before the guards got away. A few miles down the road I came across a camp for Jewish women and children. There are 800 Polish, Russian and Hungarian Jewesses among them, all with a yellow cross painted on their coat on the back and a number tattooed on their arms. Some of them were only 14 and were weeping and plaintively hysterical. They had been working at nearby timber factories. The German practice was to tear families asunder, and most of these women had been separated for five years from homes, husbands and children.'

This was the first graphic description in a British newspaper. Through April, the Allies' advance discovered more despicable suffering. And soon there were photographs. The Express explained:

'It becomes a solemn duty to publish at least part of the photographic evidence which reaches the newspapers of the vileness of the creatures we are fighting. The pictures for the most part are too horrible to print at any time. The atrocities of the concentration camps overrun by the Allied armies are beyond words and pictures when it comes to the task of bringing home to ordinary, kindly, gentle people the depths of sadistic brutality to which the German has reverted.

'This is no propaganda. It is blunt, spine-chilling fact, testified by trained and responsible cameramen and reporters. These compounds of torture and death stand close by pleasant and smiling towns, smug, rich and prospering from the loot of plundered countries. Ease and comfort and complacency on the edge of such calculated, bestial cruelty. Social life proceeding undisturbed, almost within earshot of torture and murder!

'The soul of every decent human being confronted with this evidence must rage at his own impotence to conceive a just and fitting punishment for those who committed and those who condoned these horrors.'

The Daily Express and Daily Mail decided against printing most of the horrendous images in their papers, and instead displayed them at their offices or in libraries, some in book form.

None of the Allied bombing of the Third Reich was motivated by knowledge of the concentration camps. The despicable compounds were only discovered after 99.9% of the ordnance had been dropped on Nazi Germany.

On VE Day, The Times contained the report of a Russian commission which had been investigating Oswiecim camp (Auschwitz) in Polish Silesia where a million had been killed, included citizens of the Soviet Union, Poland, France, Belgium, Holland, Czechoslovakia, Yugoslavia, Hungary, Italy and Greece:

'The commission describes Oswiecim as the worst in its experience. Departments were maintained where experiments of a revolting character were conducted by German doctors. Most of the deportees who arrived at the camp were killed at once in gas chambers. On an average, one in six was selected for work. The camp covered more than 1,100 acres and accommodated up to 250,000 people. Seven tons of women's hair was found, ready for dispatch to Germany. Human teeth, from which gold fillings had been extracted, were piled several feet high.'

Six million Jews were murdered by the Nazis, along with another six million people whom the Third Reich psychopaths considered were political or social threats, or merely just a nuisance.

Hold the front page

Through the first five months of 1945, Fleet Street's prime topic was, understandably, experiences from the front lines in western Europe; the matter closest to most hearts. On 12th March, journalists from the Daily Telegraph, the Mail and Express were being escorted close to the action when a shell exploded nearby, killing Peter Lawless of the Telegraph and injuring the others. But those papers did not print this incident at the time, presumably recognising that their readers had their own fears and shocks to deal with. British journalism concentrated on bringing news of prospective victory for those at home.

On 26th April, the Mirror reported:

R.A.F. SCORE 6-TON HITS ON HITLER'S HIDEOUT

On Saturday 28th, the Express announced:

THIRD REICH DEAD

Then on Wednesday 2nd May:

HITLER IS DEAD

The Telegraph was more tentative:

HITLER'S DEATH ANNOUNCED

As usual, The Times allocated its front page to Classified messages, the most prominent of which on this day was:

'R.A.A.F. Would anyone who knew or has information of Aus 411060 Pilot Officer Bert Tuck posted missing on September 28, 1943, kindly communicate with his cousin, L.F. Tuck, R.A.F. Wigsley, Notts.'

However, in the top right corner was squeezed: HITLER DEAD. And the journal of record made a break from tradition by devoting Page 2 to an extensive obituary of the dictator, which included:

'Few men in the whole of history and none in modern times have been the cause of human suffering on so large a scale. From the time he became master of Germany he made lies, cruelty and terror his principal means to achieve his ends; and he became in the eyes of virtually the whole world an incarnation of absolute evil.'

Next day, page 2 of The Times returned to normal with Home News, including revelations about flourishing wild flowers on London bomb sites, brought by the wind or in horses' nosebags. Meanwhile, the Express highlighted 'The most tremendous news night of the war':

ARMY OF 1,000,000 SURRENDER
'HITLER AND GOEBBELS SUICIDE'
HOLLAND, NORWAY END IS NEAR

On Saturday, the Telegraph announced:

SURRENDER: THIS IS THE END

Monday 7th May, the Mirror explained:

GERMANY OFFERS SURRENDER TO SOVIET, BRITAIN, U.S.

The Telegraph was now more circumspect :

GERMANY'S FINAL SURRENDER IS IMMINENT

Next day, the Mirror proclaimed:

VE-DAY!
'It's over in the west, after 5 years 8 months and 4 days.'

On Page 2 they presented one of the finest cartoons of the war period: Zac's sketch of a universal soldier holding a symbol of Peace with the advice: "Here you are – don't lose it again"

The Telegraph proclaimed:

GERMANY CAPITULATES

And The Times again modified, allocating page 2 to a long article detailing the RISE AND FALL OF THE THIRD REICH, the last paragraph stating:

'The final surrender came yesterday. So perished the monstrous regime of the Third Reich under the accumulated hatred provoked by its crimes.'

Page 7 provided some Opinion:

'Never in the history of war has the entire fighting strength of a great military State been more decisively ground into fragments and overwhelmed in the uttermost catastrophe of defeat. In a score of great cities of Germany scarcely a building stands intact.'

Numbers

One morning in February 1945 the Americans sent 1,000 bombers to Berlin and so reduced the population there by 25,000 in a single day. On 22nd February, a week after Dresden, the Third Reich received its largest ever air raid - from 2,000 USAAF and 500 RAF crews.

During the war, Bomber Command dispatched around 350,000 sorties to attack Germany or German-occupied territory with 1.2 million tons of ordnance. During these missions more than 8,000 aircraft were lost. 135,000 men flew on BC combat missions. Forty-one per cent failed to return.

5,582 BC air crew were known to have been killed on operations. A further 42,000 were presumed dead - of whom almost 10,000 were Canadians. Around a hundred planes were destroyed in air collisions. In non-operations, 8,000 died and 4,000 were wounded. Five hundred ground crew were killed. Total RAF personnel losses amounted to more than 90,000.

The USAAF lost 60,000 aircraft during the war. More than 50,000 American airmen died on north European operations, another 25,000 around the Mediterranean and another 14,000 in the Pacific.

61,000 British citizens died from German bombs, 67,000 French people were killed by aerial ordnance. Half a million Soviet citizens died from Luftwaffe bombing. Five million German servicemen were killed in the European war; nine million male or female Soviet military personnel.

Rejoicing

'Victory, complete and rarely paralleled in war for its decisiveness, is in the grasp of the conquering Allies... the goal is all but reached. It is a story of courage and splendour which will warm mankind's heart for ages to come.'

... declared the Daily Express on 14th April 1945. With a print run of three million, the 'world's biggest selling newspaper' was received in a quarter of British homes wherein a daily was read. Increasingly, the Opinion column concentrated on congratulations. On 23rd April, imminent success warranted:

'This is the harvest of vast endeavours in the workshops and the factories, on the airfields, in the conference chambers. It is the harvest of the bravery and the skill and the endurance of myriads of men, of many nations, on the seas, in the skies and on the shell-torn, bomb-scarred earth, all doing their damnedest towards a great common end. This penetration into the very lair of the wounded beast is a triumph for the whole of the sane, civilised world.'

On Saturday 26th April:

'The time for rejoicing over final victory in Europe is near at hand. The armies of the west and east are firmly linked up. In Europe the soldiers are almost at the end of their task. In San Francisco the statesmen are at the start of theirs. Pray that they will succeed; that the unity of the battlefield will be carried into a lasting peace.'

And:

'Hitler is reported to be dead. That particularly appetising piece of news about an unsavoury wretch will become official only when the Red Army have found his remains in Berlin and satisfied themselves of his true identity. Was there ever such news? Was there ever such a triumph? How can we rejoice enough at the triumph of our men in arms? There will be no future occasion of greater moment, no more fitting time for the celebration – of the world's release from tyranny.'

By 5th May:

'This is the greatest moment of exultation for the British people in their long and arduous and adventurous history. These are the days of their greatest glory.'

And on 7th May, in a five-column wide feature on page 2:

'The glory is upon us. The war in Europe is won; the mighty effort to which we set our hands on that September Sunday of blue skies and air-raid alarms so long ago is accomplished. This is Victory-in-Europe-Week. Now is the springtime of all spring times, the time for laughter and dancing and singing. Through the valour of her sons the world has won for herself another chance to prove that justice and righteousness are not empty words, but living imperishable ideals in the heart of Man.

'And we, the people of Britain, have been privileged beyond all other peoples in the part we have taken in the struggle from the beginning to the end. It has been our war. Let us never be ashamed to remember that we declared war on Germany, recognising then the vileness of Nazi ambitions and pledging ourselves, with cool heads and level minds, to overthrow it. The great shadow which might have shrouded the whole world in barbarism and misery for a thousand years is lifted, dispersed, ended. And great glory is upon us.'

Which did not mean the whole matter was yet concluded:

'The Japs have only had a foretaste of what Germany has been through. The rest is now on the way to them.'

Two days later, acknowledgement of the key role of an ally:

'The British people need no prompting to remember the contribution of the Red Army to victory, or the suffering of Russia. They know, and will never forget, that every bomb rained down square by square on Stalingrad was one that some British city was spared.'

And soon the other vital player with 'their mighty and brilliant conception of air war' got a mention:

'Day bombing... was thorough; it was swift and remorselessly efficient. It was carried out unflinchingly, even when losses were 60 or more bombers, each with a crew of 10, on a single raid. The men of the Eighth Air Force believed in their mission, and the utter breakdown of the huge German war machine when the test came proved how right they were. The tribute and gratitude of the free world goes with the valiant Eighth as they cross the oceans again for new missions against Japan.'

Your vote counts

The big plan for the future of the world was for the three major Allied leaders to figure out a better way of handling international affairs, and to determine how the defeated Axis powers should be policed in the short term, re-politicised in the longer term; admirable, vital goals, to be signed off by the trio of champions, Roosevelt, Stalin and Churchill. But a week is a long time in politics, and suddenly it wouldn't be Roosevelt representing the U.S.A. The President had been sickly and crippled for a long time. His public appearances had become limited, with presentation of the top American carefully managed for public consumption. He would be helped into a chair to sit alongside his two strategic partners; only then would photographers have access.

After making phenomenal progress on a huge range of political issues at home and abroad, Roosevelt died on 12th April 1945. His deputy Truman immediately took the reins. A couple of weeks later, Hitler committed suicide. Soon after that, aero-engine factories in Coventry were being turned over to car production, dozens of soldiers were blown up on British beaches while trying to defuse mines, and a General Election was declared in the United Kingdom, which Prime Minister Churchill assumed he would win.

On 24th May, one British newspaper laid its cards on the table:

'In the four-page battledress to which it is still restricted, the Daily Express will play its part in the election campaign. In its news columns, all sides will be reported. In this column, the Daily Express will battle unceasingly to make converts to its point of view. Its opinions are put forward in the firm and steady conviction that they are in the best interests of the nation. Its weapons are argument, information and the spread of knowledge. With this powerful armoury, the Daily Express hopes to carry conviction amongst the people.'

But the Daily Mirror was equally full of conviction:

'Defeatism is not the mood in which the people of Britain face their future. They have conquered the Nazi evil. They are confident they can conquer the evils of poverty and slum-dom. They expect a party which claims to speak for them to share and be the exemplar of their proud faith in themselves. Now it's up to Labour.'

As soon as the RAF had ferried back 10,000 POWs from Germany aboard BC craft, demobilisation began. The aim was to downsize the personnel complement by a third, at a rate of 5,000 people a week. Celebrity aviator Douglas Bader had no plans to leave, but he almost got chucked out by campaigning in uniform for the Conservative candidate in west Fulham, which was against the rules. Ignoring the extraordinary capacities of recently treasured Soviet allies, the Daily Express warned of electoral dangers:

'The Socialists want to nationalise all our industries, and that includes the aviation industry. De Havillands, makers of the world-famous Mosquito – the creation of free enterprise – received orders during the past three years for aircraft, engines, and propellers totalling £59,000,000, and their net profit was £140,000 – less than 3/4d in the pound. How would a State-owned aircraft industry have managed? And would it have produced the Mosquito?'

The Daily Mail made clear its instincts with a cartoon showing a handsome Winston striding forward arm-in-arm with a beautiful, purposeful Britannia. But would women vote as they had before the war? There were clues in north London in the middle of May when 25 WAAFs went on strike, refusing to provide household management for a bunch of important Germans held in RAF barracks, including the man who created the Messerschmitt planes: yes, Messerschmitt himself. These girls had had enough.

Voting took place early in July, but votes were not collated until the end of the month to allow for the returns from overseas troops. Did service in the RAF help a fellow win political hearts and minds? Group Captain Ward stood for the Conservatives in the constituency of Worcester. The officer had influential contacts in the city: his brother was the Earl of Dudley. How would he fare against Labour's J. Evans? The votes were counted again and again and again. And eventually it was declared that the RAF man had captured the seat by four votes. Elsewhere across the country, a dozen RAF personnel standing for Labour won majorities:

'A tidal wave has swept over Britain. The Daily Express does not conceal its disappointment with the result.'

The new Labour Government announced its top three priorities: winning the war against Japan; an intensive house-building campaign; and the speeding up of demobilisation to make manpower available for the reconstruction drive; 50,000 bomb-damaged houses, not classified as "total loss", would be re-built or restored with funds from the War Damage Commission in the next two years:

'The limit to repair costs will be raised to £1,200, sufficient for most London suburban houses.'

(By September, these ambitions were abandoned.) The Times was exercised by pressing concerns of its esteemed readership, not least inadequacies of the nation's telephone services:

'Lady Eleanor Smith writes: "In my view the situation has become progressively more disgraceful since the cessation of hostilities".'

At the top table, Stalin was joined by US President Truman, then Labour Prime Minister Clement Attlee, to agree the big deals. And the world was left wondering how and why a nation could so abruptly cast aside the extraordinary man who had done so much to keep it free and democratic. The Telegraph surmised:

'The coming year will pass judgement on the electoral decision that dispensed with Mr. Churchill's services at a moment when that decision was at strange variance with the warm gratitude which every man and woman in the country felt toward him. Even as he passes from office there is clear recognition that will continue undimmed into history of his supreme achievement in the darkest hour which he made our finest.'

And so to Tokyo

On 9th March, 250 planes had undertaken the USA's most formidable bombing mission, dropping 1,600 tons of incendiaries on Tokyo, killing 84,000 and injuring 100,000. Fifteen square miles of urban area were destroyed, making one million people homeless. In mid-May the Americans mounted a press conference in London to announce:

> 'The air war against Japan will be on a greater scale than that in Europe, and as many as 3,000 Super Forts may be used if the Japs continue to resist.'

Next day, 900 carrier-borne U.S. aircraft assaulted the Japanese mainland. A week later, Tokyo experienced its biggest raid so far when 500 Super Forts dropped 700,000 incendiaries, weighing 4,000 tons. Many of the 2,000 new bombers emerging from U.S. factories this month - and not now required in Europe - were assigned to mining the seas around Japan to hamper imports of food and raw materials. Meanwhile, a million leaflets were scattered across urban areas recommending citizens to surrender.

The Land of the Rising Sun responded in one curious fashion: releasing giant paper balloons full of helium over the Pacific, so prevailing winds would carry them to the United States, where bomblets suspended below the balloons would drop off. One quaint item of oriental ordnance descended on a family picnic in California killing five children. Some drifted north into Canada.

American airmen were told they would have to undertake at least 30 missions over Japan. On 26th May, the Express headlined:

4,000 TONS CARPET HEART OF TOKYO

By the middle of June, the USA had more or less destroyed half a dozen Japanese cities. At the start of July, the biggest incendiary raid ever was undertaken. The Express noted:

> 'Total air war hits Japan: The greatest air war in history has now been let loose on Japan, which, up to today, has had 32 days of non-stop attacks, destroying 120 square miles across 26 cities.'

Through July, a thousand bombers decanted 43,000 tons of napalm, burning a million people.

Over in New York, a USAAF aircraft in poor visibility rammed into the 79th floor of the Empire State Building. And in Britain, fourteen American airmen, travelling home from Prestwich Airport, died when their plane crunched on to the Isle of Skye.

In London, new Ministers were pressing civil servants to create mechanisms to bring utilities into public ownership; and to establish a National Health Service. Meanwhile Bomber Command continued to lose aircraft on training flights or in ground incidents. Mrs Allen of Totteridge received a letter from the Air Ministry reporting that her son, Leonard, had been killed in an air accident. But in the same post was a letter from Leonard telling the family all was well: there were two Leonard Allens in the RAF - the Ministry had written to the wrong Mum.

At Freckleton near Preston, a year after one of their bombers had crashed on the school, American servicemen presented the village with a children's playground.

August saw the USAAF's biggest ever ordnance mission: 6,000 tons in one day. An American Admiral stated that Japan would be invaded by "the most overwhelming forces ever concentrated in military history". The Emperor's hierarchy advised him this might happen in September. But a week later the atomic bomb was given its first outing.

Navigator Theodore Van Kirk had undertaken 58 Flying Fortress flights from England to Germany before being assigned to training back in the USA. Now he was asked to take on one more special mission aboard the Boeing B29 Enola Gay - to find Hiroshima in Japan, flying from the Mariana Islands in the western Pacific. He would be travelling at a great height, so was unlikely to encounter any of the 600 remaining Japanese suicide fighter pilots. He was told the target city had not been previously bombed. Only the pilot, Colonel Paul Tibbetts, knew exactly what they were carrying aboard this aircraft - a four ton bomb, a version of which had been successfully tested underground in the USA just three weeks earlier.

Theodore was aware that most Japanese aircraft factories had been destroyed; many of their aircraft carriers were disabled and devoid of planes. He did not know that across many square miles of devastated Japanese cities hundreds of orphaned children ran through the remains, no adults to care for them.

Theodore's final combat flight took more than six hours to reach the aiming point - a 350 year old city of 280,000 inhabitants, plus 40,000 military personnel. The weapon was released at 8.15 in the morning. It exploded 2,000 feet above the ground, generating temperatures in excess of 3,000 degrees Centigrade. This killed around 70,000 people instantly, and about the same number died from injuries or radiation over the following twelve months.

On Tuesday 7th August, the Daily Express declared:
THE BOMB THAT HAS CHANGED THE WORLD
'The Allies disclosed last night that they have used against Japan the most fearful device of war yet produced – an atomic bomb. One atomic bomb has the destructive force equal to five 1,000 plane raids. Experts estimate that the bomb can destroy anything on the surface in an area of at least two square miles.'

The Daily Mirror revealed:
ATOMIC BOMB IN USE AGAINST JAPS
– TOTAL RUIN SOON

The Daily Telegraph headlined:
ALLIES INVENT ATOMIC BOMB
FIRST DROPPED ON JAPAN
2,000 TIMES THE BLAST POWER OF R.A.F. 11-TONNER
ENEMY THREATENED WITH "RAIN OF RUIN"
'The Allies have made the greatest scientific discovery in history: the way to use atomic energy.'

The Times stuck to its format: Page 2 announced that Bank Holiday crowds were scattered by storms on a record day of sport, Page 3 updated a court case in France, and page 4 revealed:
FIRST ATOMIC BOMB HITS JAPAN

Next day, President Truman warned, "In their present form, these bombs are now in production." Meanwhile, in a different part of Japan, 600 Super Forts obliterated another industrial city.

And still the war continued.

Saving lives

On 8ᵗʰ August, the Daily Mail explained:
> CITY OF 300,000 VANISHED IN VAST BALL OF FIRE
> 'Bomber crew in black spectacles. Heat felt 10 miles away.'
> 'Hiroshima ceased to exist on Monday morning. While going about its business in the sunshine of a hot summer day, it vanished in a huge ball of fire and a cloud of boiling smoke – obliterated by the first atom bomb to be used in the history of warfare.'

The Mirror went for:
> CITY VANISHED IN A MUSHROOM OF FIRE

The Telegraph offered eye-witness accounts:
> "There was a flash as brilliant as the sun. What had been Hiroshima became a mountain of smoke that rose to 7 miles. The flash was seen 170 miles away."

The newspaper noted that train services in Hiroshima had been cancelled, which showed that Allied claims for the new bomb 'have probably not been exaggerated.'

The Mail pointed out:
> 'For many years scientists have dreamed of the possibility of harnessing atomic energy, that apparently infinite and inexhaustible power which exists in all matter. It has been said that the atomic energy in a handful of stones would be sufficient, if properly controlled, to drive a heavy express train from London to Glasgow.'

The Express asked:
> 'How can you begin to grasp the implications of this atomic bomb in which for the first time a vast, latent force has been released, controlled and harnessed for specified destruction?'

The Telegraph added:
> 'The Allied leaders could not justify any sacrifice of Allied lives which abstention from the use of the new weapon might involve…
> The rain of ruin cannot be indefinitely restricted.'

And as the world reeled from the scale and significance of the Hiroshima experiment, Russia declared war on Japan.

Now the Express considered:
'While Japan remains an outlaw and an enemy of civilisation, the atomic bomb may be used against her to shorten her resistance to the forces of law. But when there is no more resistance anywhere in the world to the United Nations, their first task must be to establish a world order, with atomic energy as the prime instrument for the preservation and fostering of the ideals of peace.'

The Times offered some Opinion on the 'Darkness over Hiroshima':
'All that can be said with certainty is that the world stands in the presence of a revolution in earthly affairs as least as big with potentialities of good and evil as when the forces of steam or electricity were harnessed for the first time to the purposes of industry and war. That the new power be consecrated to peace and not to war is a choice before the conscience of humanity; and in a terrible and most literal sense it is a choice of life or death.'

The Express asked:
'How many more cities must be destroyed before the leaders of Japan are brought to recognise the criminal folly of further resistance?'

The next day, colleagues of Theodore Van Kirk undertook a similar monumental flight to another previously unharmed Japanese city, Nagasaki. A massive bang, thousands of instant deaths, a mushroom cloud, acres of agonising injuries. In parallel, 1,200 Super Forts released conventional weapons on other destinations; while the Soviets seized five towns in Manchuria.

And still the war continued.

On Friday 10th August, all US bomb raids on Japan were put on hold in order to evaluate proposed terms of surrender. On Saturday, the Telegraph gave modest front page space to:
NAGASAKI WENT UP IN FLAMES
'Airmen reported a huge ball of yellow and orange fire which shot 8,000 feet into the sky.'

The Editorial column asked:
'Who can doubt that its use, which has saved the lives of countless fighting men, and put a sudden term to the suffering inflicted over vast areas, was fully justified?'

On Sunday the Americans resumed their devastation of Tokyo with 800 planes - taking care to avoid the Imperial Palace. Inside, rival factions of politicians and military men pestered the Emperor. Some were for sheathing their samurai; others clamoured to battle on. But the debate was behind closed doors; ordinary citizens were kept in the dark about negotiations. So the Americans printed a million copies of the correspondence to date between them and Japan's ruling elite, and scattered these across Tokyo - which triggered the decision-makers to act, the surrendering cabal first. Despite threats of mass suicides and palace coups, the Emperor's instincts eclipsed his warriors' manic tendencies.

On 14th August, 800 Super-Fortresses again hurled tons of napalm on everything below and, down the road, the leadership announced they'd had enough - though not everyone accepted the Emperor's edict: there was sulky destruction of remaining aircraft, a few futile kamikaze flights and bloody clusters of ceremonial suicides.

1,347 days on from the shocks of Pearl Harbor, the Express had a wonderful message:
PEACE ON EARTH

The Daily Mirror declared:
'The democracies have destroyed the dictatorships; the power of the common man, harnessed to freedom's cause, has triumphed over the mechanised savages who sought to rule the world by quenching every quality of heart and mind.'

Meanwhile, Lord Newborough told Daily Telegraph readers:
'The atomic bomb produces results over a far larger area than would be possible for scores of our ordinary bombers to achieve, thus saving the lives of many hundreds of our gallant men.'

The Express offered a prayer:
'Peace is settling on earth again. Glory to God, the blooding of our youth is ending. Any lad now, from 18 years upward, for the first time in many years, can rise with the lark in the morning and know that he will not untimely die before nightfall.'

The Mail revealed that the New Mexico atomic bomb test had turned sand dunes into a speckled-green, glass-like substance, and entrepreneurs were planning to make the material into atomic jewellery called "Atomsite", which will be "beautiful and safe". However, on 5th September, the Express ran an article by the first foreign journalist, an Australian, to be allowed into Hiroshima:

THE ATOMIC PLAGUE

'30 days after the first atomic bomb destroyed the city and shook the world, people are still dying – mysteriously and horribly – people who were uninjured in the cataclysm – from an unknown something which I can only describe as the atomic plague. Hiroshima does not look like a bombed city. It looks as if a monster steam-roller has passed over it and squashed it out of existence.'

(The valiant reporter lived to his seventies.) For several weeks, Allied aircraft towing huge white banners had been leafleting the news that hostility had ended down to pockets of troops in jungles. So as not be shot at, Japanese generals flying to meetings with their conquerors travelled in aircraft painted white. Allied planes sometimes passed over sites where the Japanese had been using and abusing thousands of prisoners. The air crews waved at the fragile fellows below, who realised their suffering could soon be over. When they were rescued, the POWs were advised not to tell their relations or anyone else what had been experienced, and, equally, their families were asked not to question the men about their months or years in captivity.

Sir John Hammerton, editor of 'War Illustrated' contemplated the significance of the atomic weapon:

'Without that stupendous instrument, war against Japan might still have been going on. The fact that no more than two of these bombs were required to reduce the fire-eating race of greedy and envious Nipponese to submission is the best proof of value of this great discovery. We can restrain our tears for the large destruction of two populous cities of a people who have shown themselves to be as cruel and barbarous as the Western Huns and even more treacherous. There can be little doubt that these bombs have saved at least a million lives of the Allied armies by bringing the Mikado and his war-mongers to their knees when confronted with their impending fate. Moreover, they have probably saved far more Japanese lives than they have taken.'

Theodore Van Kirk later described his fellow crewmen as "a bunch of civilians they put uniforms on" whose collective ambition was to get the war over and get out of the USAAF. Living to the age of 93, proud he had done his bit, he gave lectures about his experiences, and confidently defended the Hiroshima bomb as having saved lives.

Our thanks

On 8th August 1945, the Telegraph recalled:

'Five years ago today about 300 enemy aircraft attacked several British convoys off the South Coast. It was the opening assault in a campaign designed to install Hitler in Downing Street before Christmas. On Oct 31 the Luftwaffe, grievously mauled, retired in disarray from the attempt to secure the daylight mastery of the air over Britain.'

While one might argue about the dates, no-one would deny the perception that the RAF managed to repel Germany's attempts to advance against Britain that autumn; though most of the blitz bombing continued until the spring, when Third Reich forces were shifted east to shock the Russians. Nevertheless, in the midst of evaluating the extraordinary impact of the newly-released atomic bomb, the Daily Telegraph saw fit to reflect on a key period from the early days of the Nazi menace.

Let us consider Hitler's demonic trajectory. Looking at old German newsreel footage (carefully edited by PGG and co.), it would seem the high point in his career had been that glorious July 1940 day, shortly after defeating the French and gloating at what was now his Eiffel Tower in his Paris: he returns to Berlin and hundreds of girls scatter flowers in front of his ceremonial car.

At that moment Adolf undoubtedly felt chuffed to bits. He'd conquered most of mainland western Europe – like he'd said he would try to do all those years previously in beer gardens in Munich. Now he anticipated the subjugation of Britain and the seizure of Russia, after which he and every other decent German could have a good rest and enjoy themselves. As those pretty blossoms cascaded across his cavalcade, anything – everything - seemed possible.

But it didn't work out as he envisaged. By the spring of 1945, in the face of onslaughts from all sides, Adolf was thoroughly depressed. Was it feasible the Fuhrer might sink so low that he could no longer identify a way forward for himself? On 9th April, the Daily Mail reported that Hitler's new, personal, long-distance aircraft – well-armed and armour-plated – had crashed on its first test flight. In effect, the door had slammed on prospects for quick, private exit. The main man was stuck in town.

Take a look at the TV mini-series, 'The Bunker', in which Anthony Hopkins plays Hitler, cowering under reinforced concrete, hearing gunfire from the approaching Russians and bomb bangs from American and British aircraft when he's trying to concentrate on what to do for the best. The Fuhrer is aggravated by his gloomy Generals; telling them to try harder, but they're saying they've done their best, and he reckons there are traitors among them - here in The Bunker - who don't believe Germany is going to win.

That drama captures the end of the arc. Adolf got so cheesed off: no hope of a seaside ice cream - when he'd promised so much, and so many people had admired his goals – which, of course, were never for him alone, but were for the Reich nation. Those relentless and unrelieved bomb raids on HQ – that was it. He'd had enough.

So, Thank You. A great big thank you to the Allied air forces – from the top brass to the tea ladies – who pursued in every possible way to contribute to the policy and practice of dropping explosives on Germany – for so long, despite the agonising and deadly challenges of doing so.

A great big thanks to every Russian who was pushed to the front in order to provide overwhelming difficulties for the Third Reich war machine, which eventually started to run out of planes and tanks and oil and ammunition and sense of purpose.

Massive thanks to all western soldiers, sailors and civilians who persevered with their daunting endeavours for so long.

"Un grand merci" to all the underground partisans across Europe who undertook deadly activity in the middle of the night to derail German plans - often spectacularly derailing munitions trains.

A giant thanks to Churchill who pushed and pushed and pushed and pushed to sustain the fight against the Nazi regime.

Immense gratitude to the U.S.A. for sending over so many excellent men and machines.

Because the frustrating disappointments a tyrant encounters whilst trying to conquer Europe - when the world hates you and wants you stopped somehow or other – those things eventually got to Hitler, who concluded that suicide was the only remaining appropriate action.

By 15th April, the USAAF was so confident about the forthcoming conclusion that they allowed returning bombers to fly low over London on their way back to East Anglia, hence enabling the public to see the marvellous Yankee machines that were hammering Hitler into the ground. The RAF soon joined in these low-flying passes over built-up areas, but the British chaps were quickly told to stop frightening old ladies.

A Daily Mail editorial considered that:

'... even the death of Hitler does not necessarily bring nearer the date on which hostilities in Western Europe can be said to end.'

They were wrong about that. It did end within days.

The Times reflected that:

'The people of this country and the civilised world will receive the news with profound thankfulness when the Government of the allied Powers announce that the war in Europe is ended. It will be a day to observe and to celebrate in a manner that reflect a swift lightening of the heart and the lifting of a great oppression, but... to many the day will be a time of tragic personal memories and for many others the anxieties that have centred on the battlefields of Europe will be transferred to other battlefields far distant overseas.'

The Daily Express asked:

'How many fighter planes did we have in reserve when the Battle of Britain was won? It has been said that there were only nine – a few Spitfires and Hurricanes. At any rate there were not a great many more. And it was from that ridiculous nucleus that the strength of Britain was built.'

Once peace reached the Pacific, it was appropriate to fully profile the work of 'our boys'. The Express explained:

> 'Nearly 100 R.A.F. stations will throw their gates open to the public on Saturday, September 15, when the country will mark the fifth anniversary of one of the greatest days in the Battle of Britain. The following day, Sunday September 16, a special service of thanksgiving will be held in Westminster Abbey, preceded by a march – including workers from the aircraft industry – from Wellington Barracks.'

On Wednesday 5th September, alongside the first detailed photograph of the remains of Hiroshima, the Daily Telegraph announced that its Pageant of the Royal Air Force would be staged at the Royal Albert Hall later in the month. It would depict:

> '…the growth of the R.A.F. from its earliest days. The entire arena of the hall, with the help of every modern lighting and mechanical effect, is being used to show in dramatic sequence, from the Battle of Britain, the great attacks on Germany, the Middle East campaigns, the Battle of the Atlantic and the Invasion of Europe'.

Ten days later, the Daily Mail presented:

BATTLE FOR BRITAIN

> 'It is September 15 – anniversary of "the great day". On this day in 1940 the Battle of Britain was decided. It was won by Britain and lost by Germany. The enemy, seeking to strike down this country by another of the giant blows which had laid Europe prostrate at its feet, lost 185 of his aircraft. The Royal Air Force lost 25 machines, from which 14 pilots were saved. These figures give some measure of the triumph of that band of very gallant gentlemen – the immortal Few. We shall remember them today when a remnant of their company joins in a flight over London. They should be remembered too by all other nations. On this day five years ago the world was freed from extinction. To us, in this small island, belongs the pride and honour of that mighty achievement. It is fitly commemorated by the opening in London today of Thanksgiving Week.'

The Telegraph featured an article about the 'RAF's Greatest Day', when:

> 'Londoners could see for themselves aircraft falling in flames and pilots floating to earth on parachutes.'

The paper recorded that there were two large-scale raids on the 15th, but noted they did not result in the greatest weight of German bombs dropped in a single day, nor on the most Luftwaffe daily casualties.

Visitors to Hyde Park could examine a selection of Luftwaffe aircraft that had been downed across the previous five years. The Daily Mirror published a finely-executed sketch of a sophisticated tableau in which a male and female worker jointly hold up a pilot who is strangling a Nazi eagle he has grasped from the air.

The following day - Fighting Services Day, organised by the National Savings Drive - church services were held to commemorate Air Force achievements and losses. The Pageant, funded by the Daily Telegraph, took place on 19th and 20th of September, with 'Cabinet Ministers, Service Chiefs and flying aces' in attendance - a full house on both nights; ticket proceeds going to the RAF Benevolent Fund and the RAF Association. The evening ended with a reading by the Poet Laureate John Masefield, then a speech from Lord Trenchard, who pointed out "the RAF had saved the country in the Battle of Britain". He hoped that the work of the RAF would now help bring peace and happiness on earth. Finally, 2,500 airmen and airwomen and the audience of 6,000 rose to sing the National Anthem.

The commemoration of the Battle of Britain had first taken place in September 1942 in the form of a small lunch party for a dozen of the surviving participants. This gathering grew a little in September 1943, and the next year a number of church services were held to acknowledge the critical undertakings.

Prior to the September 1945 commemorations, one of The Few told the Express:

> "Those who fought laid a path for complete co-operation between the free nations. September 15 should be a permanent monument to that co-operation, so that it remains as strong in peace as in battle."

Undoubtedly, the event and the date were then and thus cemented into British history.

9

SO WHAT HAVE WE LEARNT?

Two million people in the British aircraft industry between 1939 and 1945 manufactured 125,000 aircraft. They were at their busiest in 1944, turning out 2,400 a month. Eighty million incendiary bombs were dropped by Bomber Command. A third of all the Command's casualties were suffered in 1944, when 3,527 of its aircraft were lost. However, of the year's 160,000 missions, only 1.9% did not return, with 2,000 air crew becoming POWs. The RAF and USAAF caused an estimated 350,000 civilian deaths in Germany during the war.

The Commonwealth War Graves Commission maintains nine large cemeteries in Germany, accounting for more than 17,000 airmen. Max Hastings considers that Bomber Command's casualties were:

'... the lowest possible stake that Britain could be seen to throw on the tables of Europe when the Russians were counting their dead in millions.'

55,500 Command aircrew lost their lives. 5,800 Coastal Command crew died, as did 3,600 Fighter boys. Following D-Day, 8,000 British invasion troops died on the continent.

Russia and Germany each lost around 100,000 aircraft. A third of a million Luftwaffe personnel died. Total European deaths from aerial ordnance were 600,000. Seven million people were rendered homeless by Allied bombing. Meanwhile, twelve million individuals were murdered by the Nazis; half because they were Jewish.

Total British deaths caused by the war were 450,000. For the Americans it was 420,000. For Germany: seven million. For Russia: twenty-seven million. For a full dimension of the toll, read the final chapter of Max Hastings's 'All Hell Let Loose'.

In March 1945 General Eisenhower thanked Commander Harris for so effectively bombing German cities. The airman replied:

'My crews have been sustained by the sure knowledge that the path of the Allied armies on all fronts would be smoothed.'

A couple of months later, Harris thanked his personnel:

"As the count is cleared, those of Bomber Command who gave their lives will be found not less than the total dead of our invasion armies now in Germany. Never have so small a band of men been called to support for so long such odds. You indeed bore the brunt."

In parallel, the Fighter Command Chief told the rest of the RAF:

"We have made it possible for the Allied forces to deliver the knock-out blow. Your great deeds will be remembered in history."

Towards the end of August, Arthur Harris left the RAF, and the UK, feeling he had not been given much official thanks - though the Daily Express offered a fine send-off:

'Bomber Harris gave the victims of the blasted and battered towns of Britain what they wanted – a chance to hit back harder. But reprisals were not in his mind. Bomber Harris had other ideas. He believed in the annihilation of the enemy by the "saturation" raid. The technique was known as area bombing. Could that policy have succeeded on its own? Certainly no man could have prosecuted it with greater determination. Harris's Lancasters took a splendid part in the smashing down of Germany's resistance, alongside the American Forts and Liberators, who came later with their precision bombing. After these combined night and day attacks on the sources of production came the tactical or close-support bombing, of direct assistance to the ground forces. And then Germany cracked.

Have any of these methods of warfare a future? Probably not. The day – or the night – of vast bomber fleets has gone. The atom bomb is here. But the place of Bomber Harris is unique in history.'

Who'd live there?

Wikipedia hosts an array of formulae for comparing World War Two bombing impact, including quantities of ordnance, frequency of targeting and mayhem caused. One can also examine the mushrooming timeline. Before the war, Guernica was first to experience 300 deaths delivered from the sky. Three other Spanish cities registered similar or higher figures the next year. Meanwhile, Chinese cities had populations reduced by four figures from Japanese assaults.

Warsaw in Poland lost 4,000 citizens in September 1939; Rotterdam, 800 on one May day in 1940. London became prominent on 7th September with 450 fatalities, then Coventry in November with 600.

In April 1941, 4,000 people of Belgrade in Yugoslavia died from Axis bombing. In June, similar numbers perished in a Chinese city. Leningrad suffered a thousand deaths from the Luftwaffe in September; Rangoon in Burma, an equal number from the Japanese in December.

1942 saw terrible assaults on Paris, Cologne and Stalingrad. 1943 brought the first US contributions, then combined UK and American forces headed for Hamburg to cause a death toll greater than the total of British blitz casualties. The RAF's mission to Kassel in the autumn resulted in a five figure toll. Darmstadt suffered similarly the following year, then in 1945 Dresden eclipsed those fatalities.

Nuremberg was bombed on ten occasions, receiving 14,000 tons of explosive in all. Stuttgart and Hamburg each experienced eighteen raids. Cologne was attacked on twenty occasions. Essen (home to the Krupps complex) was targeted on thirty nights, during which were delivered 40,000 tons. Duisberg would prove to be the most bombed place in Germany with 300 air raids; through one grim night, then day, it was subject to 2,000 sorties. Berlin suffered 24 major raids - and received the greatest quantity of explosive: 60,000 tons, causing 60% of buildings to be badly damaged.

A few years earlier, London had suffered Luftwaffe visits on 70 occasions, though many were minor affairs. In total, the British capital had received 20,000 tons. Liverpool was the second most bombed British city, suffering 2,000 tons over eight raids, causing 4,000 fatalities. Birmingham, Plymouth and Bristol were next in severity; then Glasgow, Southampton and Portsmouth. Hull had the irritation of being a navigation point for some German crews returning home, so any unreleased ordnance was heaved out above the port, eventually killing 1,000 below.

Stratifying city deaths globally, above Stalingrad, we find Warsaw, then Dortmund, London, Essen, Cologne, Hamburg, Nagasaki, Hiroshima and Tokyo, with Berlin on top.

700,000 people perished in Japanese cities through the spring and summer of 1945, then along came the atomic weapons. Hiroshima's toll was particularly high because the authorities, having seen one plane overhead now flying away, broadcast that the raid was over, so people could safely re-occupy the streets. No-one knew that the device was descending slowly on a parachute and would suddenly....

Tit for tat

One schoolchild snatches a toy from another, who hits out and so receives a punch back. Suddenly there is a scrap behind the bike sheds. Would adults behave better?

At the start of the war, the major nations signed Statements of Intent to avoid bombing civilians. Six years later, millions of town dwellers were dead. All governments contemplated the repercussions of failing to restrict aerial activity. Hitler ignored the criteria upon ordering the invasion of Poland, where brutal advances by his army and air force killed hundreds, few in uniform. However, between the UK and the Third Reich, the validity of aiming only at military targets stood for some time. Whitehall initially saw fit to explain that bombing industrial sites in Germany's Ruhr valley would not be permitted because those factories were private property.

On New Year's Eve 1939, the Archbishop of Canterbury warned:

> 'As the war goes on and just indignation rises against some of the methods of the enemy, there will be angry demands to pay them back in their own coin. We must be on our guard against an unrestricted competition in atrocities. Surely there will be limits below which, at whatever cost, honour will forbid us to fall?'

On 16th March 1940, Luftwaffe aircraft bombed Scotland's Scapa Flow harbour and accidently released a bomb above a cottage which killed the occupant, a council employee. Churchill (not yet Prime Minister) seized on this violation and proposed that the RAF drop bombs on Berlin. A few days later, a handful of British aircrews unloaded a few canisters of explosives above the German capital, which damaged some buildings and killed a couple of German citizens and, ironically, an English woman. It was the first clear case of Tit for Tat. When the Luftwaffe killed hundreds in Rotterdam on 14th May, Churchill - five days into No 10 - approved an attack by a fleet of planes against the factories of the Ruhr valley. Now the RAF laid aside scruples and got over there, but failed to disperse ordnance on to any appropriate structures.

On 3rd June, 200 Luftwaffe planes dropped 1,000 bombs across Paris. Two days later, the Express could report:

R.A.F. RAIN BOMBS ON RUHR
Hit oil tanks, aircraft works and an arsenal
Allied airmen exact vengeance as Paris raid deaths mount to 254

On 24th August, a Londoner was the victim of a stray Luftwaffe bomb that had been meant for a Thames oil tank. The RAF immediately sent eighty aircraft to Berlin, but only a few planes reached the city to scatter canisters through heavy cloud.

Incensed by this further violation of domestic air space, Hitler ordered retaliation raids on London, most of which took place on 7th September when a large Luftwaffe force dropped 300 tons. The Germans lost 36 planes on this mission, while 28 RAF defenders went down.

Now the RAF was told to bomb anything in the German-occupied territories. Churchill wrote to the Air Ministry:

'I believe moral advantage would be gained in Germany at the present time if on two or three nights in a month a number of minor, unexpected widespread attacks were made upon the smaller German centres. You must remember that these people are never told the truth, and that wherever the Air Force has not been, they are probably told that the German defences are impregnable.'

He was alarmed by the Luftwaffe releasing explosives on parachutes above London:

'This proves the "act of terror" intention against the civilian population. My inclination is to say that we will drop a heavy parachute mine on German cities for every one he drops on ours.'

'I wish to know by Saturday night what is the worst form of proportionate retaliation, i.e. equal retaliation, that we can inflict upon ordinary German cities for what they are now doing to us…'

The RAF's interruption of the Munich knees-up on 9th November rattled Hitler, resulting in the 400 aircraft raid on Coventry. In turn, the RAF mounted retaliatory attacks on Mannheim on 16th December - the first British attack specifically on an urban area, killing 50 citizens, damaging 500 buildings and leaving a thousand homeless. Churchill later recalled:

'German thoroughness had enabled a complete system of bomb-proof shelters to be built, into which all were forced to go by iron routine. When eventually we got to Germany we found cities completely wrecked, but strong buildings standing up above the ground, and spacious subterranean galleries where the inhabitants slept night by night, although their houses and property were being destroyed above. But in London, although the attack was less overpowering, the security arrangements were far less developed. If the bombs of 1943 had been applied to the London of 1940, we should have passed into conditions which might have pulverised all human organisation.'

He reflected that:

'London, which was certainly unconquered, was not also unconquerable.'

Arthur Harris's early thrust against cute little Lubeck triggered Hitler to order attacks on handsome old centres such as Exeter, Bath, Norwich, York and Canterbury. A German press spokesman described these as the Baedeker raids, as if the travel guide book had determined targets.

Why did Hitler never assault Oxford or Cambridge? Perhaps he anticipated a time when those iconic locations would be part of a great Germanic empire: the Ashmolean re-named the 'Adolfian'?

Richard Overy observes:

'The ruins of Europe in 1945 were mute testimony to the remorseless power of bombing and the inevitability of escalation.'

Was it inevitable or avoidable? Hastings considers that, for the Allies:

'...the cost of the bomber offensive in life, treasure and moral superiority over the enemy tragically outstripped the results that it achieved.'

But the goal was to remove the Nazi regime. Was there another way? In the last month of the war, Hitler screeched that all Allied air force POWs must be executed as retaliation for the intensive bombing they and their colleagues had imposed on his cities. Mercifully, his commanders ignored this order.

And there were other limits to tit-for-tat: back in 1940, Churchill secretly commissioned the production of gas bombs, to release poison over recipients. But he never sought their use, because the enemy had not deployed such weaponry.

So it could have been worse.

Turning point?

The 15th of September is designated as Battle of Britain Day because around this date in 1940 Hitler put his plans for the proposed invasion of England on hold – again. It was a possible window for the seaborne assault on the British Isles, requiring, in advance, domestic air forces to be sufficiently diminished to not impede the barges in the Channel.

German navy and army officers kept warning the Fuhrer about the difficulties of putting troops and gear aboard boats to cross water quickly without special training or equipment. With tired airmen and troubled planes working from unfamiliar airfields in France, Belgium and Holland, the Luftwaffe pressed on with harming the RAF and the Royal Navy's air arm, while losing a lot of craft and crew in accidents. Many went down in the sea on the way out, or on the way back. German pilots monitored their fuel carefully to make sure they could return to base. If they were forced to land in England, for them the war would be over - until invading German troops reached them, of course.

The Luftwaffe was certainly taking its toll on British aircraft: some Tommies were definitely going down in flames. Yet, somehow, next day, there seemed to be as many, if not more, English machines to meet the intruders in the skies. By the end of August, Goering was telling Hitler that his flyers were close to extinguishing the RAF menace; but the Reich Admirals needed more time to prepare sufficient craft to transport thousands of soldiers and hundreds of tanks over sea; while

Wehrmacht Generals feared what might lie beyond the beaches - assuming they avoided the big guns of Dover, and dismounted sharply from their improvised vessels.

Of course, we will never know to what degree Third Reich westward ambitions were inhibited by concerns about Britain's Royal Navy emerging in some form – surface ships or undersea – from Portsmouth and Chatham the moment any logistics activity appeared on the continental shoreline.

Nothing was clear as September proceeded, and so Hitler saw sense - one of the last occasions when a sliver of sanity prevailed - the big launch was delayed, for a few days at least. The 15th came and went, and the barges stayed in their harbours. But the Luftwaffe carried on buzzing over to bash the Brits.

A few weeks later, the Fuhrer recognised the weather was worsening (as his Admirals had said), and the days were getting shorter (as the Generals had explained) and the RAF was not eliminated (as Goering had promised), so decided it would be better to hold off until the spring.

So what we are commemorating on 15th September is that a mad dictator did not send over his invaders in the autumn of 1940 because it looked too problematic, given the circumstances. The RAF and its associates had not failed. They kept taking up more planes to challenge the Luftwaffe, which caused the enemy to delay plans by a week or two, then a few months. The British and allied flyers had not defeated the Third Reich or even the Luftwaffe, but they had defended English skies sufficiently well and for sufficiently long to cause Hitler to recalibrate.

By October 1940, the Luftwaffe more or less gave up flying across the Channel in daylight. Instead they came at night. And, in the dark, Britain had no realistic means of inhibiting such intrusions. Radar was in its infancy. There was no device or institutional system to guide British planes towards night bombers. Fighter Command could do nothing, and ground-based defences were horribly ineffective. Hence the Luftwaffe spat at UK urban areas for months on end, only abandoning this harassment in May 1941. Why? Because they were re-assigned to eastern Europe, there to invade Russia.

In the autumn of 2015, there seemed to be almost a fetish for the Spitfire in the media. Fly pasts and memorial events for The Few proliferated, witnessed by the few remaining gentlemen who had survived extraordinary days of courage 75 years before.

It is patently an honour to attend ceremonies of Remembrance for the achievements of Battle of Britain airmen and their machines. They contributed to a change in the early events of an appalling global conflict, but whenever we contemplate those heroic sons, always recall they totalled just 1% of the Allied airmen who went on to die in the skies.

Only way out

Falling on their swords was a tradition amongst military commanders who devised and/or executed a battle plan that resulted in dreadful failure. As the Second World War blundered on, this career conclusion acquired a role in the upper ranks of the Luftwaffe. Most prominently, Udet, who bore the title Generalluftzeugmeister no less, shot himself on 17th October 1941 when he became overwhelmed with the complexities of deploying forces against Russia while maintaining a belligerent aerial presence over the English Channel, across the Mediterranean and along north Africa.

Studies of the highs and lows of the German air force reveal squabbles over departmental responsibilities and priorities. The service had many excellent pilots, impressive training, and formidable determination, but was frequently hampered by conflict between senior officers. Next to see himself off was Jeschonnek, Chief of General Staff, who felt terrible after the RAF blasted the Peenemunde rocket plant in 1943.

Before the war, Luftwaffe Commander Hermann Goering boasted that he would not expose Berlin to a single bomb from enemy aircraft. For the next six years Goering continued to get things wrong and always blamed others. His final major error was to recommend he take control of Germany's prospects when Russian tanks were approaching the capital. On 23rd April 1945, from Luftwaffe HQ, he sent a message to Hitler's bunker:

> "My Fuhrer, in view of your decision to remain in Berlin to defend the city, do you agree to my now assuming command of the Reich with full authority in domestic and foreign policy?"

This didn't go down well. The recipient replied that his second-in-command deserved the death penalty and would be immediately stripped of all titles and responsibilities. Within hours, Goering was arrested by the SS, who in turn were soon captured by the Allies. Hence the Luftwaffe top man was put on trial for his war crimes. But someone slipped the prisoner poison. The Birmingham Mail of 16th October 1946 explained:

GOERING'S SUICIDE IN HIS CELL

Crunching a glass phial of cyanide in his mouth, Hermann Goering cheated the hangman by committing suicide in Nuremberg Gaol last night – two and a half hours before his ten fellow war criminals were hanged one by one in the floodlighted gymnasium of the prison.

Among the many theories being discussed is the possibility that Frau Goering could have passed the phial to her husband when kissing him (through the bars). Another theory is that the German barber may have slipped the phial between Goering's collar and neck.

The prisoner had previously confided to a Nuremberg psychiatrist:

"I wish I had surrendered to the Russians; they would have either killed me outright or treated me like a hero. I never dreamed you Americans would treat a Marshal like a common criminal.

"You remember the Mussolini incident? We got pictures of Mussolini dead in the gutter with his mistress, and hanging in the air upside down. They were awful. Hitler went into a frenzy. He seized the picture and went up and down shouting, "This will never happen to me.".."

Another pilot also brought his career to a self-inflicted conclusion. Remember Rudolph Hess, Hitler's deputy, who took a secret flight to Scotland to try to strike a peace deal? Stuck in Welsh security hospitals reading newspapers for the rest of the war, by February 1945 it all looked so gloomy that he tried stabbing himself with a bread knife.

Six months later, Hess was shipped over to Nuremberg to face trial for conspiracy to 'commit crimes against peace and humanity'. Rudolph played the amnesia card, forgetting all those terrible things he had done before the war, so the tribunal screened old newsreels of him strutting around Berlin with Hitler, which helped him remember for a while.

Hess got off with a life sentence in Spandau Prison in Berlin. Once all the others Nazis had died or been released, the absent-minded absconder could move freely in the building, doing what he liked as long as it didn't require a bread knife.

When he became infirm, the kindly jailers installed a lift so he could get down to the garden. Less sympathetic observers noted it was costing a fortune to keep alive the old bastard who had signed death warrants for millions of Jews. Then, at the age of 93, he yanked the cable from his reading lamp and hung himself out of a window.

It's official

How had the Fatherland become Rubbleland? In 1946, the UK Chiefs of Staff Intelligence Committee reported that:

> 'So long as the Germans were fighting against weak nations or enjoying overwhelming superiority, it may be said that their air strategy, as adopted, justified itself by results. Their great failure lay in the incredible optimism and over-confidence in high places, particularly on the part of Hitler himself and his political entourage, which could envisage nothing but easily-won success, and was incapable of foreseeing the strength and resources of the Powers to which they became progressively opposed, in what they refused to regard as a long-term struggle.'

The Committee noted:

> '… during the last six months of the war, relations between Hitler and the air staff increasingly deteriorated. The air staff became unable either to exert their influence in the necessary quarters or to pursue policies based on their own judgement in the light of operational experience.'

The Third Reich assigned one million people to anti-aircraft defences, two million for aircraft manufacture, but this wasn't enough. Biggest weakness was fuel shortages - once the Americans had finessed bombing the factories that could produce oil from brown coal. Air training was cut back, so new pilots were unprepared for front line challenges. Just 700 night-fighters tried to keep the western Allied bombers at bay, while experienced flak crews were filleted by demands for fresh soldiers for the eastern front.

Some captured Luftwaffe administrators revealed 'major mistakes' in their organisation, not least:

> 'Goering permitted no realistic reflection on the loss of air superiority, but squandered time and energy in the most disgusting insults of the fighter force.'

The British Chiefs concluded:

'The failure of German air strategy was part and parcel of the failure of German military strategy as a whole; the result of the blind optimism and confidence of Hitler and his entourage in final victory, and their wilful refusal to foresee and prepare against the consequences of military commitments undertaken far beyond their resources. The failure to build up German air power on a scale commensurate with their military commitments, even at the expense of other arms, played a leading part in the downfall of Hitler's Reich.'

'I see they got you too'

This is the title of the final chapter of a memoir penned by a once-handsome Australian who fought in the Battle of Britain until he was shot up by a Messerschmitt over the Channel. Richard Hillary's craft was burning fiercely and he struggled to release himself from the cockpit. Unconscious, he fell free and dropped into the water, where he was rescued by a Margate lifeboat crew. He was extremely badly burnt and spent many months recuperating until he was well enough to be considered for skin graft operations that might allow his eyes to blink properly once more, and for his face to look less misshapen.

He was assigned to a special surgery unit in Surrey run by a brilliant New Zealand doctor, Archie McIndoe. A succession of painful sessions saw Hillary become less disfigured and more functional; skin shaved off his legs for re-building his hands and face. He was sorely aware of how grotesque he appeared, and at one point hoped a German bomb would fall and kill him.

The hospital procedures eventually enabled him to take trips into London to admire the architecture and girls. In the spring of 1941 he was in a Soho bar when a Luftwaffe plane flew over and bombed the building. He struggled from the debris and was then elated when a fireman treated him as normal, asking him to help dig someone else out of rubble. Hillary uncovered an injured woman, who looked up at her rescuer and said: "I see they got you too".

Despite his appearance, and the inadequacy of his hands, the Aussie pressed the RAF to allow him to fly again. Not long after his memoir was published in 1942, Hillary was training for night-fighting when his craft crashed, killing him and another airman.

Hillary had been an early member of The Guinea Pig Club, an association of survivors of extreme burns from flying service who enjoyed social events with Mr McIndoe's talented staff at the Queen Victoria Hospital in East Grinstead. The first service participants were from Fighter Command; later, the Club became dominated by BC airmen. By 1945 there were more than 600 in the odd-looking gang, and most managed to move on to a conventional life.

One of them became a Physics teacher at Gosforth Grammar School, Newcastle on Tyne. I wish, looking back, I had had the confidence and decency to politely enquire of my tutor what he had done for his country during the war.

Declassified

For anyone who may have got the impression that flying between 1939 and 1945 was inherently dangerous, consider one man who racked up more than 400 hours as a passenger aboard aircraft and lived to tell the tale. Mr W. S. Churchill had good reason again and again to hop on a plane to travel somewhere or other. Never a leisure flight; no holiday trips for this fellow; all work-related aerial transportation. But he did it. The British Prime Minster logged all that flying, trouble-free - admittedly often with an escort of RAF fighters to ensure his journey was not intercepted by maverick Luftwaffe craft.

Appearing in the travel manifest as passenger 'Colonel Warden', Churchill enjoyed sitting in the cockpit and monitoring the controls. One of his longest trips had been to Persia in 1942 to meet Stalin for the first time. An American pilot flew the PM in a Liberator from England to Gibraltar, across the Sahara, through Egypt, then north over the Kurdistan mountains. When they landed in Teheran, the politician told the pilot that his altimeter needed adjusting because, as the plane touched down, the instrument was reading 4,000 feet above sea level. The diplomatic Yank explained that the display was correct - this was the registered height of the airfield. Undaunted, on the way back, the distinguished frequent flyer told the young fellow at the controls to gain more height as they approached Gibraltar, otherwise they might collide with the famous Rock.

Press censorship in Britain ended on 2nd September 1945, exactly six years after it had commenced. Now journalists, military managers and scientists could expose some of the secrets they had been obliged to keep away from Joe Public. The next edition of the fortnightly 'War Illustrated' revealed the 'magic' of radar, with photographs of kit in action alongside commentary that promoted a perception of boffins having broken through unbelievable barriers at early stages in the war, thus helping Britain win:

> 'On green spaces around London two acres of wire-netting were erected on small posts as a sort of giant's spider's web close to the ground. In the centre was a small wooden hut. It can now be told that these webs were the Gun and Light Laying (G.L.) system which very rapidly helped the Anti-Aircraft network to beat the blitz.'

The article added that 'within the next 24 months amazing progress was made', though some elements of the aerial systems had to be sourced from Japan. But for these machines:

> 'Britain might have been bombed to surrender-point.'

People could now be told about the hoax ships deployed along the British coast to lure enemy reconnaissance aircraft and bombers towards wooden targets, moored well away from docks. Air-sea rescue successes were announced: 3,723 British and 1,998 American air men were pulled from the drink around the British coastline.

A German journalist revealed that, following Dunkirk, Hitler had confided to him that a few heavy bombing raids on London would force the English to beg for peace. A copy of the Third Reich plans for occupied Britain was unearthed in Berlin. The document included judicial procedures:

> 'Severe punishment will be passed by military courts on civilians who associate with prisoners of war, make slurring remarks about the German Army of Occupation or its commanders, circulate pamphlets or organise meetings.'

In the early days of the war, the British Government had devised contingency plans for evacuating London in the face of approaching German ground troops. A major concern was what to do with the Royal Family. One intention was to drive them up to Worcestershire, to secretly install them in a big private house in big private grounds –

Madresfield Court. Then they could be moved further north and extracted by aircraft from Scotland for a low-profile trip to Canada. To support this scenario, a Ministry van delivered lots of tinned food to Madresfield to be kept under lock and key until the arrival of the distinguished guests. Lady Morrison recently told the author that, when it became clear the king and queen would not turn up on their doorstep, her family contemplated utilising the larder full of goodies, but resisted the temptation - which was fortunate, for in the summer of 1945, Ministry men returned to Madresfield to carefully cross-check the original delivery manifest and load all the cans back in a van again.

Strike unsure?

Bomber Command had endeavoured to help bring about the defeat of the Third Reich as quickly as possible. How? By dropping high explosives and incendiary devices on that regime until it was sufficiently damaged, devastated and death-strewn to have no appetite or capacity to continue menacing its neighbours or even defending its own territory, and would instead surrender unconditionally.

This required lots of big aircraft capable of conveying large quantities of ordnance across the North Sea to decant above German assets. The work needed thousands of courageous people with the skills and constitution to operate in dreadful conditions with a high likelihood of an abrupt death in horrible circumstances.

Every airman was a volunteer, who in effect made a pact between himself and his country – to anticipate an imminent, traumatic death to help unleash weaponry on enemy facilities, then bring the planes back in order to repeat the procedures as quickly as possible. Prospects for painless survival were extremely poor; 25 new recruits were required every day, because that was the average loss rate for the sons undertaking the tasks.

Typically, five Allied bomber aircraft failed to survive their required journey each day or night. The inadequacy of the early machines became swiftly, sharply, apparent. But the process of supplying better craft could take years. Meanwhile, the management had to make the best of what they'd got. And they did. Bombing what they could, when they could.

The fine monument to Bomber Command in Green Park in London features the force's motto, 'Strike Hard, Strike Sure'. But the notion of surgical targeting was unrealistic through most of the war. Those boys were simply tipping out the contents of a flying lorry full of explosives.

And the Allies never really comprehended the Germans' capacity to return to some sort of normality after a raid. The British should have known better, because they had evidence from their own bombed industrial areas during the winter of 1940-41. They knew that in the aftermath of an assault, the rescue and civic services acted swiftly to extract the injured, put out fires, remove the bodies, shore up structures, repair utilities, tidy rubble and re-open the street or factory. Those not directly affected wanted to return to relative normality: go to work, earn their wages, bring home food. The factories needed to re-commence production and meet orders.

German regional authorities were extremely efficient at supporting the recovery of a bombed street. They would commission re-building work and assign destitute families to houses that had belonged to Jewish people.

After the war, the occupying Allies discovered that much of daily life had continued uninterrupted in many German cities. Factory production was generally only disturbed for a few days. Of course, the cruel irony of such recovery capacity and survival instincts was that the war went on and on, so the density of destruction and death became ever more severe. Still those populations did not abandon their neighbourhoods, their workplaces, but struggled on. Max Hastings points out that in ruined cities German people queued at temporary offices to pay their taxes. Area bombing did not fragment the German populace. The citizens never rioted, revolted or rose up en masse against their leadership – which was what the Allies had anticipated.

Why did so many cathedrals and churches remain upright, defiant, proud, amidst the smouldering rubble? This was not necessarily evidence of the work of God. The places of worship were better built than the surrounding offices and houses. Generally they had sloping roofs supported by strong stone walls and pillars. Bombs and incendiaries would generally roll off such structures, their robust survival making for a compelling picture.

When the United States reviewed their European bombing campaign they were stunned by the statistics: the Third Reich war machine continued to expand munitions production right to the end of 1944. This was because most of the work was not based in the sixty cities which the RAF had recommended targeting. All that bombing, all the blood spilled by the deliverers and the receivers, had made only a small dent in the capacity of Hitler's armaments industry.

By March 1945, when so much of Germany was in ruins, so many people were dead, injured or in mourning, the anticipated resolution of the bombing war had still not come about. Many citizens rationalised that the havoc in their town was retribution for having permitted the Nazis to come to power, and having turned a blind eye to the removal of their Jewish neighbours.

As Allied ground troops battled towards Germany, concentration camp guards hid evidence of their despicable work by forcing surviving prisoners to dig up the dead from the mass graves with their bare hands in order to burn the remains. Allied forces brought about the termination of such inhuman behaviour: the holocaust, the murdering of innocent people on an industrial scale. This had never been the motive for all that bravery and determination, but what an achievement.

Overy's study of 'The Bombing War' concludes that the American concentration on damaging oil supplies most effectively delimited the Nazi regime. Blanket assaults by the RAF caused merely 3% of the damage to German economic capacity. The Nazi conquest of Europe had provided the regime with eight million forced workers, while 20 million more within the occupied zones slaved on orders for Third Reich war demands:

> 'For most of the Allied bombing offensive these factors were either insufficiently known or not understood, and bombing, as a result, was relatively ineffective.'
>
> '...even if the estimated total of 350,000 German dead from bombing were all workers, that would still have represented only 1.6% of the German industrial and rural workforce...'

However Professor Overy does acknowledge that the relentless bombing of the Fatherland by the RAF, and later the Americans, did force Germany to assign military assets to challenge that offensive which in turn weakened the Reich's army capacities. For the Allies:

'Bombing could be used to maintain domestic morale and to exert leverage on the enemy in ways which were rendered easily visible in the democratic media. That the campaign could have been conducted differently, at lower cost (to both sides) and with greater efficacy, is not in doubt, but it is evident from the historical record why these opportunities, strategic and technical, were missed or ignored or misunderstood, or incompetently attempted. War is always easier to fight looking backwards.'

Overy's analysis makes clear how lucky you and I are not to have lived through those terrible times; not to have had to choose agonising political or military decisions, or been obliged to undertake terrifying military service.

I would add that Bomber Command essentially succeeded with its grim responsibilities, because the lunatic who had started it all was driven to kill himself. Thanks in part to the monumental endeavours of the Command, the fundamental job was done. Europe's recent seventy-plus years of peace and prosperity are due in part to those many, many thousands of Bomber Command airmen who executed their tasks with unending determination and extraordinary courage. Let us always respect and remember them.

Remains

A British bomber which crashed on icy mountains in Sweden remained lost for more than thirty years until the craft was encountered by hikers who found the frozen bodies of some of the airmen still inside. It is estimated that a quarter of a million incendiary canisters are still buried in German soil. Every year ordnance devices are unearthed, sometimes exploding and injuring or killing the disposal experts. Three members of an extraction team died together in Cottingen in 2010. Not every dug-up object is handled with care. Birmingham's rubbish disposal plant has received rusty bombs that people have found in their gardens and just dumped in their bins.

After the war all nations had huge quantities of munitions that were no longer necessary. RAF units were assigned to detonate unused stocks of German ordnance. Thousands of aircraft were scrapped; just a few examples preserved for museums.

In Britain, remnants of radar stations have become shrines of respect. East of Ipswich is The Transmitter Block which housed part of 'the world's first operational radar station' that enabled 'a numerically inferior RAF to intercept and defeat the Luftwaffe'. Old airfield control towers are treasured and promoted, also often with degrees of contrivance as to their specific role in advancing the Allied cause. A few runways were given new purpose in the 1970s with the construction of the motorway network. A length of the M4 sits across an old RAF base; the M5 utilises a strip that served a Gloucester aircraft factory.

All over Britain are museums displaying military aircraft. Most substantial collections are the RAF centres at Hendon in London and Cosford in the Midlands, and the Imperial War Museum's site at Duxford in Cambridgeshire. Hendon's ambition is:

'... to ensure that the RAF story endures for future generations.'

An excellent research library enables people to dig out detail on personnel, aircraft, sites and missions; though certain squadrons:

'... only mention flights which involved combat. Some units had to destroy their records, for example, when retreating during the Battle of France in 1940.'

And in some busy training units:

'... only events such as accidents would be deemed worthy of note.'

The Museum's quarterly glossy magazine, Radar, covers many matters aerial, from historical research to collectible prospects. One recent edition profiled war-time RAF Caribbean volunteers alongside a recommendation for Spitfire cufflinks as a Valentine's Day gift.

Duxford holds a fine range of British aircraft and an original V1 rocket ramp. One big modern building is intricately packed with a cross-section of USAAF machines.

Most European countries hold some remnants of air combat. In the middle of Sweden is the Bofors Industrial Museum where:

'...visitors can find out about the famous Bofors 40-mm anti-aircraft gun which, amongst other things, helped to defend London during the Second World War'

The literature makes no reference to the many bigger guns made for Germany, or those manufactured under licence in the USA, or how the economy was affected by such exports.

Hamburg still contains vast concrete constructions built to protect soldiers and citizens from Allied bombing, including several huge flak towers which look like features from a Batman movie. These ten-storey monsters were commissioned by Hitler to demonstrate that his regime had the capacity to defend itself: reinforced walls three metres thick, topped by massive guns, collectively able to fire 8,000 shells a minute at enemy aircraft 14 kilometres away. The macabre towers remind all who see them of the determination of a deranged psychopath to fend the heart of his grotesque empire from aerial enemies – and that's the idea. German schoolchildren are taught about the Fuhrer and his atrocities, and shown evidence of those dark days. A Hamburg church holds a museum showing how the country experienced Allied bombing. A Cologne museum is in a building that was used by the Gestapo. Visitors can examine the prison cells and contemplate their purpose.

In Berlin are many admirable museums. The Jewish Museum is a fine, sensitive institution, where you can consider the experiences of a young Jew who escaped from Berlin, got to the U.S.A., joined the army, was posted to Europe, and so helped liberate the city - where he eventually found a few of his relatives, but learned that the rest had gone to concentration camps.

The Technik Museum holds 40 aircraft and:

'....portrays the rise and fall of the Luftwaffe and shows how the National Socialists misused the fascination with flying for their own purposes.'

Visitors can also see one of the freight trucks used to transport Jews.

A Berlin railway station retains remnants of its façade as destroyed in November 1943. The German town of Wallberg keeps on show a pile of rubble created by area bombing. Until the Berlin wall came down, there were acres of rubble to its west, but now the whole area has been re-built, without any indication of the spot below where Hitler shot himself.

For a sense of the enormity of the tasks undertaken by Bomber Command, visit Lincolnshire where the greatest concentration of squadron airfields lay. When the Americans were allocated to East Anglia, this flat county became the next best place for BC bases.

Twenty airfields held half the Command, and some sites are still active RAF centres, many housing accessible history features. Local cemeteries often have War Grave sections commemorating airmen. Pubs and cafes display signed photographs of aircraft. The village of Woodhall Spa has memorials to BC Squadrons in its square, near the Petwood Hotel which was a centre of Command officer activity, formal and informal. At RAF Coningsby is the hangar for the Battle of Britain Memorial Flight – the Lancaster, Spitfires and Hurricanes delivering popular air displays in the summer months.

Remnants of old stations have been preserved. Most evocative is East Kirkby where two young farmers - inspired by the loss of their brother on a bombing sortie - gathered rare artefacts from BC missions. Without public sector grants, they collected paperwork and equipment to present tableaux capturing squadron life and times. One complex interpretation panel shows the array of target locations for Lancaster flights from here. 164 of those aircraft did not come back: nine lost over Berlin, a dozen around Stuttgart. Eight crashed somewhere else in Germany, four went down in France. Eight sank in the North Sea, ten had fatal problems close to base, and fourteen disappeared without trace.

Representation

Germany's biggest military museum is in Dresden. Holding thousands of guns and a set of rockets, it pre-dates the war and was not damaged in February 1945. There is little evidence of the Nazi regime, except for a few tanks, a soldier's helmet displaying a tiny swastika, a battered 'Adolf Hitler Street' sign, and a small bust of him:

> 'The Museum has made an effort to distance itself from the visual presentations of military history. Instead of glorifying war and armies, the museum tries to present the causes and consequences of war and violence.'

Peenemunde's Technical Museum at the old rocket test site takes pride in German scientific prowess, but acknowledges the 'ambivalent nature of technological progress'.

Several museums in Canada profile that country's considerable and vital input to the work of RAF Bomber Command. One houses a Lancaster.

Tangmere – a critical Battle of Britain airfield near Chichester - is a rich centre of RAF appreciation run by enthusiasts. A hangar panel explains:

> Today it is 'a peaceful scene under an English heaven', but as you look, remember the many thousands of men and women who worked, fought from and sometimes died here. Whose efforts helped ensure the peace and freedom we take for granted today. Let them not be carelessly forgotten.

The RAF museums do a first class job in presenting examples of aircraft, with explanatory panels about the machine, and where and when it was mostly used. One of the first features visitors encounter at Hendon and Cosford is the sophisticated set of vertical panels displaying information on the development of flying over consecutive years. Hendon's Milestones of Flight occupies one long wall opposite a selection of exhibits. Each of the 100 panels is nearly three metres tall and a third of a metre wide. The first features 1903 and, in particular, the Wright Brothers first powered flight. At the far end, the year 2002 panel includes a paragraph respectfully noting the recent death of the Queen Mother.

The format means each year has exactly the same space to display a magazine-like mix of images and information. Typically ten paragraphs of text pick out interesting or important phenomena of that year: new planes, special events, memorable achievements - all of which, at first sight, seems satisfactory. But the design formula causes the development and endeavours of the Royal Air Force to be presented in a very strange way, due to each year getting equal space. It makes 1903 seem as significant as 1943 and 1983. To the casual viewer it looks convenient and digestible, but if you consider how many planes took off in 1903 compared with forty years later; how many people worked in the aircraft industry (if you could call it that) at the start of the 20th century compared with 1943; how many professionals died in air crashes in each of those periods that lie four decades apart - surely 1943 deserves more space? The traumatic continental war years are only distinguished from less troubled times by a slight change in the background colour of the panels. That staggering density of commitment, responsibility, activity and significance of those shocking periods of last century's history are almost invisible. I would contend that very few people stop to study the panel for 1944 and read through the ten paragraphs of snippets to discover:

'The RAF reached its peak personnel strength in July: 1,185,833.'

Staff tell me that many visitors don't know even know what the initials R.A.F. stand for. Cosford's version, 'Aviation Timeline', consists of similar but smaller panels covering 1912 to 2006, squeezed into a small room.

Evaluation and re-interpretation of the war continues with vigour, not least while servicemen and women from those years are still with us. The RAF Museums run research programmes and lecture series, often supported by teaching staff from university war history departments. I hope some student of conflict is studying the power of image to impact on one's perception of history. I was shocked at a large bust of Adolf Hitler on display in a military museum in Spain. No interpretation detail, but one immediately recognised the profile and felt unease.

Across Britain these days we can find many images of war aircraft, especially Spitfires and Lancasters, on sale, frequently without context. The pictures alone convey valour and victory. In Duxford's shop I counted 80 items featuring a Spitfire image. I recently met a Second World War pilot who was regularly asked by a picture salesman to sign copies of Spitfire prints. The old chap did this in exchange for a few free samples. Perhaps he should have requested that a donation be made to a service charity for each of his valuable signatures.

Hendon's Bomber Hall holds a Lancaster that survived more than 130 missions across the North Sea. I suspect few visitors see the small panel of text on an adjacent wall:

'Bomber Command was the RAF's main UK-based strategic striking force during the Second World War.

A total of 364,514 individual sorties were flown by Bomber Command crews, and approximately 955,044 tons of weapons dropped. No fewer than 8325 Bomber Command aircraft were lost on operations, with 55,500 men killed and 8,430 wounded.

Many of those who gave their lives in combat were from the Commonwealth, including 8209 Canadian Royal Air Force, 3412 Royal Australian Air Force and 1433 Royal New Zealand Air Force personnel. Additionally, a further 8305 air and ground crew were killed in non-combat accidents.'

At rest

Imagine you are crewing a bomber over enemy territory when something goes seriously wrong with your aircraft: the skipper decides it will not travel as far as a neutral country or even the sea and there is no alternative but to get out now.

If you manage to exit with your parachute and it opens and functions like they promised, then you are descending on to enemy soil. You may be aware or unaware of the circumstances of your fellow crew members. They could be gently dropping somewhere nearby, or might still be aboard your plane. As you descend, you have a few minutes to collect your thoughts, contemplate your situation; anticipate what may lie ahead. This seems to me preferable to being blown to smithereens inside the fuselage. But someone may have spotted you on your way down. If they have a gun, they may be tempted, or instructed, to shoot you. If you land in one piece, can you unclip your harness and hide the chute and run for cover, or are people going to grab you? Will these captors be sympathetic to your plight? Or will they harbour bitterness against you and all foreign airmen who have recently caused such trouble, damage and pain to their neighbourhood, family, friends, nation? Your fate could be protracted and horrible - the price of that benign descent and those precious moments to evaluate your life and, if inclined, to say your prayers.

Dozens of airmen who fell from bombers were assaulted by furious folk, uninhibited by any formal procedures regarding the handling of enemy servicemen. A lynching party could gather; some locals relishing participation, others wary. Technically, a fatal assault might be a crime, but there was every chance officials would not fret about one less prisoner-of-war to process. However that ugly flurry of vindictive activity might not be lost in the fog of war, because witnesses who harboured reservations about the angry gang could see fit, when peace was achieved, to alert authorities of the dark deeds. In August 1944, six American airmen parachuted down in Darmstadt to be murdered by the people who surrounded them. Then, in June 1945, Allied occupation laws came into effect and members of that lynch mob were identified and arrested. Five men and two women were found guilty of war crimes and sentenced to death by hanging.

Of course, most airmen in troubled planes never met their opponents face to face. Instead they died in or around their craft when it broke up or blew up in the sky. These boys, or bits of them, dropped fast. Germanic authorities were diligent at recording Allied deaths and organising the burial of the remains of victims with some sort of dignity. Once the Allies were managing the country, considerable effort was applied to dealing afresh with the war dead, which meant most bodies were moved to new locations; many American victims taken back to the USA at the request of their families.

Cemeteries across Europe, including 200 in the UK, hold the remains of airmen. The Kiel War Cemetery has nearly 1,000 Allied crewmen lost in bombing raids. Berlin's 1939-1945 War Cemetery is primarily occupied by airmen: 2,700 British, 530 Canadian, 220 Australian, 60 New Zealanders, 50 Indians and 30 South Africans. Reichswald Forest Cemetery manages more than 4,000 graves of Allied flyers. The distinguished American Cemetery outside Cambridge holds almost 4,000 men who died in air crashes in East Anglia. However, the biggest concentration of deceased US service personnel is at Manila in the Philippines where 53,000 men are remembered, many thousands of whom were air guys.

I counsel you to visit War Graves Commission sites in England and ponder the gravestones. Sobering, stark reminders of the price paid by so many sons.

Memorials

How can you mislay 20,000 people? That is one discrepancy between different sources on war dead in Britain. The US Battle Monuments Commission Memorial booklet states:

> 'When the Strategic Bombing Campaign ended on April 12, 1945, the Americans had dropped 1,388,000 tons of bombs and the British 988,000 on Germany - at the cost of 110,000 airmen from both nations lost in action.'

Whereas RAF Hendon's Souvenir Guidebook tells readers that Bomber Hall is:

> '...a memorial to the 131,000 young men who died during the combined bombing offensive.'

Have the Americans left out the Commonwealth, and perhaps extracted deaths from accidents? The US Air Museum at Duxford records:

'At its peak strength in 1944, USAAF employed 450,000 Americans in Britain. Nearly 30,000 never made it home.'

The Air Forces Memorial at Runnymede near Windsor is dedicated to 20,456 men and women from air forces of the British Empire lost in air and other operations during World War Two and who have no known grave. We can appreciate the possibilities for overlap or exclusion*.

A trio of Russian War Memorials in and around Berlin commemorate the 80,000 Soviet personnel who died during the capturing of Berlin in April and May 1945, when western Allied air forces were winding down. Luftwaffe crew who died battling Britain have a memorial plaque at Shoreham Aircraft Museum. Sites of individual German plane crashes in the UK are sometimes marked and maintained.

One of the first memorials to World War Two RAF personnel was unveiled in Denmark in July 1945, where a Mosquito had crashed the previous September. On the Cocos Islands in the south Pacific is a memorial established by an ex-Bomber Command officer who moved to New Zealand after the war and learnt about a crew of six who had died on the Cocos in an unfortunate take-off.

It is very easy to ignore memorials. Most lie in defined locations that one does not need to encounter. But many sit in public space where people can consider the plaques. One of the simplest but most effective I know nestles at a minor road junction south of Worcester and reads:

'Does it mean nothing (to you) – ye who pass by?'

I hope this book will incline more people to contemplate such tributes.

Easy to miss is a modest statue in front of St Clement Danes church on the Strand in London. The plaque reads:

'Marshall of the Royal Air Force
Sir Arthur Harris BT GCB OBE AFC.
In memory of a great commander and of the brave crews of Bomber Command, more than 55,000 of whom lost their lives in the cause of freedom. The nation owes them all an immense debt.'

It was unveiled by the Queen Mother in 1994 in a ceremony disturbed by people who considered Harris a war criminal. I suspect the hecklers were unaware of the reflections in War Illustrated, 28th September 1945:

> 'In this war Harris fought for his Command and the boys who flew the bombers. He had to fight those who opposed the bombing strategy, and they were many. In his heart Harris mourned the loss of the gallant fellows whose lives were lost flying his bombers because Hitler and some other fools had plunged the world into war.
>
> Some day, little pig-tailed Jacqueline Harris will grow up and realize that her daddy was a great war leader. Perhaps the British public will grow up, too, and understand that Harris's policy saved countless lives in the Army and the Navy and that no one man contributed more to the reduction of Allied casualties in the Second World War.'

As we know, the Kent coast dog-fights took place in August and September 1940. The next year there was little appetite to reflect on that combat - RAF units were bombing in the Baltic and other squadrons had just arrived in Russia to aid our new allies. But in September 1943 a lunch was held in London for some of the airmen who had survived the Battle of Britain, and ex-Home Secretary Sir John Anderson emphasised the importance of those skirmishes:

> 'Surely there was never such a marvellous year as 1940, witnessing as it did those absolutely shattering events in just a few weeks. Surely there never was a greater battle, never one in which more stupendous issues depended. The fate of our Empire was at stake, and with it the liberties of free nations. Likewise there was never a battle more decisively won. Before the enemy had to admit defeat he had lost no fewer than 2,400 machines in some 10 weeks.'

The following year, services remembering the struggle were held at St. Paul's Cathedral and Westminster Abbey. After the war, Lord Trenchard lobbied to create a Battle of Britain chapel in the Abbey. His ashes were interred there in 1956. Fifty years later, a magnificent sculpture of fighter airmen was established on the Thames Embankment half-a-mile from the Abbey.

Recently, a statue commemorating women who worked in the steel industry during the war was unveiled in Sheffield. Hearing the proud testimony of those elderly ladies on BBC Radio Four's 'Women's Hour' brought a lump to my throat.

A new memorial in Lincoln is bringing fresh attention to air war endeavour. On a hill across from the Cathedral, the International Bomber Command Centre has being developed to:

> 'Educate future generations about those who served with the Command and the sacrifices they made to preserve our freedom.'

Designed to complement the East Kirkby Aviation Heritage Centre, it inscribes the names of the 26,500 BC fatalities listed at Lincoln Cathedral whose squadrons were based in the county, and will also add the further 30,000 who saw service from other stations. An archive centre has been built close to the tasteful commemorative panelling that forms an array around the base of a handsome wing-like spire:

> 'We owe it to those who have never before been properly recognised to put the record straight.'

Birmingham was the third most heavily bombed British city, experiencing 2,000 tons of Luftwaffe ordnance which killed 2,241 people and seriously injured another 3,000. In all, there were 77 air raids, destroying around 13,000 buildings. In 2005, Birmingham erected a memorial to the victims of the blitz bombing. 'Tree of Life' is a modest affair, attracting little attention in a busy shopping district, close to temporary market stalls, including, occasionally and innocently, one for a German barbeque butcher.

A more powerful reminder of those shocking times in Brum would be to re-consider the 15,000 aluminium discs stuck on the side of a new shopping mall. The big round panels were never meant to symbolise anything; just a neat way of decorating a large curving structure. If we saw fit to imagine each disc representing either a person or a building in Birmingham that was eliminated by bombing assault, the shiny circles could take on historic significance.

*9,000 British airmen had died in World War One. Between the wars, accidents saw off 3,700. Since 1945, a further 16,000 RAF air men have perished.

Showing off – again

"Aren't planes great. Look what they can do!"

The RAF's hardware is its best recruiting tool. Who doesn't want to get close to such impressive things. Fast and powerful; sleek and sexy. The admiration of magnificent flying machines dates from their first tentative elevations off the ground. Soon after the start of the annual Hendon displays, the newly-constructed Wembley Stadium staged 'London Defended - a stirring Searchlight Spectacle'- wherein planes swooped over the football pitch firing blanks and dropping mock bombs on ground crew pretending to blast up shells.

We have noted the first peacetime victory parades and fly-pasts. By 1946 the appetite for putting on a show had grown: 38 RAF squadrons mustered 330 planes to cross London, then head over coastal towns from Portsmouth to Exeter for the sixth anniversary of the Battle of Britain. Meanwhile, alongside a factory in Hertfordshire, the Society of British Aircraft Constructors had staged a commercial flying programme. The Times reported:

> 'Amongst the interesting demonstrations was refuelling in the air. Two Lancasters took off almost together and one refuelled the other over the aerodrome with a long pipe.'

The summer had also seen British European Airways commence its new regular service between London and Ankara. Civil aviation was on the up.

In 1947 the September commemoration fleet was reduced, perhaps because of scheduling difficulties amidst mushrooming passenger flights. The fly-past was part of 'Battle of Britain Week', which included a tableaux of planes parked in Horse Guards parade, and another Daily Telegraph sponsored pageant at the Albert Hall, entitled 'Festival of Reunion', aiding the RAF Benevolent Fund - which, by December 1946, had helped 80,000 families and were dealing with 19,000 new cases. A supportive member of the House of Lords pointed out:

> "It still cannot be seen when the calls for help will substantially diminish."

The aerial parade of 130 planes, including examples from the Royal Navy, the USA and Czechoslovakia, was led by a Hurricane, described in The Times as:

'... symbol of the men and aircraft of the Battle of Britain.'

So, at this stage, the Spitfire had yet to move into the limelight.

By 1952 the confederation of British Aircraft Constructors had settled into Farnborough, and the challenges of handling prototypes were horribly demonstrated: a new type of jet was flying towards the site when it broke up, propelling one of its engines into the crowd. The two men at the controls died, as did 25 members of the public, with a further 60 injured. St Johns' Ambulance crews removed the bodies - then, amazingly, the air show continued. This surely reflected the culture of a time when war was still strong in memories. People were used to planes crashing: you got on afterwards the best you could. In fact, the next day's show drew a bigger crowd. 'Flight' magazine considered the test pilot:

'...a steadfast champion of the progress which is being so perilously won. It is the clear responsibility of everyone concerned to "press on", giving constant thought to the pilots who render this advancement possible. Such men are the pathfinders of the supersonic age upon which, for better or worse, we now enter.'

The inquest concluded that the airmen 'died accidentally in the normal course of their duty', and that the deaths of spectators were also accidental. A week later the flyers were posthumously awarded the Queen's Commendation for Valuable Service in the Air, while 'Flight' mused on the Farnborough first-aid parties, who were:

'... helped beyond measure by the steadiness, calmness and quiet refusal to panic of the crowd of some 120,000. No tribute could be too high for the man-in-the-street and his wife and family who came that afternoon to watch the great demonstration of British aviation and would not be deterred from staying to the end.'

On their way home, survivors had discovered clumps of dried blood on their clothing. Seemingly, none of them, nor the relatives of the dead, saw fit to try to sue the Society of Constructors, or the aircraft manufacturers, or the event managers - the Ministry of Supply - for their misfortunes on that Saturday.

The following year, a prang over the Grand Canyon resulted in more order being applied to the utilisation of air space. American civil aviation was highly competitive. Customers needed to be won and stroked. Operators wanted full planes making pleasant journeys that would encourage repeat business. Sometimes a little de-tour would allow travellers a better view of what lay below, which was the intention of two crews from different companies as they flew their charges over the famous gorge. Alas, while everyone was gazing at rock formations, the two craft collided. After this, the sky began to be regulated: air space defined vertically and horizontally, monitored to isolate individual flights.

In Britain, the concept of dedicated war planes passing over public events was consolidated. Instead of you going to a memorial, the memorial would come to you. Negotiations with civil airline operators allowed one vintage fleet to vector over a huge spread of sites on a single afternoon.

Almost all aircraft have a "Wow!" factor, not least modern jets. The design, noise, power and handling capacity are what you register when a machine appears. No-one needs to know anything about the RAF or aeronautics to be impressed, awed, by their presence.

The Red Arrows were formed in 1964 to replace various RAF display fleets. Here is a marketing device that needs no text. The wonder of their elegant, breath-taking swoops are sufficient to respect their builders and users. 60,000 people recently watched the boys zoom over Cosford. The Official Programme, part sponsored by Rolls Royce, presented a sanitised and glorious summary of the Force, past, present and future. The author hopes this publication will provide some context for everyone who loves a great plane.

2015 brought opportunities to show planes to the Royal Family. On Saturday 11th June, Her Majesty's 90th Birthday saw fifteen craft over Buckingham Palace. A month later, another Palace crossing marked the 75th anniversary of the Battle of Britain which, the RAF's press release explained:

'... ranks alongside the battles of Trafalgar and Waterloo as one of the most significant in British history. It was the first major battle to be fought entirely in the air and was the first significant strategic defeat for the Nazis during World War II. The RAF's victory enabled the western

Allies to later liberate Western Europe and compel the Nazis to fight on two fronts, leading to their consequent defeat.'

Who would have time to question this summary? A few weeks later, a jet performing a Saturday air show routine near Brighton (where, 75 years ago, there would have been RAF and Luftwaffe fighters overhead) swerved down towards a major road, slicing across the carriageway, hitting cars, and casting metal against spectators. This proved perfect timing for Sunday newspaper editors, with witnesses supplying graphic images of flaming wreckage. The Sun then campaigned to have old jets banned from flying displays, and the Civil Aviation Authority soon amended its rules. How fortunate we are that such horrors have become so exceptional.

In September 2015, one UK broadcaster screened a pair of programmes about the Battle of Britain, the second of which featured a fly-past of WW2 fighters. The presenters took some liberties with their explanations of the significance and ordering of the original events. Perhaps to a degree this was to justify the commissioning budget and to capture audience attention. Some critical factors never reached the screen, but simply appeared within the Radio Times supporting text. Viewers were given a very simplified and somewhat misleading picture of what those wonderful machines and men had done. Does it matter? I think so. (Further examples on our website section: 'As seen on TV'.)

Big hitters

There are more than 100 books about the Spitfire - patently an endless appetite for examining and appreciating this fine machine. Reading Amazon reviews posted by purchasers, one can identify obsessions over glorifying the aircraft. Amateur critics pick holes in certain titles for failing to respect a particular marque; not acknowledging aspects of evolving characteristics or circumstances. Most UK library bookshelves offer a selection of these volumes, amidst general or specific studies of war and aviation. Not all provide satisfactory insights. One coffee table book of 'The Blitz' consists of 1940-41 photographs taken for national newspapers: 160 choreographed images providing an impression of Luftwaffe bombing impact. Severe damage is profiled, yet in the background we can see that most buildings are intact; the photographers could not find an angle to show devastation to the horizon.

Plenty of images of plucky folk cheerily making efforts to return to normality; not least a bunch of Cockneys conducting a sing-song round a rescued piano on a pavement - all conveniently facing the camera. Most contrived is a dog being theatrically rescued from a hole in the ground. One wonders how many times the animal was lifted up before the picture-maker was happy with the shot. Members of the Royal Family are seen visiting happy people amidst the rubble. No dead bodies are shown; there is just one image of distress: a woman in tears. The message: citizens survived despite the destruction, and found ways to re-establish normality; demonstrating the Brits could not be beaten by the Nazis. The narrative does not mention what the RAF was doing, or not doing, to resist the raids.

For a digestible yet comprehensive narrative on the whole conflict, I counsel you to absorb Antony Beevor's superb 'The Second World War'. His chapters on the mass, horrific, inhuman behaviours following Germany's invasion of Russia make much of the air war seem civilised and trifling.

A big champion of Bomber Command is Denis Richards, who gives a positive spin to horrible outings in 'The Hardest Victory'. After recounting one early ghastly sortie, he considers: 'For this operation the balance sheet showed nothing on the credit side for Bomber Command except gallantry.' Mr Richards does not hide troubles and tragedies, but acts as a great advocate for the necessity of what the Command set out to do. Two 'areas of weakness' were aircraft heating systems and the 0.3 inch machine guns. Achievements include bombing invasion barges, bolstering British morale, sea-mining, helping defeat U-boats and the German surface fleet, knocking out Italy and reducing the V-weapon menace. He acknowledges the Command failed to make much of a dent in enemy munitions production.

But when faced with such critical circumstances, what could the Armed Forces do but try and try again to hurl their assets at the enemy in the belief that combat would in some way inhibit the menace? Our political and military leadership never lost sight of the essential task of maintaining a perception at home and abroad that Britain could fight on and was fighting on. The Americans appreciated evidence of that - which might sooner or later incline them to support western Europe's efforts to overcome the Nazi regime. Stalin wanted to see the greatest possible military force being brought to bear against the western side of German-occupied territory - to draw a degree of pressure away from Soviet army orders to stand ground in the face of hugely powerful and determined offensives. Subjugated citizens across Europe, being treated brutally by Third Reich psychopaths, could draw a fragment of comfort from knowing their oppressors were being challenged elsewhere. The millions across the British Empire wanted evidence that the home nation was doing everything possible to defend itself before responding to requests for help. And Britons needed to believe that there were schemes afoot, resources being deployed, initiatives being undertaken to lessen the trouble they were experiencing or, more likely, learning about.

Newspaper editors required a front page lead that was not a wail of desperation or despair, gruesome news of citizens' deaths, or house and street destruction; rumours of possible national defeat. The role of the RAF was to contribute as much as possible to sustaining and advancing the capacity to cause trouble for the enemy – sink their ships, cripple their aircraft, impede their troops, flatten their factories. Deliver as much inconvenience, damage and pain to that abrasive regime as assets would allow. That was why they went out there again and again, often in less than satisfactory planes with less than satisfactory equipment in less than satisfactory conditions. Those volunteer airmen were defending British airspace and intruding into hostile territory to provide regular evidence that here was a nation committed to succeed against whatever odds.

I trust our range of newspaper headlines provide a useful context for the activity and its evaluation. The major publications were inclined (not just because of censorship) to consider all missions as necessary; and were therefore respected. Their capital letter presentation is a valuable prism for considering the social impact of cataclysmic events which historians sometimes cloud over by coldly extracting facts and figures.

Most approved RAF histories tend to swiftly skate over the thin ice of troubled days or nights. In contrast, we have been enlightened on our journey by acute observations from the two military historians who have most forensically examined the astounding trajectory of Bomber Command: Sir Max Hastings and Professor Richard Overy. I am very grateful to both of them for allowing me to generously quote from their formidable analyses.

For documentation of the material and human loss on individual Bomber Command missions, turn to William Chorley's six volumes listing the demise of each aircraft. The first book covers 1939 and 1940; four are devoted to one calendar year of the war, the final volume to 1945. They constitute a sobering catalogue of aerial tragedy. Each year's edition is thicker than its predecessor, up until 1945 - because more aircraft were destroyed each successive year.

The entries document the last flight of each aircraft - who was aboard and what is known or is suspected to have caused the demise. Most crew are logged as having died, but if they became prisoners, that is accounted for; and any other anomalies or relevant information is briefly noted - each son generally warranting a single line entry. Chorley's work deserves space in any decent library in Britain for evermore.

Worcester's Hive – where this author has spent much time - has a thousand titles on World War Two, thanks in part to related University courses. The City of Birmingham Library holds 1,500 books on military matters and aviation. The nearby Ian Allen bookshop has 1,000 Aviation titles. A few streets away, Waterstones offers 500 books on World War Two - 30 of which have a Spitfire image on their cover. Every one of these books acts to some extent as an antidote to the perception of those school children who told me that "Hitler took over Europe and bombed Britain, but the RAF shot down his planes, and Hitler was defeated - then England won the World Cup". (More recommended reads in our website section: 'Find out more'.)

Where are we now?

The era of blundering around in the dark in the skies, trying to release ordnance that might do something to discourage the enemy from proceeding with their prosecution of the war, whilst not falling out of the sky yourself is long gone - replaced by high tech, 'surgical' strikes, controlled from a console far from the front line, with the capacity to eliminate specific troublesome individuals. On 8th September 2015, seventy five years on from the RAF's initial failure to deflect Luftwaffe bombing raids on London, the Daily Telegraph's front page headline was:

RAF KILLS BRITISH JIHADISTS IN SYRIA TO SAVE THE QUEEN

Bizarre science fiction? No, true, but clearly worded to maximise the triumph of the Royal Air Force. A couple of renegade British citizens fighting with Isis terrorists in war-torn Syria had been using the internet to encourage associates in England to mount attacks on the Royal Family during the events marking the 70th anniversary of VJ Day. GCHQ had identified the messages and their sources. The locations of the senders were monitored, and when the men drove a car across a desert track they became isolated and thus a clear target for a drone missile attack. One RAF 'pilot', sitting in a room in Lincolnshire, flew a drone towards the vehicle then, using the camera pictures from aboard the drone, unleashed missiles to blast the occupants. And it worked.

Big Facebook-type photos of the victims showed them as swarthy, gun-wielding guerrillas. The Telegraph headline was sculpted from a complicated political statement by David Cameron, designed to offset criticisms of dither from No 10 in the wake of difficult issues stemming from Middle East crises, not least the horror and embarrassment of many refugees dying near Mediterranean beaches as they endeavoured to escape from conflict.

Most British newspapers relished this elimination of renegade citizens without collateral damage to people nearby. The Conservative Prime Minister has saved the Queen, thanks to the RAF. At a stroke, the Royal Air Force achieved a boost to its profile, capacity and achievements - with impeccable timing for, just a day later, Her Majesty became Britain's longest serving monarch, and a week later presided over the anniversary celebrations for the Battle of Britain.

100 years ago, Hugh Trenchard began advocating, then initiating, the aerial bombing of troublesome foreigners in distant parts. Patently, there remains an appetite for convenient-seeming solutions to international problems - all of which are vulnerable to potential media manipulation and distortion.

The summer of 2015 saw political squabbles over the numbers of civilians accidentally killed during US-led coalition attempts to defeat Islamic State. In September, the British defence secretary claimed that the RAF had eliminated 330 ISIS members without causing a single civilian casualty. However Simon Jenkins in the Guardian argued:

> '... dropping bombs is politically cosmetic. It is trying to look good to a domestic audience; a cruel delusion, a pretence of humanity, ostentatious, immoral, stupid.'

One year on, emotive evidence of Syrian government assaults on Aleppo was propelled worldwide with pictures of a battered and bloody boy pulled from the wreckage of his bombed home. Unlike World War Two, when few people had cameras, and images took days to reach Fleet Street, we now have immediate public surveillance of the target scene. How does this impact on the values of the bombers? Recently it has been suggested that bomb aimers based in front of computers in Britain deserve war service medals.

* * * * * *

Coventry prides itself on absorbing the lessons of war, and thus being now well placed to promote international harmony. Visitors approaching the conurbation are greeted by signs reading 'City of Peace and Reconciliation'. In November 2015, 2,000 people attended the Remembrance Service and 50 large wreaths were laid at the War Memorial. After this admirable event, I visited the Tourist Information Centre that sits in a corner of the shell of the old cathedral. Attractions being publicised included 'War Games', a Museum exhibition examining 'the role of war in childhood play and strategic games through a series of intriguing and immersive activities'. One could also attend a 'Second World War Family Day: 'a Blitz experience and sing along, ARP training, a salvage sorting centre, make-do-and-mend crafts and much more' – all part of the city's Festival of Peace.

Tourist Centre personnel told me that the Luftwaffe had not intended to destroy the cathedral - it just happened to be close to munitions factories. In fact, they considered the Germans had done the city a favour by eliminating so many "awkward little streets of old buildings", to be replaced by "one of Britain's first pedestrianised shopping malls".

The old cathedral displays a 'litany of reconciliation' panel which recommends we condemn:

'The hatred which divides nation from nation, race from race, class from class. The covetous desires of people and nations to possess what is not their own. The greed which exploits the work of human hands and lays waste the earth.'

In the new cathedral, a trio of new paintings represented three WW2 bombed cities: Coventry, Dresden and Hiroshima. Each picture was the same size, yet the bombing of Hiroshima was much more deadly than at Dresden, which had been fifty times worse than that of Coventry.

On the evening of Saturday 14th, the city council mounted an event to convey solidarity against military violence - exactly 75 years on from the night of the major blitz bombing. It was to mirror annual events in Dresden when citizens hold hands and light torches to indicate their appreciation of peace each February. (Modern Germany has done a wonderful job in re-instating and enhancing its many handsome cities.)

In Coventry's University Square, a thousand people turned up. A local BBC journalist was master of ceremonies, presenting children singing between clips from radio documentaries on bomb survivors. Then the crowd shone torches or mobile phone lights through a two-minute silence. The size of the gathering acknowledging their city's past troubles in this way was surely disappointing. The number of people holding up lights roughly matched the figures of those killed by German bombs in Coventry during the winter of 1940/41.

Does one conclude that the publicity failed to work, that people had better things to do, or that British society has moved to a point whereby it takes peace for granted? The Dresden event has its detractors; police often have to control pro-Nazi demonstrators who seek to disturb the gathering. Doubtless every school around Coventry undertook special lessons to assess the horrors of warfare. But can we change behaviour for the better? We are reliant at the end of the day on our politicians who have in their grasp the possibility of advancing peace or aggression. But maybe one cannot have peace without a preceding period of aggression. Churchill's forthright stance against Nazi Germany eventually brought peace to most of Europe. Tony Blair is rightly decried for having caused and stimulated violence across the Middle East, but he also helped bring an end to violence in the UK with his contributions to the peace effort in Northern Ireland.

Amongst the peace demonstrators in Coventry that Saturday evening was a man discreetly handing out flyers exposing current munitions manufacture in the city. Around this time, most newspapers were presenting conflicting statistics over the proportions of the British population who would approve further bombing of Syria, and were condemning new Labour leader Jeremy Corbyn for resisting the renewal of the Trident nuclear missile deterrent system.

* * * * * *

"It is a gut-wrenching display. I don't see how anyone could forget the images, the evidence, the re-creations of what happened. It reminds everybody of the extraordinary complexity of choices of war, and what war does to people, to communities, countries, the world."

US Secretary of State John Kerry's response to visiting the Hiroshima peace park in April 2016. The following month, President Barack Obama went there and was lobbied by a Japanese version of the Campaign for Nuclear Disarmament to acknowledge that dropping the atomic bombs had been a war crime, and to apologise. Instead, the first serving American President to see the shrine met survivors of August 1945 and delivered fine oratory:

"Seventy one years ago, on a bright, cloudless morning, death fell from the sky and the world was changed. We come to mourn the dead, including 100,000 Japanese men, women and children, thousands of Koreans and a dozen Americans held prisoner. We have a shared responsibility to look directly into the eye of history and ask what we must do differently to curb such suffering again. Today, the children of this city will go through their day in peace. What a precious thing that is."

* * * * * *

Every war-time squadron has incredible stories of unique and startling courage, grit and audacity; proud testimony and tributes to brave men. I have endeavoured to approach the subject of military flying from a perspective well removed from standard-issue enthusiasm. I am sure many RAF people will be scathing of my shallow compression of complicated aeronautical matters and examples, but I am trying to reach a different and larger constituency – who don't know and perhaps therefore have not cared.

It seems to me that all war-time RAF airmen were heroes - undertaking terrifying tasks that might result at any moment in their violent deaths. They believed they could help bring the war to a fruitful end, but they had no idea how it might all turn out. They just got on with their bit of it. They did their bit.

Of course the dropping of explosives from planes has many arbitrary consequences. Hitler eventually managed to propel thousands of rockets across the Channel, each of which, statistically, killed one Briton - not a war winning strategy. Hitler and his henchmen had grasped power with the heated votes of 37% of the electorate. Hence, close on two-thirds of Germans had not chosen the Nazi regime, but they suffered it all the same. Allied bombing missions forced Hitler to withdraw vital resources away from the east to protect Berlin and the Ruhr, which patently helped defeat a nation that had been mesmerised by a madman.

How long does it take to get over a national societal trauma? Several generations? One of the churches devastated in Dresden was only re-built a decade ago. Wounds are still being healed.

I hope this account of flying through World War Two has impacted on you in a constructive way. Thanks for travelling with me. I was shocked when I first listened to Ted Miles explain what his colleagues were obliged to do each evening from those Lincolnshire airfields. My sense of shock has grown and grown as I have studied the extraordinary parameters of endeavour, commitment, courage and destruction generated by air forces at war in those terrible years. I was born a year after the end of hostilities and have therefore had the pleasure and privilege of growing up in a safe, secure, healthy, prosperous and generally happy country - thanks to all those soldiers, sailors and airmen who fought to defeat the menace of the Nazi dictatorship; and thanks to the politicians who steered the course of strategy, negotiation and presentation of staggeringly complex and often horrific events.

In December 2016, Japanese prime minister Shinzo Abe, reciprocating President Obama's visit to Hiroshima, flew to Pearl Harbor to look at the 1941 memorial. He declared:

> 'We must never repeat the horrors of war again. This is the solemn vow we, the people of Japan, have taken.'

So what have we learnt? Keep a grip on democracy. Reject racism. Beware of communications becoming dominated by a few malignant manipulators, presenting inflamed, distorted pictures of the world to propagate their own agenda and mislead the masses as to where their best interests lie.

Through the war, across the globe, more than 600,000 sons were lost in the skies. If you have forgotten what you were told at school, or have been bemused by curious films that fail to provide a context, I trust this book will help you assess this phenomenally important element of our recent history.

ACKNOWLEDGEMENTS

The author is immensely grateful to everyone who helped steer him toward the completion of this project. For explanations, my thanks to the staff and volunteers at the RAF Hendon and Cosford museums, the Imperial War Museum at Duxford, the Battle of Britain Memorial Flight Visitor Centre, and the Aviation Heritage museum at East Kirkby in Lincolnshire.

For guidance to relevant literature, thanks to staff at Worcester's Hive library, the City of Birmingham Library, and the National Aerospace Library, Farnborough. For help with accessing newspaper archives, I am very grateful to personnel at the National Library of Wales.

For inspiration and revelations, I will always be indebted to ex-RAF pilots John Featherstonhaugh and Graeme Wormold. For great tolerance of my endeavours, so much thanks to John's daughter, Gil Jackson.

For help with individual chapters, many thanks to Peter Sutton, John Elkington, Polly Bowles, John Burton, Roger Tapping, Kay Stevens, John Bentley, Ryc Smith, Gerald Brooke, Brian King, Maureen Panton and Griff Holliday. For examining the whole text for correct comprehension of military and aviation matters, huge thanks to Brian Boulby. All remaining narrative shortcomings and curiosities are mine.

I greatly appreciate the feedback from Ledbury's WEA History Group and the Worcestershire Industrial Archaeology & Local History Society. For guidance on publishing and marketing, thanks to Bernard Cartwright, Jo de Vries, Susanne Lumsden, Jim Storr and Andrew Wille.

For academic input, I have been very fortunate to gain invaluable insights from staff at the Universities of Birmingham, Exeter and Wolverhampton. Particular thanks to Professor Richard Overy for generously evaluating my text and allowing me to quote from his published work.

My thanks to Simon Read for permission to quote his powerful passage on bombing experience. And I am extremely grateful to Sir Max Hastings for agreeing to my use of his analyses on so many aspects of the subject.

ROUTE MAP

Our thanks to the relevant newspaper and publishing organisations for permissions to quote text.

If we have inadvertently failed to acquire appropriate permissions to utilise copy, please advise in order that we may remedy such a shortcoming.

Many thanks to Independent Design for our book cover.

And to Jennifer Fish for our website.

www.ofsonsandskies.com

25083334R00186

Printed in Poland
by Amazon Fulfillment
Poland Sp. z o.o., Wrocław